R. Gupta's®

GENERAL ENGLISH
for
Competitive Exams

Objective Multiple Choice Questions

An Extremely Useful Book for
Mastering General English
for All Competitive Examinations

By: RPH Editorial Board

Ramesh Publishing House, New Delhi

Published by
O.P. Gupta *for* Ramesh Publishing House

Admin. Office
12-H, New Daryaganj Road, Opp. Officers' Mess,
New Delhi-110002 ☎ 23261567, 23275224, 23275124

E-mail: info@rameshpublishinghouse.com
Website: www.rameshpublishinghouse.com

Showroom:
- Balaji Market, Nai Sarak, Delhi-6 ☎ 23253720, 23282525
- 4457, Nai Sarak, Delhi-6, ☎ 23918938

© *Reserved with the Publisher*

No Part of this book may be reproduced or transmitted in any form or by any means, electronic or mechanical including photocopying, recording or by any transformation storage and retrieval system without written permission from the Publisher.

Indemnification Clause: This book is being sold/distributed subject to the exclusive condition that neither the author nor the publishers, individually or collectively, shall be responsible to indemnify the buyer/user/possessor of this book beyond the selling price of this book for any reason under any circumstances. If you do not agree to it, please do not buy/accept/use/possess this book.

4th Edition: Printed in January, 2020

Book Code: R-1762

ISBN: 978-93-5012-651-6

HSN Code: 49011010

CONTENTS

1. Spelling Test ...3
2. Grammar Test ...11
3. Sentence Corrections ...59
4. Sentence Improvement ...68
5. Jumbled Words ...79
6. Jumbled Sentences ...92
7. Fill in the Blanks ...104
8. Cloze Test ...115
9. Comprehension Passages ...130
10. Synonyms and Antonyms ...155
11. Words Commonly Confused ...165
12. One Word Substitutes ...173
13. Idioms, Phrases & Proverbs ...186
14. Change of Voice ...202
15. Change of Speech ...208
16. Verbal Analogies ...215
17. Punctuation ...222
18. Figures of Speech ...229
19. Clauses ...234
20. Foreign Words ...239
21. Odd Words Out ...243
22. Do as Directed ...252

Preface

English is an international language. It is a medium of communication for the whole world and an effective tool to one and all. English is in demand everywhere and he who commands over it has the upper edge and gets better opportunities than the rest of the competitors.

English holds the key to the world of success. Good knowledge of English improves the expression of your mind, reassures you, builds your self-confidence and improves your personality. Thereby, it opens many an opportunities of success in your life. The one who knows good English, is impressive, effective, confident and successful.

Though there is no dearth of books on General English but it is a book with a vast difference. It wholly enjoys stupendous superiority in every aspect in comparison with any other book on the subject available in the market.

The book has been especially designed and planned as a practice book in order to cater to the long-felt needs of the prospective candidates for competitive examinations conducted by the Union Public Service Commission (UPSC), Staff Selection Commission (SSC), Banks and many other agencies for recruitment to various services under government, government undertakings, autonomous bodies, and so on. Besides, the book will fully serve the purpose of the students studying at colleges and universities.

It goes without saying that the power to use English in an accurate, effective, lucid, graceful, concise, precise and pleasant manner, whether in writing or in speaking, is indisputably one of the most important achievements which a well-educated person can possess in this world of constantly growing competition relating to various aspects of life. Know it for certain that you cannot achieve your objective in this regard unless you possess a sound knowledge of General English, its applications and proper usage. This is the book that will indubitably serve your purpose.

—**Publisher**

General English
for Competitive Exams

Spelling Test 1

There are thousands of words in English language.
It is difficult to remember the spellings of all at once.
Try to learn as many as you can. Use a dictionary regularly.

Directions: *In each of the following questions, four words are given of which only one is correctly spelt. Find the correctly spelt word.*

1. A. Accompalish
   B. Ackmplesh
   C. Acomplush
   D. Accomplish

2. A. Acommodation
   B. Acomodation
   C. Accomodation
   D. Accommodation

3. A. Astonished
   B. Astronished
   C. Astoneshed
   D. Asstonished

4. A. Abandon
   B. Abanddon
   C. Abendon
   D. Abbandon

5. A. Amandable
   B. Amendable
   C. Amenddable
   D. Amendablle

6. A. Adequate
   B. Edequate
   C. Adaquete
   D. Edaquete

7. A. Ameteur
   B. Amateur
   C. Amataur
   D. Amateor

8. A. Antiquated
   B. Antiqueted
   C. Antequated
   D. Antiquatted

9. A. Adalescent
   B. Addescant
   C. Adolescent
   D. Adolascent

10. A. Archeic
    B. Arcaic
    C. Archeic
    D. Archaic

11. A. Aristocracy
    B. Arestocracy
    C. Arestocracy
    D. Aristocrecy

12. A. Antitode
    B. Antedote
    C. Antidote
    D. Autitote

13. A. Audeble
    B. Audible
    C. Audcble
    D. Audebli

14. A. Aceelerate
    B. Accilerate
    C. Accelerate
    D. Accelerati

15. A. Accedental
    B. Aceedent
    C. Accidantle
    D. Accidental

16. A. Ageonise
    B. Agonise
    C. Agonice
    D. Agonisee

17. A. Benefeted
    B. Benefitted
    C. Benifited
    D. Benefited

18. A. Belligerent
    B. Beligirent
    C. Belligarant
    D. Belligerrent

19. A. Boquet
    B. Bouquet
    C. Bouquete
    D. Bouquette

20. A. Bueyant
    B. Buoyant
    C. Bueeyant
    D. Buoyent

21. A. Bombastic
    B. Bombestic
    C. Bombostic
    D. Bombastie

22. A. Bellicose
    B. Billicose
    C. Bellecose
    D. Belicose

23. A. Chancelery
    B. Chancellery
    C. Chancellary
    D. Chancelary

24. A. Cataclysm
    B. Cataclism
    C. Catacilysm
    D. Cataclesm

25. A. Chettering
    B. Chaterring
    C. Chattering
    D. Chatering

26. A. Conjectore
    B. Conjecture
    C. Cenjecture
    D. Cenjectire

27. A. Curageous
    B. Courageous
    C. Courrageous
    D. Couregeous

28. A. Corrigible
    B. Corigible
    C. Corregible
    D. Corrigiblle

29. A. Contrebution
    B. Contribution
    C. Contributtion
    D. Conterbution

30. A. Cuttiveted
    B. Culltrivated
    C. Cultivated
    D. Caltivated

31. A. Compansation
    B. Compensetion
    C. Compensotion
    D. Compensation

32. A. Claustrophobia
    B. Cloustrophobia
    C. Claustraphobia
    D. Claustrophabia

33. A. Connoiseur
    B. Connaisseur
    C. Connaissour
    D. Connoisseur

34. A. Commetti
    B. Commitee
    C. Committee
    D. Comitte

35. A. Chauvinism
    B. Chouvinism
    C. Chevinism
    D. Cauvinism

36. A. Cumpartment
    B. Compartment
    C. Compartant
    D. Comportent

37. A. Continuous
    B. Cuntinuous
    C. Continus
    D. Contineuous

38. A. Courteous
    B. Curteous
    C. Corteous
    D. Courtus

39. A. Cheapiness
    B. Chaepness
    C. Chepness
    D. Cheapness

40. A. Colusion
    B. Collision
    C. Colision
    D. Collison

41. A. Discriminate
    B. Discremineta
    C. Discrimenate
    D. Discriminat

42. A. Discourage
    B. Disscourage
    C. Discourege
    D. Discaurage

43. A. Despponding
    B. Despending
    C. Desponding
    D. Dessponding

44. A. Desgrace
    B. Disgrece
    C. Disgrice
    D. Disgrace

45. A. Darogate
    B. Derogate
    C. Derogeta
    D. Deragate

46. A. Darmatologist
    B. Dermatologist
    C. Dermetologist
    D. Dermatologest

47. A. Dormetory
    B. Durmitory
    C. Dormitori
    D. Dormitory

48. A. Dosier
    B. Doseir
    C. Dossier
    D. Dosseir

49. A. Desparge
    B. Disparage
    C. Disperage
    D. Disparege
50. A. Efficiant
    B. Effecient
    C. Efficient
    D. Eficient
51. A. Extravagant
    B. Extreragent
    C. Extreregant
    D. Extravegent
52. A. Efflorascence
    B. Eflorescene
    C. Effllorescence
    D. Efflorescence
53. A. Equinimity
    B. Equanimmity
    C. Equannimity
    D. Equanimity
54. A. Exeggerate
    B. Exaggerate
    C. Exadgerate
    D. Exagerate
55. A. Excesive
    B. Excessive
    C. Exccessive
    D. Exccesive
56. A. Entrepraneur
    B. Entreprenuer
    C. Entrapreneur
    D. Entrepreneur
57. A. Endication
    B. Endicaltion
    C. Indication
    D. Indicetion
58. A. Excllusion
    B. Exclussion
    C. Exclusion
    D. Exclosion
59. A. Embarassment
    B. Emberrassement
    C. Embarrassment
    D. Embbaresment
60. A. Eccintric
    B. Eccentrie
    C. Eccentric
    D. Eccintrie
61. A. Exttirpate
    B. Extirpete
    C. Extirpate
    D. Exterpate
62. A. Exparienced
    B. Experianced
    C. Experienced
    D. Experrienced
63. A. Ephameral
    B. Ephimeral
    C. Ephemeral
    D. Ephemerel
64. A. Econemist
    B. Economest
    C. Economist
    D. Econimist
65. A. Epitaph
    B. Epetaph
    C. Epiteph
    D. Epitoph
66. A. Epicurean
    B. Epecurean
    C. Epicurian
    D. Epicorean
67. A. Effeciency
    B. Efficiency
    C. Eficiency
    D. Efficency
68. A. Exemplary
    B. Eximplary
    C. Exemplari
    D. Examplary
69. A. Expidite
    B. Expedeti
    C. Expedite
    D. Expedit
70. A. Eradicated
    B. Erradicated
    C. Eradecated
    D. Eradiceted
71. A. Farmament
    B. Farmement
    C. Fermament
    D. Fremament
72. A. Fariegn
    B. Forein
    C. Foriegn
    D. Foreign
73. A. Forcaust
    B. Forcast
    C. Forecast
    D. Forecaste
74. A. Fulfilment
    B. Fulffilment
    C. Fulfilmient
    D. Fullfilment
75. A. Flatering
    B. Fletering
    C. Flattering
    D. Fletaring
76. A. Fanaticism
    B. Fenaticism
    C. Faneticism
    D. Fanatecism
77. A. Falicitate
    B. Felicitate
    C. Falecitate
    D. Falecetate
78. A. Formedable
    B. Formidable
    C. Formidabul
    D. Formdable

79. A. Febulous
    B. Fabulus
    C. Fabulous
    D. Fibulous

80. A. Feud
    B. Fued
    C. Fiud
    D. Feued

81. A. Grieff
    B. Grief
    C. Grieef
    D. Grrief

82. A. Guarantee
    B. Garuntee
    C. Guaruntee
    D. Gaurantee

83. A. Garulous
    B. Garrulaus
    C. Gorrulous
    D. Garrulous

84. A. Guellible
    B. Guiellible
    C. Guillibel
    D. Gullible

85. A. Gelactic
    B. Galectic
    C. Galactic
    D. Galactec

86. A. Hypocritical
    B. Hypocretical
    C. Hypocriticel
    D. Hypocirticel

87. A. Humurous
    B. Humorous
    C. Humoreus
    D. Humorrous

88. A. Harassment
    B. Herassment
    C. Harasment
    D. Harassmient

89. A. Honorary
    B. Henorary
    C. Honerary
    D. Honorery

90. A. Haphazard
    B. Hapahazard
    C. Haphzard
    D. Haphazrd

91. A. Itenerary
    B. Itinarery
    C. Itinarary
    D. Itinerary

92. A. Indipenseble
    B. Indispansible
    C. Indispensable
    D. Indipensable

93. A. Imprecticability
    B. Impracticebility
    C. Impracticibility
    D. Impracticability

94. A. Incradulous
    B. Incredulous
    C. Incridulous
    D. Incredalous

95. A. Insolvent
    B. Insolvant
    C. Insollvent
    D. Insolvvent

96. A. Imaginative
    B. Imeginative
    C. Imagenative
    D. Imaginetive

97. A. Illiterate
    B. Iliterate
    C. Illitarate
    D. Illiterete

98. A. Inemitable
    B. Inimitable
    C. Inimetable
    D. Inimitabli

99. A. Immortal
    B. Emortal
    C. Immortel
    D. Immortol

100. A. Inibriated
     B. Enibrited
     C. Inebriated
     D. Inubrited

101. A. Impassi
     B. Impasse
     C. Impase
     D. Inpassi

102. A. Imbibision
     B. Imbision
     C. Embibition
     D. Imbibition

103. A. Juddicious
     B. Judiceous
     C. Judicious
     D. Judiceus

104. A. Kleptomonia
     B. Kleptemonia
     C. Kleptomania
     D. Klaptomania

105. A. Loquacieous
     B. Lequacious
     C. Loquacious
     D. Lequocious

106. A. Lackdaisical
     B. Lackadaisical
     C. Lckadaisicle
     D. Lackadisical

107. A. Licentious
     B. Licontious
     C. Licenttious
     D. Licientious

108. A. Lagislature
     B. Legislature
     C. Lageslature
     D. Legesleture

109. A. Logecal
B. Logical
C. Lagical
D. Logicle

110. A. Lonesome
B. Lonsome
C. Lonesum
D. Lonsum

111. A. Livity
B. Levity
C. Levety
D. Levite

112. A. Meddicine
B. Medicine
C. Medicene
D. Medicinne

113. A. Meritricious
B. Merefrecious
C. Meretricious
D. Merritricious

114. A. Missunderstood
B. Miesunderstood
C. Misunderstood
D. Misunderstod

115. A. Materialistic
B. Materielistic
C. Meterialistic
D. Matterialistic

116. A. Magnanimity
B. Megnanimity
C. Magnenimity
D. Magnanimety

117. A. Mersenary
B. Marcenary
C. Marcenery
D. Mercenary

118. A. Misogynesm
B. Mesogynism
C. Misogynism
D. Misosogesim

119. A. Maegre
B. Meager
C. Meagre
D. Megre

120. A. Neggardly
B. Nigardly
C. Niggerdly
D. Niggardly

121. A. Newrologist
B. Neurologist
C. Neurologest
D. Newrologest

122. A. Neucteus
B. Neucleus
C. Nucleus
D. Neocleus

123. A. Negotcate
B. Negociate
C. Negotiate
D. Nagotiate

124. A. Neuralgia
B. Nuraliga
C. Neurolgia
D. Neuraltia

125. A. Occurad
B. Occurred
C. Ocurred
D. Occured

126. A. Osttentatious
B. Ostentetious
C. Ostentatious
D. Ostenttatious

127. A. Obnosious
B. Obnoxeous
C. Obnoxious
D. Obnoseous

128. A. Omenous
B. Ominous
C. Ommineous
D. Omineous

129. A. Ocasion
B. Occassion
C. Occasion
D. Ocassion

130. A. Occasional
B. Occassional
C. Occesional
D. Occesional

131. A. Obstatrician
B. Obstitrician
C. Obstetrician
D. Obstetracian

132. A. Omnevorous
B. Omnivorous
C. Omniverous
D. Omnivarous

133. A. Pecification
B. Pacification
C. Pecifacation
D. Pecefication

134. A. Progressive
B. Progressive
C. Progresive
D. Prograsive

135. A. Pasiveness
B. Passiveness
C. Passeveniss
D. Passivines

136. A. Polyendry
B. Poliendry
C. Pollyendry
D. Polyandry

137. A. Puerille
B. Puerrile
C. Puerile
D. Purrile

138. A. Pesanger
B. Passenger
C. Pessenger
D. Pasanger

139. A. Paralleled
    B. Paralelled
    C. Parralleled
    D. Parallelled
140. A. Praiceworthy
    B. Peiseworthy
    C. Praiseworthy
    D. Praisaworthy
141. A. Philanthropist
    B. Philenthropist
    C. Phelanthropist
    D. Philanthropest
142. A. Profesional
    B. Professionel
    C. Professional
    D. Profissional
143. A. Philenderer
    B. Philandarer
    C. Philanderer
    D. Philonderer
144. A. Posthumaus
    B. Posthomous
    C. Posthumous
    D. Pasthumous
145. A. Pletocray
    B. Plitocracy
    C. Plotocracy
    D. Plutocracy
146. A. Perrhic
    B. Pyrrhic
    C. Pyrrhec
    D. Porrhec
147. A. Pilferage
    B. Peliferage
    C. Pilfarege
    D. Poliferage
148. A. Psycologist
    B. Sychologist
    C. Psychologist
    D. Psychogist

149. A. Prophecy
    B. Phropecy
    C. Propecy
    D. Propheci
150. A. Pselm
    B. Slam
    C. Psalm
    D. Salm
151. A. Petchy
    B. Patchy
    C. Patchi
    D. Patche
152. A. Prudint
    B. Prudient
    C. Prudente
    D. Prudent
153. A. Peevishness
    B. Pievishness
    C. Peivishness
    D. Peeveshness
154. A. Querrelsome
    B. Quarrelsame
    C. Quarrelsome
    D. Querralsome
155. A. Querrel
    B. Querral
    C. Quarrel
    D. Quarel
156. A. Quadruplets
    B. Quedruplets
    C. Quadroplets
    D. Quadruplats
157. A. Rigourous
    B. Rigerous
    C. Rigorous
    D. Regerous
158. A. Rennaissance
    B. Rennaisance
    C. Renaisance
    D. Renaissance

159. A. Regecide
    B. Regicide
    C. Rigecide
    D. Ragicide
160. A. Rumenate
    B. Ruminote
    C. Rimunote
    D. Ruminate
161. A. Ribut
    B. Rebit
    C. Rebut
    D. Rebute
162. A. Reluctant
    B. Riluctant
    C. Reluctent
    D. Relictunt
163. A. Survellance
    B. Surveilance
    C. Surveillance
    D. Survaillance
164. A. Schedule
    B. Schdule
    C. Schedale
    D. Schedeule
165. A. Sepalchrle
    B. Sepalchral
    C. Sepulchrle
    D. Sepulchral
166. A. Sympathetic
    B. Smypathetic
    C. Sympothetic
    D. Sympethetic
167. A. Sincerely
    B. Sencerely
    C. Sincerelly
    D. Sincerrely
168. A. Satellite
    B. Sattellite
    C. Satelite
    D. Sattelite

169. A. Splendour
     B. Spllendour
     C. Splandour
     D. Splendeur

170. A. Suficient
     B. Suficiant
     C. Sufficient
     D. Sufficiant

171. A. Schezophrenia
     B. Schizaphrenia
     C. Schizophrenia
     D. Schizophrania

172. A. Superanuation
     B. Superennuation
     C. Superannuation
     D. Superannuetion

173. A. Skelled
     B. Skilled
     C. Skiled
     D. Skillid

174. A. Subsequent
     B. Subsiquent
     C. Subsequint
     D. Subquent

175. A. Sanguini
     B. Sangune
     C. Sangiune
     D. Sanguine

176. A. Sycophants
     B. Sicophants
     C. Sycopants
     D. Sycophints

177. A. Superfluons
     B. Superfleos
     C. Superflous
     D. Superfluous

178. A. Teracherous
     B. Treacherous
     C. Treacheraus
     D. Treachereans

179. A. Tacciturnity
     B. Taciturnity
     C. Taciturrnity
     D. Tacitturnity

180. A. Tranquilitty
     B. Tranquility
     C. Trenquility
     D. Tranquillity

181. A. Tranquil
     B. Trenquil
     C. Tranquel
     D. Trinquil

182. A. Transperency
     B. Transparency
     C. Transpirency
     D. Tranporency

183. A. Thioretical
     B. Theoretical
     C. Theoratical
     D. Theoritical

184. A. Uncivilized
     B. Uncevilized
     C. Uncivillized
     D. Uncevelized

185. A. Unfevourable
     B. Unfevaurable
     C. Unfavourable
     D. Unfivourable

186. A. Vaingloriaus
     B. Vainglorious
     C. Vaniglerious
     D. Vaingloreus

187. A. Vulnarable
     B. Valnerable
     C. Velnerable
     D. Vulnerable

188. A. Valuptuous
     B. Volluptous
     C. Voluptuous
     D. Volupttuous

189. A. Veneration
     B. Venration
     C. Venneration
     D. Venerration

190. A. Vorecious
     B. Varacious
     C. Voarcious
     D. Voracious

191. A. Verteran
     B. Viteran
     C. Veterain
     D. Veteran

192. A. Valuable
     B. Valueable
     C. Valuabel
     D. Valoble

193. A. Vendictive
     B. Vindective
     C. Vindictive
     D. Vindictivi

194. A. Worranty
     B. Warronty
     C. Warranty
     D. Warannty

195. A. Workholic
     B. Workeholic
     C. Workoholic
     D. Workaholic

196. A. Xinology
     B. Xenulogy
     C. Xunology
     D. Xenology

197. A. Xanophobia
     B. Xinophobia
     C. Xenophobia
     D. Xunophobia

198. A. Yoghurt
     B. Yughort
     C. Yougurt
     D. Yoghart

199. A. Yoguslavia B. Yugoslavia
  C. Yugaslovia D. Yugoslovia

200. A. Zoparasite B. Zooparaset
  C. Zooparasite D. Zoprasite

Answers

1	2	3	4	5	6	7	8	9	10
D	D	A	A	B	A	B	A	C	D
11	12	13	14	15	16	17	18	19	20
A	C	B	C	D	B	B	A	B	B
21	22	23	24	25	26	27	28	29	30
A	A	C	A	C	B	B	A	B	C
31	32	33	34	35	36	37	38	39	40
D	A	D	C	A	B	A	A	D	B
41	42	43	44	45	46	47	48	49	50
A	A	C	D	B	B	D	C	B	C
51	52	53	54	55	56	57	58	59	60
A	D	D	B	B	D	C	C	C	C
61	62	63	64	65	66	67	68	69	70
C	C	C	C	A	A	B	A	C	A
71	72	73	74	75	76	77	78	79	80
C	D	C	A	C	A	B	B	C	A
81	82	83	84	85	86	87	88	89	90
B	A	D	D	D	A	B	A	A	A
91	92	93	94	95	96	97	98	99	100
D	C	D	B	A	A	A	B	A	C
101	102	103	104	105	106	107	108	109	110
B	D	C	C	C	B	A	B	B	A
111	112	113	114	115	116	117	118	119	120
B	B	C	C	A	A	D	C	C	D
121	122	123	124	125	126	127	128	129	130
B	C	C	A	B	C	C	B	C	A
131	132	133	134	135	136	137	138	139	140
C	B	B	B	B	D	C	B	A	C
141	142	143	144	145	146	147	148	149	150
A	C	C	C	D	B	A	C	A	C
151	152	153	154	155	156	157	158	159	160
B	D	A	C	C	A	C	D	B	D
161	162	163	164	165	166	167	168	169	170
C	A	C	A	D	A	A	A	A	C
171	172	173	174	175	176	177	178	179	180
C	C	B	A	D	A	D	B	B	B
181	182	183	184	185	186	187	188	189	190
A	B	B	A	C	B	D	C	A	D
191	192	193	194	195	196	197	198	199	200
D	A	C	C	D	D	C	A	B	C

Grammar Test 2

Grammar is the science of the right use of a language, or we can say, it is an art of speaking or writing a language correctly.

NOUNS & PRONOUNS

Directions: *In the following questions choose the correct options to fill the blanks.*

1. Your .... proved false.
   A. statement   B. state
   C. status   D. None of these

2. The .... of nouns should be done carefully.
   A. classification B. classify
   C. class   D. None of these

3. The way he treats us is an .... of discrimination.
   A. act   B. action
   C. active D. None of these

4. .... of water should be checked.
   A. Leak   B. Leakage
   C. Leaking D. None of these

5. To save iron from rusting, it must be ....
   A. galvanisation B. galvanised
   C. galvanising   D. None of these

6. .... is the time when everyone feels courageous and vigorous.
   A. Boy   B. Boyhood
   C. Boyish D. None of these

7. .... begets enmity.
   A. Enemy B. Enmity
   C. Enema D. None of these

8. About a dozen old men were admitted to the .... asylum.
   A. lunatic B. lunacy
   C. lunar   D. None of these

9. Being .... he could not mix up with the common people.
   A. arrogant   B. arrogance
   C. arrogantly D. None of these

10. She was .... to know the reality.
    A. curious   B. curiosity
    C. curiously D. None of these

11. .... is the key to happiness.
    A. Innocent   B. Innocence
    C. Innocency D. None of these

12. The king was liked by the people for his ....
    A. decent   B. decency
    C. decently D. None of these

13. The boy who was .... minded could not follow the teacher.
    A. absent   B. absence
    C. absently D. None of these

14. .... brings about a lot of problems in the end.
    A. Listless   B. Listlessness
    C. Listlessly   D. None of these

15. A .... girl is full of vim and vigour.
    A. vivacious   B. vivacity
    C. vivace   D. None of these

16. .... must do one's duty honestly.
    A. He   B. One
    C. You   D. None of these

17. She cried but .... heard her.
    A. nobody   B. anybody
    C. somebody   D. None of these

18. .... can solve this difficult sum.
    A. All   B. Everyone
    C. No one   D. None of these

19. .... like the size of a cat jumped over his head.
    A. Something   B. Anything
    C. Nothing   D. None of these

20. .... wants to be rich.
    A. Nobody   B. Everybody
    C. Anybody   D. None of these

21. .... likes to live a miserable life.
    A. Nobody   B. Anybody
    C. Everybody   D. None of these

22. He is not choosy. He will eat .... you give him.
    A. nothing   B. something
    C. everything   D. None of these

23. Is there .... home?
    A. somebody
    B. anybody
    C. everybody
    D. None of these

24. I think there is .... at home.
    A. nobody   B. anybody
    C. all   D. None of these

25. .... were happy at the child's birthday celebrations.
    A. Everyone
    B. Everybody
    C. All
    D. None of these

26. The boy .... broke the chair was punished.
    A. whose   B. whom
    C. who   D. None of these

27. This is the girl .... father is a scientist.
    A. whose   B. whom
    C. who   D. None of these

28. He .... nobody ever loved became a saint later.
    A. who   B. whose
    C. whom   D. None of these

29. The snake .... we saw in the forest was a cobra.
    A. who   B. which
    C. whom   D. None of these

30. The books .... you gave me are interesting.
    A. which   B. whom
    C. who   D. None of these

31. The birds .... have long tails are liked by all.
    A. who   B. whom
    C. which   D. None of these

32. This is the boy .... uncle is an army officer.
    A. whom   B. whose
    C. which   D. None of these

33. That boy .... father is a doctor is an intelligent one.
    A. whose
    B. which
    C. whom
    D. None of these

34. Those .... love violence finally bow down to the more powerful.
    A. whose B. whom
    C. who D. None of these
35. She is the girl .... we saw in the theatre.
    A. who B. whom
    C. whose D. None of these
36. The place was so dirty that ..... wished to run away from there.
    A. everybody B. anybody
    C. few D. some
37. ..... was there to help me.
    A. Somebody B. Anything
    C. Anybody D. Nobody
38. Is there .... to eat?
    A. some B. something
    C. any D. few
39. ..... of the students were making a great noise.
    A. Anyone B. Somebody
    C. Many D. Nobody
40. ..... of the students can solve this sum.
    A. Someone B. Anybody
    C. Somebody D. None
41. ...... of us should try our best to make India a heaven.
    A. Any B. Somebody
    C. Anybody D. All
42. .... of us do not know the real meaning of our lives.
    A. Any B. Something
    C. Several D. Many
43. My .... black.
    A. hairs are B. hair is
    C. hairs shall D. hair will
44. She saw two .... on the last Sunday.
    A. thiefs B. theifs
    C. thieves D. theives
45. My sister is a ....
    A. bacheloress B. bachelor
    C. unmarried D. spinster
46. One is supposed to do ....
    A. our duty B. their duty
    C. one's duty D. his duty
47. Take anything .... you want.
    A. that B. which
    C. than D. then
48. I cannot tolerate ....
    A. separated you
    B. your separation
    C. separation from you
    D. you separated
49. He is .... faithful partner.
    A. yours B. you
    C. your D. your's
50. Ajay is more smart than ....
    A. her B. hers
    C. herself D. she
51. Vivek works harder than ....
    A. me B. I
    C. her D. his
52. They should help ....
    A. the poor people
    B. the poor
    C. the poor persons
    D. the poor peoples
53. .... are mad.
    A. All his sons
    B. His all sons
    C. Sons all his
    D. All sons his
54. The poor fellow .... to fate.
    A. resigned
    B. resigned himself
    C. resigned itself
    D. resigned themselves

55. Nobody will help you but ....
    A. I   B. me
    C. ours   D. his
56. It is a good chance, You must avail .... this opportunity.
    A. of   B. yourself of
    C. for   D. from
57. The person who is elected .... my relative.
    A. is   B. he is
    C. his   D. him
58. He made ....
    A. yours mention
    B. mention of you
    C. mention for you
    D. mention about you
59. .... I know, he is quite faithful.
    A. As far as
    B. So far as
    C. So far this
    D. So far so
60. It is a duty of a person to take .... for his family.
    A. pain   B. pains
    C. pain-killers D. pained
61. She does not love .... husband.
    A. his   B. her
    C. its   D. their
62. Let .... work together.
    A. him and me
    B. he and I
    C. he and him
    D. I and me
63. Copper, Silver and Gold ....
    A. each will do
    B. either will do
    C. any one will do
    D. any will do
64. Jessica and Roma are very irregular .... habits.
    A. in her   B. in their
    C. in its   D. in every
65. One likes to enjoy .... who was a great poet.
    A. The sonnets of Shakespeare
    B. Shakespeare's sonnets
    C. Sonnets
    D. Shakespeare
66. That is the boy ...... everybody loves.
    A. whom   B. who
    C. that   D. whose
67. That is the girl .... won the first prize.
    A. whom   B. who
    C. whose   D. which
68. That is the man ..... purse was lost.
    A. who   B. whom
    C. whose   D. their
69. I have got .... I wanted.
    A. which   B. whose
    C. that   D. what
70. .... man has his own will.
    A. All   B. Any
    C. Each   D. Many

Directions (Qs. 71-100): *In each of the following questions a sentence is given which may or may not be correct. Select the option which is the correct form of the sentence. If you think none of the options is correct, your answer is 'D'.*

71. I, he and you are class fellows.
    A. I, you and he are class fellows.
    B. You, he and I are class fellows.
    C. He, you and I are class fellows.
    D. None of these
72. Both didn't go.
    A. Both of you don't go.
    B. Neither of you didn't go.
    C. Neither went.
    D. None of these

73. They and you can go outside.
    A. You and they can go outside.
    B. They and you can goes outside.
    C. You and they can goes outside.
    D. None of these
74. John, Peter and Micky help each other.
    A. Peter, John and Micky help each other.
    B. John, Peter and Micky help one another.
    C. John, Peter and Micky helps one another.
    D. None of these
75. Distribute these apples between four friends.
    A. Distribute these apples between four friend.
    B. Distribute these apples among four friends.
    C. Distribute these apples among four friend.
    D. None of these
76. Every boy was in their best mood.
    A. Every boys were in their best mood.
    B. Every boy was in his best mood.
    C. Every boy was in his best moods.
    D. None of these
77. The two friends like one another.
    A. The two friends like each other.
    B. The two friend likes each other.
    C. The two friends likes each other.
    D. None of these
78. Who do you like the best?
    A. Who does you like the best?
    B. Whom do you like the best?
    C. Whom does you like the best?
    D. None of these
79. Either Satish or Rakesh has been ordered to bring their books.
    A. Either Satish or Rakesh has been ordered to bring his books.
    B. Either Satish or Rakesh have been ordered to bring his books.
    C. Either Satish or Rakesh have been ordered to bring their books.
    D. None of these
80. One must do his duty.
    A. One must do their duty.
    B. One must do your duty.
    C. One must do one's duty.
    D. None of these
81. Distribute these sweets among two brothers.
    A. Distribute these sweets between two brothers.
    B. Distribute these sweet among two brothers.
    C. Distribute these sweets between two brother.
    D. None of these
82. It is one of the best novels that has been written by Leo Tolstoy.
    A. ... the best novel that have been written...
    B. ... the best novels that have been written...
    C. ... the best novel that has been written...
    D. None of these
83. The books are for he and I.
    A. These books are for him and me.
    B. There books are for I and he.
    C. These books are for his as well as mine.
    D. None of these

84. Any of these two books will serve my purpose.
    A. Any of these two book...
    B. Each of these two book...
    C. Either of these two books...
    D. None of these
85. He availed of that chance.
    A. He availed himself of that chance.
    B. He availed him of that chance.
    C. He availed his of that chance.
    D. None of these
86. We went in the garden and enjoyed.
    A. We went in the garden and enjoyed there.
    B. We went in the garden and enjoyed ourselves.
    C. We went in the garden and enjoyed themselves.
    D. None of these
87. Neither of your five brothers have helped you.
    A. None of your five brothers have helped you.
    B. None of your five brothers has helped you.
    C. Neither of your five brothers has helped you.
    D. None of these
88. This is the book whose pages have been torn.
    A. This is the book whose pages has been...
    B. This is the book whom pages have been...
    C. This is the book the pages of which have been...
    D. None of these
89. He kept himself away from the dog.
    A. He kept away from the dog.
    B. He kept the dog away from himself.
    C. He kept himself from the dog.
    D. None of these
90. It was her, who stole your purse.
    A. It was she, who stole your purse.
    B. It was hers who stole your purse.
    C. It was herself who stole your purse.
    D. None of these
91. Neither Sohan nor his friends attend his class.
    A. ...his friends attend him class.
    B. ...him friends attend his class.
    C. ...his friends attend their class.
    D. None of these
92. None of the four boys were there.
    A. Neither of the four boys was there.
    B. None of the four boys was there.
    C. None of the four boy were there.
    D. None of these
93. He was happy at his brother arrival.
    A. He was happy at his brother's arrival.
    B. He was happy at him brother's arrival.
    C. He was happy at himself brother's arrival.
    D. None of these
94. If I was him, I would not abuse him.
    A. If I were he, I would not abuse him.
    B. If I were him, I would not abuse him.
    C. If I was he, I would not abuse him.
    D. None of these

95. Whom do you think will win the match?
    A. Whose do you think will win....?
    B. Whom does you think will win...?
    C. Who do you think will win....?
    D. None of these
96. He abstained himself from the meat.
    A. He abstained from meat.
    B. He abstained his from the meat.
    C. He abstained he from the meat.
    D. None of these
97. The rabbit hid itself behind a bush.
    A. The rabbit hid himself behind a bush.
    B. The rabbit hid behind a bush.
    C. The rabbit hid herself behind a bush.
    D. None of these
98. He absented from the meeting.
    A. He absented itself from the meeting.
    B. He absented himself from the meeting.
    C. He absented hisself from the meeting.
    D. None of these
99. Whom do you think he is?
    A. Who do you think he is?
    B. Why do you think he is?
    C. Whom do you think he is?
    D. None of these
100. Everyone of us should do our duty.
    A. Everyone of us should do her duty.
    B. Everyone of us should do their duty.
    C. Everyone of us should do his duty.
    D. None of these

Answers

1	2	3	4	5	6	7	8	9	10
A	A	A	B	B	B	B	A	A	A
11	12	13	14	15	16	17	18	19	20
B	B	A	B	A	B	A	C	A	B
21	22	23	24	25	26	27	28	29	30
A	C	B	A	C	C	A	C	B	A
31	32	33	34	35	36	37	38	39	40
C	B	A	C	B	A	D	B	C	D
41	42	43	44	45	46	47	48	49	50
D	D	B	C	D	C	A	C	C	D
51	52	53	54	55	56	57	58	59	60
B	B	A	B	A	B	A	B	A	B
61	62	63	64	65	66	67	68	69	70
B	A	C	B	A	A	B	C	D	C
71	72	73	74	75	76	77	78	79	80
B	C	A	B	B	B	A	B	A	C
81	82	83	84	85	86	87	88	89	90
A	B	A	C	A	B	B	C	A	A
91	92	93	94	95	96	97	98	99	100
C	B	A	A	C	A	B	B	C	C

ARTICLES

Directions: *Fill in the blanks with suitable articles, if required.*

1. He looks as foolish as .... ass.
   A. a B. an
   C. the D. No article
2. Did you go to .... prison to visit him?
   A. a B. an
   C. the D. No article
3. I found .... one-rupee note in the market.
   A. a B. an
   C. the D. No article
4. It is a pleasure to meet such .... efficient man.
   A. a B. an
   C. the D. No article
5. The sage lived in a cave in .... Himalayas.
   A. a B. an
   C. the D. No article
6. There is .... union in our factory.
   A. a B. an
   C. the D. No article
7. He hit his wife on the head with .... umbrella.
   A. a B. an
   C. the D. No article
8. I caught him by .... collar.
   A. a B. an
   C. the D. No article
9. Child is .... father of man.
   A. a B. an
   C. the D. No article
10. He gazed at .... moon for two hours.
    A. a B. an
    C. the D. No article
11. Do you know .... boy in white?
    A. a B. an
    C. the D. No article
12. She is .... girl I am looking for.
    A. a B. an
    C. the D. No article
13. Have you read .... Mahabharat?
    A. a B. an
    C. the D. No article
14. ....rich are not always happy.
    A. A B. An
    C. The D. No article
15. Oranges are sold by .... dozen.
    A. a B. an
    C. the D. No article
16. Milk is sold by .... litre.
    A. a B. an
    C. the D. No article
17. .... Amazon is the longest river in the world.
    A. A B. An
    C. The D. No article
18. .... higher you climb, the colder it gets.
    A. A B. An
    C. The D. No article
19. She is .... untidy girl.
    A. a B. an
    C. the D. No article
20. I am .... M.A. is English.
    A. a B. an
    C. the D. No article
21. I have already spent .... few rupees I had.
    A. a B. an
    C. the D. No article

22. .... English are very hard-working.
    A. A B. An C. The D. No article
23. April is the fourth month of .... year.
    A. a B. an C. the D. No article
24. Rice is sold by .... kilogram.
    A. a B. an C. the D. No article
25. She is .... best of the three girls.
    A. a B. an C. the D. No article
26. .... man in the car is a friend of mine.
    A. A B. An C. The D. No article
27. Brevity is .... soul of wit.
    A. a B. an C. the D. No article
28. .... thing of beauty is a joy for ever.
    A. A B. An C. The D. No article
29. .... little learning is a dangerous thing.
    A. A B. An C. The D. No article
30. .... best sauce for food is hunger.
    A. A B. An C. The D. No article
31. Birds of .... feather flock together.
    A. a B. an C. the D. No article
32. He makes .... living by begging.
    A. a B. an C. the D. No article
33. It is ...... pity that he died so young.
    A. a B. an C. the D. No article
34. What .... nuisance it is?
    A. a B. an C. the D. No article
35. Delhi is .... London of India.
    A. a B. an C. the D. No article
36. Where is .... will, there is a way.
    A. a B. an C. the D. No article
37. Her father is .... physician and surgeon.
    A. a B. an C. the D. No article
38. This will benefit .... poor.
    A. a B. an C. the D. No article
39. ....bird in hand is better than two in a bush.
    A. A B. An C. The D. No article
40. As he is hard-working, he will win .... prize.
    A. a B. an C. the D. No article
41. .... water of this well is dirty.
    A. A B. An C. The D. No article
42. Only .... wearer knows where the shoe pinches.
    A. a B. an C. the D. No article
43. .... action will be taken against you.
    A. A B. An C. The D. No article

44. .... sun rises in the east.
    A. A   B. An
    C. The   D. No article
45. She was promoted to .... highest post.
    A. a   B. an
    C. the   D. No article
46. Did you see .... Taj Mahal?
    A. a   B. an
    C. the   D. No article
47. He is .... one-eyed man.
    A. a   B. an
    C. the   D. No article
48. This is .... useful book.
    A. a   B. an
    C. the   D. No article
49. Cloth is sold by .... metre.
    A. a   B. an
    C. the   D. No article
50. The sun sets in .... west.
    A. a   B. an
    C. the   D. No article
51. Amar bought......umbrella yesterday.
    A. a   B. an
    C. the   D. No article
52. Surinder is ...... honest boy.
    A. a   B. an
    C. the   D. No article
53. She wrote ...... book in French.
    A. a   B. an
    C. the   D. No article
54. ...... lion roars.
    A. A   B. An
    C. The   D. No article
55. ..... apple a day keeps the doctor away.
    A. A   B. An
    C. The   D. No article
56. John bought ...... car yesterday.
    A. a   B. an
    C. the   D. No article
57. His father is ..... engineer in the U.S.A.
    A. a   B. an
    C. the   D. No article
58. It is hard for ..... owl to fly during the day times.
    A. a   B. an
    C. the   D. No article
59. She had ..... rimmed hat.
    A. a   B. an
    C. the   D. No article
60. My uncle is ..... heart specialist.
    A. a   B. an
    C. the   D. No article

Directions (Qs. 61 to 90): *In each of the following questions a sentence is given which may or may not be correct. Select the option which is the correct form of the sentence. If you think none of the options is correct, your answer is 'D'.*

61. Ganga is a holy river.
    A. Ganga is the holy river.
    B. The Ganga is a holy river.
    C. The Ganga is the holy river.
    D. None of these
62. Hindustan Times is published from Delhi.
    A. Hindustan Times is published from the Delhi.
    B. The Hindustan Times is published from the Delhi.
    C. The Hindustan Times is published from Delhi.
    D. None of these

63. Bible is a holy book.
    A. Bible is the holy book.
    B. The Bible is the holy book.
    C. The Bible is a holy book.
    D. None of these
64. Earth revolves round sun.
    A. The earth revolves round sun.
    B. Earth revolves round the sun.
    C. The earth revolves round the sun.
    D. None of these
65. Higher you go, cooler it is.
    A. The higher you go, cooler it is.
    B. Higher you go, the cooler it is.
    C. The higher you go, the cooler it is.
    D. None of these
66. The gold is a precious metal.
    A. The gold is the precious metal.
    B. Gold is a precious metal.
    C. The gold is one of the precious metals.
    D. None of these
67. The honey is sweet when tasted.
    A. Honey is sweet when tasted.
    B. The honey is sweet when it is tasted.
    C. The honey is the sweet when tasted.
    D. None of these
68. Taj Mahal is a wonderful building.
    A. The Taj Mahal is a wonderful building.
    B. The Taj Mahal is the wonderful building.
    C. The Taj Mahal is the wonderfully building.
    D. None of these
69. Rich should help poor.
    A. Rich should help the poor.
    B. The rich should help poor.
    C. The rich should help the poor.
    D. None of these
70. The Delhi is the capital of the India.
    A. The Delhi is the capital of India.
    B. Delhi is the capital of India.
    C. Delhi is the capital of the India.
    D. None of these
71. My elder brother is a M.A.
    A. My elder brother is an M.A.
    B. My elder brother is M.A.
    C. My elder brother is M.A's.
    D. None of these
72. He is an European.
    A. He is European.
    B. He is a European.
    C. He is a European's.
    D. None of these
73. The water is a good solvent.
    A. Water is a good solvent.
    B. Water is good solvent.
    C. The water is good solvent.
    D. None of these
74. My brother is an university professor.
    A. My brother is university professor.
    B. My brother is a university professor.
    C. My brother is an university professors.
    D. None of these
75. Tony is Dhoni of our team.
    A. Tony is the Dhoni of our team.
    B. Tony is an Dhoni of our team.
    C. Tony is Dhoni's of our team.
    D. None of these

76. Punjab is richest state of India.
    A. Punjab is the richest state of India.
    B. The Punjab is the richest state of India.
    C. The Punjab is richest state of India.
    D. None of these

77. I requested the clerk to make a F.D.R.
    A. I requested the clerk to make an F.D.R.
    B. I requested the clerk to make F.D.R.
    C. I requested the clerk to make a F.D.R.
    D. None of these

78. The death is a great leveller.
    A. A death is a great leveller.
    B. An death is a great leveller.
    C. Death is a great leveller.
    D. None of these

79. Himalayas is in the north of India.
    A. The Himalayas is in the north of India.
    B. Himalayas are in the north of India.
    C. The Himalayas are in the north of India.
    D. None of these

80. A religious person worships the God and the Nature.
    A. A religious person worships the God and Nature.
    B. A religious person worships God and the Nature.
    C. A religious person worships God and Nature.
    D. None of these

81. Arpan is a honest boy.
    A. Arpan is an honest boy.
    B. Arpan is honest boy.
    C. Arpan is honest's boy.
    D. None of these

82. Shatabdi Express is fastest train in India.
    A. The Shatabdi Express is fastest train in India.
    B. The Shatabdi Express is the fastest train in India.
    C. Shatabdi Express is the fastest train in India.
    D. None of these

83. An man is mortal.
    A. A man is mortal.
    B. The man is mortal.
    C. Man is mortal.
    D. None of these

84. The poet and novelist are died.
    A. The poet and the novelist is died.
    B. The poet and novelist is dead.
    C. The poets and novelists is dead.
    D. None of these

85. The honesty is the best policy.
    A. An honesty is best policy.
    B. Honesty is best policy.
    C. Honesty is the best policy.
    D. None of these

86. The man needs the waters and the air to live.
    A. The man needs the water and air to live.
    B. The man needs water and the air to live.
    C. Man needs water and air to live.
    D. None of these

87. Water of this well is sweet.
    A. A water of this well is sweet.
    B. Water of this well is the sweet.
    C. The water of this well is sweet.
    D. None of these
88. Oranges are sold by dozen.
    A. The oranges are sold by dozen.
    B. Oranges are sold by the dozen.
    C. An orange is sold by dozen.
    D. None of these
89. Arjun walked two miles and half at stretch.
    A. Arjun walked two miles and a half at stretch.
    B. Arjun walked two miles and half at a stretch.
    C. Arjun walked two miles and a half at a stretch.
    D. None of these
90. The Delhi is the capital of India.
    A. The Delhi is capital of India.
    B. Delhi is a capital of India.
    C. Delhi is the capital of India.
    D. None of these

Directions (Qs. 91-110): *Select the correct sentence from the following. If none is correct mark 'D' as the answer.*

91. A. The old man looked at a sky.
    B. The old man looked at the sky.
    C. The old man looked at an sky.
    D. None of these
92. A. An Einstein comes to solve the problem.
    B. A Einstein comes to solve the problem.
    C. The Einstein comes to solve the problem.
    D. None of these
93. A. Rohan is a honest boy.
    B. Rohan is an honest boy.
    C. Rohan is the honest boy.
    D. None of these
94. A. Gold is an precious metal.
    B. Gold is the precious metal.
    C. Gold is a precious metal.
    D. None of these
95. A. Bible is a holy book.
    B. The Bible is a holy book.
    C. An bible is a holy book.
    D. None of these
96. A. Samudra Gupta is Napoleon of India.
    B. Samudra Gupta is the Napoleon of India.
    C. Samudra Gupta is a Napoleon of India.
    D. None of these
97. A. The Himalayas are the biggest mountains in the world.
    B. The Himalayas are a biggest mountains in the world.
    C. The Himalayas are an biggest mountains in the world.
    D. None of these
98. A. The Shyam is a good boy.
    B. A Shyam is a good boy.
    C. Shyam is a good boy.
    D. None of these
99. A. Sky knows no limit.
    B. The sky knows no limit.
    C. A sky knows no limit.
    D. None of these
100. A. He has a old head over young shoulders.
     B. He has the old head over young shoulders.
     C. He has an old head over young shoulders.
     D. None of these

101. A. The beauty needs no ornaments.
     B. Beauty needs no ornaments.
     C. A beauty needs no ornaments.
     D. None of these
102. A. Is not childhood the golden period of our life?
     B. Is not childhood a golden period of our life?
     C. Is not childhood an golden period of our life?
     D. None of these
103. A. Bravery of the Rajputs is proverbial.
     B. An bravery of the Rajputs is proverbial.
     C. The bravery of the Rajputs is proverbial.
     D. None of these
104. A. Whites are not superior to the blacks.
     B. The whites are not superior to the blacks.
     C. The whites are not superior to blacks.
     D. None of these
105. A. More, merrier.
     B. The more, the merrier.
     C. More, the merrier.
     D. None of these
106. A. Indians are industrious people.
     B. Indians are the industrious people.
     C. The Indians are industrious people.
     D. None of these
107. A. He likes apples of Kashmir.
     B. He likes the apples of Kashmir.
     C. He likes the apples of the Kashmir.
     D. None of these
108. A. He has hundred rupees in his pocket.
     B. He has the hundred rupees in his pocket.
     C. He has a hundred rupees in his pocket.
     D. None of these
109. A. He is braver of the two boys.
     B. He is the braver of the two boys.
     C. He is the braver of the two boys.
     D. None of these
110. A. Guilty must be severely punished.
     B. A guilty must be severely punished.
     C. The guilty must be severely punished.
     D. None of these

Answers

1	2	3	4	5	6	7	8	9	10
B	C	A	B	C	A	B	C	C	C
11	12	13	14	15	16	17	18	19	20
C	C	C	C	C	C	C	C	B	B
21	22	23	24	25	26	27	28	29	30
C	C	C	C	C	C	C	A	A	C
31	32	33	34	35	36	37	38	39	40
A	A	A	A	C	A	A	C	A	A

41	42	43	44	45	46	47	48	49	50
C	C	B	C	C	C	A	A	C	C
51	52	53	54	55	56	57	58	59	60
B	B	A	A	B	A	B	B	A	A
61	62	63	64	65	66	67	68	69	70
B	C	C	C	C	B	A	A	C	B
71	72	73	74	75	76	77	78	79	80
A	B	A	B	A	B	A	C	C	C
81	82	83	84	85	86	87	88	89	90
A	B	C	B	C	C	C	B	C	C
91	92	93	94	95	96	97	98	99	100
B	A	B	C	B	B	A	C	B	C
101	102	103	104	105	106	107	108	109	110
B	A	C	B	B	C	B	C	B	C

❏❏❏

ADJECTIVES & ADVERBS

Directions (Qs. 1-45): *In the following questions choose the correct options to fill in the blanks.*

1. .... water that was in the jug evaporated.
   A. Little
   B. The little
   C. Small
   D. A small

2. He has not sung .... songs.
   A. much
   B. most
   C. more
   D. many

3. Srishti has searched .... office.
   A. whole the
   B. the whole
   C. a whole
   D. some whole

4. Premchand was .... best and .... famous writer.
   A. a, the most
   B. the, a most
   C. the, more
   D. the, the most

5. William Shakespeare is famous as ....
   A. a poet and a dramatist
   B. a poet and dramatist
   C. the poet and the dramatist
   D. a poet and the dramatist

6. She returned .... than I had thought.
   A. quickly
   B. more quicker
   C. more quickly
   D. quicker

7. He is .... foolish person.
   A. rather the
   B. a rather
   C. rather a
   D. rather

8. This pen .... rupees.
   A. costs twenty
   B. twenty costs only
   C. costs only twenty
   D. only costs twenty

9. It is .... pride.
   A. nothing else but
   B. nothing else than
   C. else nothing than
   D. but

10. This tea is .... to drink.
    A. too hot
    B. very hot
    C. enough hot
    D. much hot

11. The girl whom you met is the .... sister of Ravi.
    A. eldest   B. elder
    C. older   D. oldest
12. The historical place is ....
    A. seeing worth
    B. worthy of seeing
    C. worth seeing
    D. worthy seeing
13. These flowers smell ....
    A. sweet
    B. sweetly
    C. more sweetly
    D. sweetest
14. .... aspirant cannot pass the entrance examination.
    A. Each   B. Every
    C. All   D. No
15. Prem Chand .... second Shakespeare.
    A. is a   B. is
    C. is the   D. is an
16. What does the ...... leader suggest?
    A. other   B. another
    C. others   D. anothers
17. He .... money.
    A. has few   B. have few
    C. has little D. have little
18. The .... boys are rewarded.
    A. first two   B. two first
    C. firsts two D. two's first
19. He is .... brave.
    A. stronger than
    B. stronger then
    C. more strong then
    D. more strong than
20. No sooner said ....
    A. so done   B. and done
    C. then done   D. but done
21. .... student in the class got prizes.
    A. Each and every
    B. Every and each
    C. Every
    D. Never
22. It is .... picture than the one we saw last Monday.
    A. interesting
    B. much interesting
    C. more interesting
    D. most interesting
23. She is clever ....
    A. that her mother is
    B. as her mother is
    C. to her mother is
    D. than her mother is
24. They will get ....
    A. Red, green and black paper
    B. Red, green black paper
    C. Red and green and black paper
    D. Red green black paper
25. Health is .... wealth.
    A. preferable to
    B. more preferable than
    C. more preferable to
    D. most preferable then
26. My brother is .... MBA.
    A. a   B. an
    C. the   D. any
27. Have you got .... cheese?
    A. some   B. many
    C. a few   D. few
28. No, I have not got .... cheese.
    A. many   B. few
    C. any   D. some
29. There is only .... milk left in the bottle.
    A. enough   B. few
    C. much   D. a little

30. There is .... hope of his recovery.
    A. any   B. little
    C. many   D. few
31. .... water in the jug has been drunk by Mohan.
    A. little   B. The few
    C. A few   D. Few
32. I shall play .... piano at the party.
    A. some   B. any
    C. the   D. few
33. .... labourers were found dead in the mine.
    A. Any   B. Fewer
    C. Many   D. Less
34. Could I borrow .... umbrella?
    A. our   B. your
    C. yours   D. my
35. My brother is standing in the .... row.
    A. any   B. many
    C. some   D. first
36. Give me .... rice.
    A. some   B. few
    C. a few   D. any
37. .... sheep grazing on the slope of the hill had gone away.
    A. Any   B. The few
    C. This   D. Much
38. Have you got .... magazines to read?
    A. all   B. much
    C. some   D. little
39. I have .... money that I want to spend on shares.
    A. any   B. much
    C. less   D. some
40. There is .... owl on the branch of the tree.
    A. a   B. the
    C. an   D. some
41. .... dogs were barking at the strangers.
    A. Some   B. Any
    C. Much   D. Less
42. The girl bought her father .... juice.
    A. few   B. some
    C. any   D. many
43. You should take .... honey everyday.
    A. any   B. many
    C. a little D. a few
44. .... boy was punished by the teacher.
    A. Either   B. All
    C. Any   D. Many
45. .... girl was asked to join the army.
    A. None   B. Neither
    C. All   D. Any

Directions (Qs. 46-75): *In each of the following questions a sentence is given which may or may not be correct. Select the option which is the correct form of the sentence. If you think none of the options is correct, your answer is 'D'.*

46. Harish is senior than you.
    A. Harish is more senior than you.
    B. Harish is more senior to you.
    C. Harish is senior to you.
    D. None of these
47. My shirt is more superior than yours.
    A. My shirt is superior than yours.
    B. My shirt is more superior to yours.
    C. My shirt is superior to yours.
    D. None of these

48. Sangeeta is more wiser than Sunita.
    A. Sangeeta is wise than Sunita.
    B. Sangeeta is more much wiser than Sunita.
    C. Sangeeta is wiser than Sunita.
    D. None of these

49. It is the most impossible to stay in the flames of fire for a long time.
    A. It is the more impossible to stay...
    B. It is impossible to stay...
    C. It is more impossible...
    D. None of these

50. Tony is the most happiest boy in the world.
    A. Tony is most happiest boy...
    B. Tony is the happiest boy...
    C. Tony is the most happy boy...
    D. None of these

51. Sonu is more cleverer than industrious.
    A. Sonu is more cleverer to industrious.
    B. Sonu is more clever to industrious.
    C. Sonu is more clever than industrious.
    D. None of these

52. Surjeet is better than any player in the team.
    A. Surjeet is better than any other player in the team.
    B. Surjeet is more better than any other player in the team.
    C. Surjeet is better than any players in the team.
    D. None of these

53. Rohit is my oldest son.
    A. Rohit is my most oldest son.
    B. Rohit is my eldest son.
    C. Rohit is my most eldest son.
    D. None of these

54. Sachin is more famous than any player of cricket.
    A. Sachin is more famous than any other player of cricket.
    B. Sachin is famouser than any other player of cricket.
    C. Sachin is the most famous than any other player of cricket.
    D. None of these

55. Less dresses are needed for the circus men.
    A. Lesser dresses are needed for the circus men.
    B. Fewer dresses are needed for the circus men.
    C. Least dresses are needed for the circus men.
    D. None of these

56. What is the last news?
    A. What is the newest news?
    B. What is the latest news?
    C. What is the end news?
    D. None of these

57. There are only fewer bananas left in the basket.
    A. There are only a few bananas left in the basket.
    B. There are only the few bananans left in the basket.
    C. There are only more few bananas left in the basket.
    D. None of these

58. Mukesh got cent per cent marks in Mathematics.

A. Mukesh got absolute marks in Mathematics.
  B. Mukesh got full marks *or* hundred per cent marks in Mathematics.
  C. Mukesh got up to date marks in Mathematics.
  D. None of these
59. Tony is a miser boy.
  A. Tony is miser boy.
  B. Tony is miser.
  C. Tony is a miser.
  D. None of these
60. John has spent little money he had.
  A. John has spent the little money he had.
  B. John has spend a little money he had.
  C. John has spent more little money he had.
  D. None of these
61. Sandeep is five years smaller than I *or* me.
  A. Sandeep is five years more smaller than I.
  B. Sandeep is five years smaller to I.
  C. Sandeep is five years younger than I *or* me.
  D. None of these
62. My pants are more inferior than you.
  A. My pants are more inferior than yours.
  B. My pants are inferior to yours.
  C. My pants are inferior than yours.
  D. None of these

63. My mother bought no fewer than five kilos of sugar.
  A. My mother bought no less than five kilos of sugar.
  B. My mother bought no the little than five kilos of sugar.
  C. My mother bought no little than five kilos of sugar.
  D. None of these
64. My brother needs as much as five thousand rupees.
  A. My brother needs as many as five thousand rupees.
  B. My brother needs as much more as five thousand rupees.
  C. My brother needs as more as five thousand rupees.
  D. None of these
65. Reema is the richest of all other friends.
  A. Reema is the riches of all other friend.
  B. Reema is the richest of all the friends.
  C. Reema is the richest of all the friend.
  D. None of these
66. Deepak is rather happier than you.
  A. Deepak is more happier than you.
  B. Deepak is most happier than you.
  C. Deepak is happier than you.
  D. None of these
67. I do not like these kinds of shirts.
  A. I do not like this kind of shirts.
  B. I do not like these kinds of shirts.
  C. I do not like this kinds of shirts.
  D. None of these

68. These sort of people are not liked by me.
    A. This sort of people are not liked by me.
    B. These sorts of people are not liked by me.
    C. This sort of peoples are not liked by me.
    D. None of these

69. I sat nearest to her.
    A. I sat nearer to her.
    B. I sat more nearer to her.
    C. I sat next to her.
    D. None of these

70. You are becoming clever day-by-day.
    A. You are becoming more cleverer day-by-day.
    B. You are becoming much cleverer day-by-day.
    C. You are becoming cleverer day-by-day.
    D. None of these

71. The best team won the final match.
    A. The better team won the final match.
    B. Best team won the final match.
    C. More best team won the final match.
    D. None of these

72. Open your books at nine page.
    A. Open your books in nine page.
    B. Open your books at page nine.
    C. Open your books in page nine.
    D. None of these

73. My brother bought much apples.
    A. My brother bought many apples.
    B. My brother bought much more apples.
    C. My brother bought many more apples.
    D. None of these

74. His statement is truthful.
    A. His statement is truth.
    B. His statement is true.
    C. His statement is more true.
    D. None of these

75. Whole town is under water.
    A. Whole of town is under water.
    B. The whole town is under water.
    C. Whole the town is under water.
    D. None of these

76. My brother smokes seldom.
    A. My brother smokes little.
    B. My brother seldom smokes.
    C. My brother smokes less.
    D. None of these

77. Tom is enough rich to help the poor.
    A. Tom is rich enough to help the poor.
    B. Tom is enough rich than to help the poor.
    C. Tom is rich enough than to help the poor.
    D. None of these

78. It is nothing else than pride.
    A. It is nothing else but pride.
    B. It is nothing else than a pride.
    C. It is nothing else but a pride.
    D. None of these

79. It is too cold today.
    A. It is very cold today.
    B. It is too a cold today.
    C. It is very a cold today.
    D. None of these

80. I shall come back just now.
    A. I shall come back just after.
    B. I shall come back presently.
    C. I shall come back just then.
    D. None of these

81. She works quick than you.
    A. She works quickly than you.
    B. She works more quickly than you.
    C. She works much more quick than you.
    D. None of these
82. You are so nice.
    A. You are so a nice.
    B. You are very nice.
    C. You are a very nice.
    D. None of these
83. My brother met me presently.
    A. My brother met me just now.
    B. My brother met me now.
    C. My brother met me just.
    D. None of these
84. The almirah is too much heavy for me.
    A. The almirah is too heavy for me.
    B. The almirah is too very heavy for me.
    C. The almirah is much heavy for me.
    D. None of these
85. She only spent ten rupees.
    A. She spent only ten rupees.
    B. She only spent a ten rupee notes.
    C. She only spent a ten rupee note.
    D. None of these
86. He speaks much fluently.
    A. He speaks very fluently.
    B. He speaks more fluently.
    C. He speaks most fluently.
    D. None of these
87. Mohan compelled Sonu to at once leave the place.
    A. Mohan compelled Sonu at once to leave the place.
    B. Mohan compelled Sonu to leave the place at once.
    C. Mohan compelled Sonu leave the place to at once.
    D. None of these
88. I shall tomorrow go there.
    A. I shall tomorrow went there.
    B. I shall tomorrow there go.
    C. I shall go there tomorrow.
    D. None of these
89. I visit the castle often.
    A. I visit often the castle.
    B. I often visit the castle.
    C. I visit the often castle.
    D. None of these
90. He tried to hurriedly reach the hotel.
    A. He tried to reach the hotel hurriedly.
    B. He hurriedly tried to reach the hotel.
    C. He tried to hurriedly the hotel reach.
    D. None of these
91. He ran very fastly.
    A. He ran much fastly.
    B. He ran most fastly.
    C. He ran very fast.
    D. None of these
92. Ravi is very wiser than Yogesh.
    A. Ravi is many wiser than Yogesh.
    B. Ravi is much wiser than Yogesh.
    C. Ravi is too wiser than Yogesh.
    D. None of these
93. You should speak the truth always.
    A. You should always speak the truth.
    B. You should speak always the truth.

C. You always should speak the truth.
D. None of these

94. She is wonderful beautiful.
   A. She is wonderfully beautiful.
   B. She is wonderfully beautify.
   C. She is wonderful beautify.
   D. None of these

95. It is very cold to go out.
   A. It is very too cold to go out.
   B. It is much too cold to go out.
   C. It is too cold to go out.
   D. None of these

Answers

1	2	3	4	5	6	7	8	9	10
B	D	B	D	B	C	C	C	A	A
11	12	13	14	15	16	17	18	19	20
A	C	A	B	A	A	C	A	D	C
21	22	23	24	25	26	27	28	29	30
C	C	C	A	A	B	A	C	D	B
31	32	33	34	35	36	37	38	39	40
A	C	C	B	D	A	B	C	D	C
41	42	43	44	45	46	47	48	49	50
A	B	C	A	B	C	C	C	B	B
51	52	53	54	55	56	57	58	59	60
C	A	B	A	B	B	A	B	C	A
61	62	63	64	65	66	67	68	69	70
C	B	A	A	B	C	A	A	C	C
71	72	73	74	75	76	77	78	79	80
A	B	A	B	B	B	A	A	A	B
81	82	83	84	85	86	87	88	89	90
B	B	A	A	A	A	B	C	B	A
91	92	93	94	95					
C	B	A	A	C					

❑❑❑

PREPOSITIONS

Directions (Qs. 1-50): *Fill in the blanks with suitable prepositions.*

1. Children should be able to adopt ..... harsh weather conditions.
   A. to   B. with
   C. in   D. onto

2. The boat which was rowed with only one oar went ..... in circles, only when it was rowed with both the oars, it moved.
   A. around   B. round
   C. away   D. about

3. The Sergeant was returning from a New Year eve dinner with friends when he chanced ..... five drunken passengers ..... a taxi harassing girl.
   A. upon, in   B. against, in
   C. at, inside D. on, inside

4. In most parts of the city there were huge traffic jams with vehicles backed up ..... miles.
   A. to B. at
   C. through D. for

5. The huge surge in foreign exchange reserves ..... the current financial year should be a cause ..... concern to the policymakers.
   A. of, for B. of, of
   C. in, for D. in, of

6. Celebrations transform our life of routine and boredom .... rejuvenation and rejoicing.
   A. towards B. unto
   C. into D. to

7. Miserly people are incapable of trusting life and that's why life does not open its treasures ..... them.
   A. to B. for
   C. within D. towards

8. There are so many people of Indian origin settled ..... the globe, from different professions.
   A. throughout B. across
   C. round D. wide

9. Fluctuations in business fortunes is another reason for companies going in .... a floating workforce.
   A. to B. towards
   C. through D. for

10. She hopes to be a teacher but her real talent lies in wielding the brush .... aplomb.
    A. in B. with
    C. beyond D. into

11. Thousands of young patriotic Indians responded to Vivekananda's clarion call and jumped whole-heartedly ...... the freedom struggle.
    A. for B. to
    C. in D. into

12. Today, the youth are so self-centered, they are not bothered ..... the poverty around them.
    A. about B. with
    C. to D. for

13. Many NRIs are looking ..... investing in India like buying homes.
    A. for B. to
    C. into D. at

14. The new Science and Technology Policy rightly seeks to put in place simplified administrative and financial procedures that will hopefully breathe fresh life........Indian science.
    A. within B. in
    C. into D. for

15. She is not the only artist to have faced threats from underworld but she is the only one brave to talk ..... them.
    A. about B. on
    C. relating D. upon

16. Life would be fun without any restraint imposed ..... belonging to one religion.
    A. for B. by
    C. at D. on

17. There has been a large accession of books .... the library.
    A. at B. to
    C. for D. in

18. His aggressive way of dealing ..... people will make many misconstrue his actions.
    A. of B. at
    C. with D. in

19. He felt it to be an insult .... his pride when I did not believe his words.
    A. in B. at
    C. on D. to

20. The new hospital provides ample amenities ..... the patients.
    A. for B. to
    C. through D. towards

21. Literature cannot close its eyes ..... the ambient society.
    A. upon B. on
    C. against D. to

22. The monetary help that he rendered .... the most appropriate moment was really appreciable.
    A. in B. at
    C. to D. into

23. He had no option but to resign from the office after the defamation heaped ..... him.
    A. against B. on
    C. upon D. around

24. His habit of interfering made him extremely unpopular ..... his colleagues.
    A. in B. against
    C. on D. at

25. His ignoble tastes are ..... variance with his elevated social status.
    A. in B. against
    C. on D. at

26. It is difficult for an over-scrupulous person to live ..... coarse people.
    A. in B. amongst
    C. around D. between

27. After the earthquake, the whole city appeared to be .... a shambles.
    A. at B. in
    C. on D. upon

28. ...... circumstances compelled him, the lazy refused to work for his living.
    A. Till B. Until
    C. Since D. After

29. A shocked nation was trying to come to terms ..... the sudden death of the Prime Minister.
    A. on B. at
    C. with D. after

30. .... his passing away, the nation has lost a great patriot who made an outstanding contribution to public life.
    A. With B. On
    C. In D. After

31. He never deviated .... his commitment to serve the people of India with exceptional devotion.
    A. from B. in
    C. against D. at

32. .... this park was much bigger but recently a swimming pool has been built making it shrunk.
    A. Previously B. Formerly
    C. Earlier D. In early days

33. Indian farmers might hope ..... the forecast of rain and thunder to come true as their fields are dried of drought.
    A. for
    B. in
    C. with
    D. None of the above

34. She exuded confidence as she walked ..... the board-room for the interview.
    A. to B. in
    C. into D. at

35. It is imperative for the Indian economy to sustain high rates of growth ..... many years.
    A. for B. over
    C. through D. around

36. The use of narcotics is very much ..... the increase now especially among young people.
    A. at B. on
    C. to D. with

37. He is too much of an idealist to be concerned ..... worldly matters.
    A. with B. of
    C. to D. for

38. He carried on working late ..... the night.
    A. till B. at
    C. into D. in

39. Driving ...... the sun, we had to shade our eyes.
    A. through B. into
    C. in D. with

40. There's something strange .... the whole affair.
    A. in B. into
    C. around D. about

41. I could hardly hear the song .... the music in the background.
    A. against B. for
    C. since D. above

42. The standard of your work is well ..... the average of your class.
    A. behind B. low
    C. below D. beneath

43. His dead body was found ..... the debris caused by earthquake.
    A. below B. beneath
    C. under D. within

44. You could put it ...... to nostalgia when he talks about the old days in Delhi.
    A. law B. beneath
    C. down D. under

45. He is ...... the generation that headed West in search of fame and stayed back.
    A. of B. from
    C. in D. with

46. There are so many mistakes in these books, sometimes I feel like trying my hand ..... it.
    A. on B. upon
    C. with D. at

47. I do not remember why the curfew had been imposed but I still recollect that I was very afraid ..... it.
    A. of B. to
    C. about D. against

48. We all possess a reserve of strength and fortitude ..... which we are rarely conscious.
    A. of B. about
    C. to D. at

49. We never know life ..... we have borne its trials and hardships.
    A. till B. untill
    C. since D. before

50. Delinquency is rampant .... the youth of today.
    A. in B. around
    C. amongst D. with

Directions (Qs. 51-125): *In each of the following questions a sentence is given which may or may not be correct. Select the option which is the correct form of the sentence. If you think none of the options is correct, your answer is 'D'.*

51. I agreed to you.
    A. I agreed with you.
    B. I agreed for you.
    C. I agreed on you.
    D. None of these

52. Tony reached at the station in time.
    A. Tony reached on the station in time.
    B. Tony reached the station in time.
    C. Tony reached to the station in time.
    D. None of these

53. A gang of robbers attacked on the bank manager.
    A. A gang of robbers attacked the bank manager.
    B. A gang of robbers attacked at the bank manager.
    C. A gang of robbers attacked to the bank manager.
    D. None of these

54. He accompanied with us to Mumbai.
    A. He accompanied us to Mumbai.
    B. He accompanied to us to Mumbai.
    C. He accompanied on us to Mumbai.
    D. None of these

55. He was accused with murder.
    A. He was accused for murder.
    B. He was accused to murder.
    C. He was accused of murder.
    D. None of these

56. He was accustomed on going for a walking in the morning.
    A. He was accustomed to going for a walk...
    B. He was accustomed for going for a walk...
    C. He was accustomed at going for a walk...
    D. None of these

57. He achieved on a great success in life.
    A. He achieved a great success in life.
    B. He achieved to a great success in life.
    C. He achieved for a great success in life.
    D. None of these

58. The jury acquitted Tony for murder.
    A. The jury acquitted Tony to murder.
    B. The jury acquitted Tony of murder.
    C. The jury acquitted Tony on murder.
    D. None of these

59. Ajit was anxious on his mother's health.
    A. Ajit was anxious for his mother's health.
    B. Ajit was anxious about his mother's health.
    C. Ajit was anxious at his mother's health.
    D. None of these

60. Rupesh applied for a Principal.
    A. Rupesh applied to the post of a Principal.

B. Rupesh applied for the post of a Principal.
C. Rupesh applied on the post of a Principal.
D. None of these

61. The pen was apposed on the inkpot.
A. The pen was apposed to the inkpot.
B. The pen was apposed for the inkpot.
C. The pen was apposed with the inkpot.
D. None of these

62. Your father deals with sugar.
A. Your father deals on sugar.
B. Your father deals to sugar.
C. Your father deals in sugar.
D. None of these

63. He was ashamed to himself.
A. He was ashamed of himself.
B. He was ashamed with himself.
C. He was ashamed for himself.
D. None of these

64. He was asking on you.
A. He was asking to you.
B. He was asking after you.
C. He was asking with you.
D. None of these

65. I never aspired on such grand success in life.
A. I never aspired to such grand...
B. I never aspired with such...
C. I never aspired for such grand...
D. None of these

66. A big crowd assembled to the outside.
A. A big crowd assembled on the outside.
B. A big crowd assembled at the outside.
C. A big crowd assembled outside.
D. None of these

67. The damage due to floods was assessed for £ 8 million.
A. The damage due to floods was assessed at £ 8 million.
B. The damage due to floods was assessed on £ 8 million.
C. The damage due to floods was assessed with £ 8 million.
D. None of these

68. The gambling trends are assimilated in the modern society with lightning speed.
A. The gambling trends are assimilated into...
B. The gambling trends are assimilated to...
C. The gambling trends are assimilated with...
D. None of these

69. He has been appointed on the job of a manager.
A. He has been appointed to the job of...
B. He has been appointed for the job of...
C. He has been appointed at the job of...
D. None of these

70. I have ordered for a cup of coffee.
A. I have ordered to a cup...
B. I have ordered a cup...
C. I have ordered in a cup...
D. None of these

71. Tom resembles with his father.
A. Tom resembles to his father.
B. Tom resembles in his father.

C. Tom resembles his father.
   D. None of these
72. I am tired from you.
   A. I am tired of you.
   B. I am tired on you.
   C. I am tired with you.
   D. None of these
73. He has no faith for God.
   A. He has no faith with God.
   B. He has no faith in God.
   C. He has no faith to God.
   D. None of these
74. I lodged a complaint about the arrogant clerk.
   A. I lodged a complaint for the arrogant ...
   B. I lodged a complaint against the arrogant...
   C. I lodged a complaint on the arrogant...
   D. None of these
75. Mukesh caught Rakesh from the arm.
   A. Mukesh caught Rakesh on the arm.
   B. Mukesh caught Rakesh to the arm.
   C. Mukesh caught Rakesh by the arm.
   D. None of these
76. The manager is satisfied by your work.
   A. The manager is satisfied with your work.
   B. The manager is satisfied at your work.
   C. The manager is satisfied on your work.
   D. None of these
77. The teacher was angry with your conduct.
   A. The teacher was angry to your conduct.
   B. The teacher was angry on your conduct.
   C. The teacher was angry at your conduct.
   D. None of these
78. The teacher was angry at you.
   A. The teacher was angry on you.
   B. The teacher was angry with you.
   C. The teacher was angry to you.
   D. None of these
79. They all contributed for the Relief Fund.
   A. They all contributed to the Relief Fund.
   B. They all contributed with the Relief Fund.
   C. They all contributed on the Relief Fund.
   D. None of these
80. His father died from cholera.
   A. His father died with cholera.
   B. His father died of cholera.
   C. His father died on cholera.
   D. None of these
81. Ramu's father died of overwork.
   A. Ramu's father died with overwork.
   B. Ramu's father died from overwork.
   C. Ramu's father died to overwork.
   D. None of these
82. He guarded himself at bad habits.
   A. He guarded himself against bad habits.

B. He guarded himself to bad habits.
C. He guarded himself of bad habits.
D. None of these

83. The old lady burst in tears.
A. The old lady burst into tears.
B. The old lady burst to tears.
C. The old lady burst for tears.
D. None of these

84. He was fond for music.
A. He was fond to music.
B. He was fond of music.
C. He was fond with music.
D. None of these

85. You are in the habit of quarrelling on trifles.
A. You are in the habit of quarrelling into trifles.
B. You are in the habit of quarrelling over trifles.
C. You are in the habit of quarrelling with trifles.
D. None of these

86. You should not be jealous with your friends.
A. You should not be jealous of your friends.
B. You should not be jealous to your friends.
C. You should not be jealous in your friends.
D. None of these

87. Naresh was convicted with the charge of theft.
A. Naresh was convicted of the charge of theft.
B. Naresh was convicted to the charge of theft.
C. Naresh was convicted for the charge of theft.

D. None of these

88. Tanu is suffering with fever.
A. Tanu is suffering to fever.
B. Tanu is suffering on fever.
C. Tanu is suffering from fever.
D. None of these

89. She is slow on studies.
A. She is slow at studies.
B. She is slow of studies.
C. She is slow in studies.
D. None of these

90. Usha is hard at hearing.
A. Usha is hard to hearing.
B. Usha is hard on hearing.
C. Usha is hard of hearing.
D. None of these

91. Priya wants to get rid from him.
A. Priya wants to get rid of him.
B. Priya wants to get rid to him.
C. Priya wants to get rid with him.
D. None of these

92. My examination begins from Saturday.
A. My examination begins at Saturday.
B. My examination begins on Saturday.
C. My examination begins in Saturday.
D. None of these

93. The tale begins on a pinkish youth Jack.
A. The tale begins with a pinkish youth Jack.
B. The tale begins to a pinkish youth Jack.
C. The tale begins upon a pinkish youth Jack.
D. None of these

94. A tragedy befell to his uncle.
    A. A tragedy befell on his uncle.
    B. A tragedy befell upon his uncle.
    C. A tragedy befell his uncle.
    D. None of these
95. He invited me for dinner.
    A. He invited me to dinner.
    B. He invited me of dinner.
    C. He invited me on dinner.
    D. None of these
96. He visited for the Taj twice.
    A. He visited the Taj twice.
    B. He visited to the Taj twice.
    C. He visited about the Taj twice.
    D. None of these
97. This food is unfit at the patient.
    A. This food is unfit on the patient.
    B. This food is unfit with the patient.
    C. This food is unfit for the patient.
    D. None of these
98. She knocked the door.
    A. She knocked upon the door.
    B. She knocked on the door.
    C. She knocked to the door.
    D. None of these
99. You have only added in my worries.
    A. You have only added to my worries.
    B. You have only added on my worries.
    C. You have only added into my worries.
    D. None of these
100. Sheila was born of the queen.
    A. Sheila was born the queen.
    B. Sheila was born to the queen.
    C. Sheila was born with the queen.
    D. None of these
101. Dev was born to poor parents.
    A. Dev was born of poor parents.
    B. Dev was born with poor parents.
    C. Dev was born at poor parents.
    D. None of these
102. Mr. Tony is famous to his novel.
    A. Mr. Tony is famous for his novel.
    B. Mr. Tony is famous with his novel.
    C. Mr. Tony is famous about his novel.
    D. None of these
103. Salman Rushdie is famous in Indians.
    A. ... is famous to Indians.
    B. ... is famous for Indians.
    C. ... is famous with Indians.
    D. None of these
104. The air escaped to the balloon.
    A. ...escaped from the balloon.
    B. ...escaped for the balloon.
    C. ...escaped on the balloon.
    D. None of these
105. He was bent upon mischief.
    A. ... was bent on mischief.
    B. ... was bent for mischief.
    C. ... was bent in mischief.
    D. None of these
106. I was introduced with his uncle.
    A. ...was introduced on his uncle.
    B. ...was introduced for his uncle.
    C. ...was introduced to his uncle.
    D. None of these
107. Beware from this dog.
    A. Beware of this...
    B. Beware to this...
    C. Beware for this...
    D. None of these

108. My shirt is superior than yours.
    A. ...is superior to yours.
    B. ...is superior from yours.
    C. ...is superior with yours.
    D. None of these
109. The poor beggar was blind with one eye.
    A. ...was blind from one eye.
    B. ...was blind in (or of) one eye.
    C. ...was blind to one eye.
    D. None of these
110. The captain was loyal for his country.
    A. ...was loyal to his country.
    B. ...was loyal with his country.
    C. ...was loyal upon his country.
    D. None of these
111. The room was infested to mosquitoes.
    A. ...was infested from mosquitoes.
    B. ...was infested on mosquitoes.
    C. ...was infested with mosquitoes.
    D. None of these
112. Mr. Kalia is kind with everybody.
    A. ...is kind for everybody.
    B. ...is kind to everybody.
    C. ...is kind on everybody.
    D. None of these
113. Don't laugh on the poor.
    A. Don't laugh upon the poor.
    B. Don't laugh at the poor.
    C. Don't laugh in the poor.
    D. None of these
114. The water of this tank is free on germs.
    A. ...is free from germs.
    B. ...is free for germs.
    C. ...is free with germs.
    D. None of these
115. The room was furnished to modern furniture.
    A. ...was furnished on modern...
    B. ...was furnished with modern...
    C. ...was furnished at modern...
    D. None of these
116. He is proud for his strength.
    A. It is proud of his strength.
    B. It is proud on his strength.
    C. It is proud with strength.
    D. None of these
117. Tagore is popular for the Indians.
    A. ...is popular on the Indians.
    B. ...is popular for the Indians.
    C. ...is popular with the Indians.
    D. None of these
118. Mr. Arora is married with the daughter of a minister.
    A. ...is married to the daughter...
    B. ...is married for the daughter...
    C. ...is married on the daughter...
    D. None of these
119. I was astonished with the sight of tiger in the street.
    A. I was astonished for the sight...
    B. I was astonished at the sight...
    C. I was astonished upon the sight...
    D. None of these
120. She has a great respect to her elders.
    A. She has a great respect for her...
    B. She has a great respect on her...
    C. She has a great respect with her...
    D. None of these
121. Miss Rita has a great zeal on the social works.
    A. Miss Rita has a great zeal for the social works.

B. Miss Rita has a great zeal at the social works.
C. Miss Rita has a great zeal with the social works.
D. None of these

122. She has a great regard with her parents.
A. She has a great regard for her...
B. She has a great regard to her...
C. She has a great regard on her...
D. None of these

123. Mrs. Smith was praying with God.
A. ...was praying for God.
B. ...was praying to God.
C. ...was praying in God.
D. None of these

124. They are steeped with ignorance.
A. They are steeped on ignorance.
B. They are steeped under ignorance.
C. They are steeped in ignorance.
D. None of these

125. Your proposal is void with reason.
A. Your proposal is void at reason.
B. Your proposal is void of reason.
C. Your proposal is void in reason.
D. None of these

Answers

1	2	3	4	5	6	7	8	9	10
A	D	A	D	C	C	A	B	D	B
11	12	13	14	15	16	17	18	19	20
D	A	D	C	A	B	B	C	D	B
21	22	23	24	25	26	27	28	29	30
A	B	C	D	D	B	B	B	C	C
31	32	33	34	35	36	37	38	39	40
B	C	A	C	B	B	A	C	B	D
41	42	43	44	45	46	47	48	49	50
D	C	B	C	B	D	A	A	B	C
51	52	53	54	55	56	57	58	59	60
A	B	A	A	C	A	A	B	B	B
61	62	63	64	65	66	67	68	69	70
A	C	A	B	A	C	A	A	A	B
71	72	73	74	75	76	77	78	79	80
C	A	B	B	C	A	C	B	A	B
81	82	83	84	85	86	87	88	89	90
B	A	A	B	B	A	A	C	A	C
91	92	93	94	95	96	97	98	99	100
A	B	A	C	A	A	C	B	A	B
101	102	103	104	105	106	107	108	109	110
A	A	C	A	A	C	A	A	B	A
111	112	113	114	115	116	117	118	119	120
C	B	B	A	B	A	C	A	B	A
121	122	123	124	125					
A	A	B	C	B					

CONJUNCTIONS

Directions (Qs. 1-30): *In the following questions choose the correct options to fill in the blanks.*

1. Hardly had he left .... his brother came.
   A. then
   B. than
   C. when
   D. that

2. I would rather have a copy .... a book.
   A. then
   B. than
   C. when
   D. that

3. He is no other .... my friend.
   A. then
   B. than
   C. when
   D. but

4. He saw a snake ....he awoke.
   A. then
   B. when
   C. than
   D. No word needed

5. Ten years have passed .... my grandmother died.
   A. since
   B. when
   C. then
   D. than

6. She is .... good .... bad.
   A. either, not
   B. neither, or
   C. neither, nor
   D. neither, than

7. The cellphone is both cheap .... best.
   A. than
   B. and
   C. then
   D. or

8. No sooner did the rogue see the police .... he disappeared.
   A. then
   B. than
   C. so
   D. because

9. Srishti will go .... Sanju goes.
   A. if
   B. than
   C. then
   D. although

10. She is wise .... timid.
    A. and
    B. yet
    C. but
    D. however

11. Neither he .... his friend is good.
    A. or
    B. and
    C. but
    D. nor

12. The officer asked the peon .... why he was late.
    A. that
    B. if
    C. but
    D. No word needed

13. Both Ajay .... Vijay are intelligent.
    A. or
    B. nor
    C. and
    D. No word needed

14. No Sooner did the thief see the public .... he ran away.
    A. then
    B. and
    C. but
    D. than

15. Abhinav .... his brothers was going to Mumbai.
    A. but
    B. yet
    C. together with
    D. No word needed

16. He behaves .... he were the captain of the team.
    A. as if
    B. as
    C. that
    D. No word needed

17. Either Rupali .... Sonali is going to attend the meeting.
    A. and B. but
    C. nor D. or
18. Neither Nirmal .... Ashwinee is going to listen the speech.
    A. and B. but
    C. nor D. or
19. Ravi .... Prakash are going to Kolkata.
    A. or B. nor
    C. but D. and
20. Rice .... curry is my usual breakfast.
    A. and B. but
    C. then D. than
21. Make hay .... the sun shines.
    A. though B. while
    C. after D. before
22. He is so weak .... he cannot walk.
    A. but B. that
    C. then D. so
23. Although he is rich, ... he is unhappy.
    A. but B. yet
    C. so D. still
24. Wait here .... I come back.
    A. till B. until
    C. before D. after
25. He is my friend .... I shall help him.
    A. so B. hence
    C. that is why D. therefore
26. He must go away .... he will be beaten.
    A. otherwise B. and
    C. or D. else
27. God loves good men .... good men love God.
    A. and B. or
    C. that D. those
28. He was late .... he was not punished.
    A. but B. yet
    C. still D. therefore
29. Walk slowly ...., you may fall.
    A. and B. or
    C. so D. otherwise
30. Work hard, ... you will fail.
    A. and B. or
    C. otherwise D. else

Directions (Qs. 31-50): *In each of the following questions a sentence is given which may or may not be correct. Select the option which is the correct form of the sentence. If you think none of the options is correct, your answer is 'D'.*

31. Although he is poor but he is honest.
    A. Although he is a poor but he is a honest.
    B. Although he is poor yet he is honest.
    C. Although he is the poor yet he is the honest.
    D. None of these
32. No sooner I step out of the house when it started raining.
    A. No sooner did I step out of the house than it started raining.
    B. No sooner did I step out of the house when it started raining.
    C. No sooner did I stepped out of the house than it started raining.
    D. None of these
33. Hardly had I step out of the house there it started raining.
    A. Hardly had I stepped out of the house when it started raining.

B. Hardly had I stepped out of the house then it started raining.
C. Hardly had I step out of the house when it started raining.
D. None of these

34. I had scarcely opened the door then a cool breeze rushed in.
    A. I had scarcely open the door when a cool breeze rushed in.
    B. Scarcely had I opened the door when a cool breeze rushed in.
    C. Scarcely had I open the door then a cool breeze rushed in.
    D. None of these

35. Tony is not only wise but honest.
    A. Tony is not only a wise boy but an honest boy.
    B. Tony is not only a wise boy but honest boy.
    C. Tony is not only wise but honest also.
    D. None of these

36. I and you am to blame
    A. I as well as you am to blame.
    B. I as well as you are to blame.
    C. I as well as you is to blame.
    D. None of these

37. Mohan is rich. Mohan help the poor.
    A. Mohan is rich yet he helps the poor.
    B. Mohan is rich and he helps the poor.
    C. Mohan is rich because he helps the poor.
    D. None of these

38. Unless you do not disclose the secret, I shall not let you go.
    A. Unless you do not disclose the secret, yet I shall not let you go.
    B. Unless you disclose the secret, I shall not let you go.
    C. Unless you disclose the secret yet I shall not let you go.
    D. None of these

39. She is as happy like you.
    A. She is as happy as you (are).
    B. She is as happy like you are.
    C. She is as happy so like you.
    D. None of these

40. This horse runs as fast like the tiger.
    A. This horse runs as fast as the tiger.
    B. This horse runs as fast as like the tiger.
    C. This horse runs as fast like as the tiger.
    D. None of these

41. Tony met no other but his fast friend Lucky.
    A. Tony met no other but than his fast friend Lucky.
    B. Tony met no other than his fast friend Lucky.
    C. Tony met no other than his fast friend but Lucky.
    D. None of these

42. My father likes such boys who are honest.
    A. My father likes such boys as are honest.
    B. My father likes such boys who as are honest.
    C. My father likes such boys those are honest.
    D. None of these

43. Work hard lest you may not fail.
    A. Work hard lest you might not fail.
    B. Work hard lest you are not fail.
    C. Work hard lest you should fail.
    D. None of these
44. Wait until I do not return.
    A. Wait until I return.
    B. Wait until I am not return.
    C. Wait until I not return.
    D. None of these
45. Both Raju as well as Ravi are intelligent boys.
    A. Both Raju and Ravi are intelligent boys.
    B. Both Raju or Ravi are intelligent boys.
    C. Both Raju as well as Ravi are intelligent.
    D. None of these
46. Neither did Rakhi attend the meeting nor Mohan attend.
    A. Neither did Rakhi attend the meeting nor did Mohan attend it.
    B. Neither did Rakhi attend the meeting nor Mohan did attend.
    C. Neither did Rakhi attend the meeting nor do Mohan.
    D. None of these
47. Neither did Sohan open the window nor his sister opened.
    A. Neither did Sohan open the window nor did his sister open it.
    B. Neither did Sohan open the window nor his sister did open.
    C. Neither did Sohan open the window nor his sister open it.
    D. None of these
48. My shirt is as good if not better than yours.
    A. My shirt is as good as if not better than yours.
    B. My shirt is as good as not better than yours.
    C. My shirt is as good if as not better than yours.
    D. None of these
49. Both of them not go there.
    A. Both of them was not go there.
    B. Neither of them *or* of the two went there.
    C. Neither of them did not go there.
    D. None of these
50. Immediately the car started I came back.
    A. At once the car started I came back.
    B. As soon as the car started I came back.
    C. Instantaneously the car started I came back.
    D. None of these

Answers

1	2	3	4	5	6	7	8	9	10
C	B	B	B	A	C	B	B	A	C
11	12	13	14	15	16	17	18	19	20
D	D	C	D	C	A	D	C	D	A
21	22	23	24	25	26	27	28	29	30
B	B	B	A	B	C	A	C	D	D

31	32	33	34	35	36	37	38	39	40
B	A	A	B	C	B	B	B	A	A
41	42	43	44	45	46	47	48	49	50
B	A	C	A	A	A	A	A	B	B

❏ ❏ ❏

SUBJECT-VERB AGREEMENT

Directions: *In the following questions, a sentence is given followed by four options. Select the option that replaces the given sentence or its part correctly.*

1. Slow and steady win the race.
   A. Slowly and steady wins the race.
   B. Slow and steadily wins the race.
   C. Slow and steady wins the race.
   D. None of these.

2. These news were broadcasted on Radio BBC.
   A. These news were broadcast on Radio BBC.
   B. This news was broadcast on Radio BBC.
   C. This news was broadcasted on Radio BBC.
   D. None of these.

3. Every boy and girl were given a prize.
   A. Every boy and girl were given prizes.
   B. Every boy and girl was given prizes.
   C. Every boy and girl was given a prize.
   D. None of these.

4. Everyone of them were clapping at the performance of the clown.
   A. Everyone of them were clapping at the performance of the clowns.
   B. Everyone of them was clapping at the performance of the clowns.
   C. Everyone of them was clapping at the performances about the clowns.
   D. None of these.

5. Law and order are to be maintained at all costs.
   A. Law and orders are to be maintained at all costs.
   B. Law and order is to be maintained at all costs.
   C. Laws and orders are to be maintained at all costs.
   D. None of these.

6. Five hundred rupees are a long sum.
   A. Five hundred rupee is a long sum.
   B. Five hundred rupee is a large sum.
   C. Five hundred rupees is a big sum.
   D. None of these.

7. Mohit, not his friends are to blame.
   A. Mohit, not his friends, is to blame.

B. Mohit, not his friend, are to blame.
C. Mohit, not his friends is, on to blame.
D. None of these.

8. I as well as you are to blame.
A. I as well as you, is to blame.
B. I as well as you are to blame.
C. I, as well as you, am to blame.
D. None of these.

9. The patient died before the doctor came.
A. The patient died before the doctor had come.
B. The patient had died before the doctor came.
C. The patient had died before the doctor had come.
D. None of these.

10. I knew that he will not respect his elders.
A. I knew that he would not respect his elders.
B. I knew that he shall not respect his elders.
C. I knew that he will not be respecting his elders.
D. None of these.

11. He is one of the greatest player who has participated in one day cricket matches.
A. He is one of the greatest players who has ....
B. He is one of the greatest players who have ....
C. He is one of the greatest players who have ....
D. None of these.

12. He behaves as if he is king.
A. He behaves as if he are a king.
B. He behaves as if he are kings.
C. He behaves as if he were a king.
D. None of these.

13. He laughed as if he were mad.
A. He laughed as if he was mad.
B. He laughed as if he had been mad.
C. He laughed as if he are mad.
D. None of these.

14. The white and the black dog is dead.
A. The white and black dog are dead.
B. The white and the black dog are dead.
C. The white and black dogs are dead.
D. None of these.

15. The painter and poet are dead.
A. The painter and the poet is dead.
B. The painter and poets are dead.
C. The painter and poet is dead.
D. None of these.

16. The committee has announced their decision.
A. The committees has announced their decision.
B. The committee has announced its decision.
C. The committee have announced its decision.
D. None of these.

17. I wish I am a millionaire.
A. I wish I was a millionaire.
B. I wish I are a millionaire.
C. I wish I were a millionaire.
D. None of these.

18. A large number of students is absent.
    A. A large numbers of students is absent.
    B. A large number of students are absent.
    C. A large number of student is absent.
    D. None of these.
19. Walking on the road, I met one of my old friends.
    A. When I was walking on the road, I met one of my old friend.
    B. When I was walking on the road, I met one of my old friends.
    C. Walking on the road, I met one of my friend.
    D. None of these.
20. Our only guide were the stars.
    A. Our only guide were the star.
    B. Our only guides was the star.
    C. Our only guide was the stars.
    D. None of these.
21. Renu is living in this house since 2012.
    A. Renu is living in this house for 2012.
    B. Renu has been living in this house for 2012.
    C. Renu has been living in this house since 2012.
    D. None of these.
22. Better you had not to gone there.
    A. Better you had not went there.
    B. Better you had not gone there.
    C. Better had you not to go there.
    D. None of these.
23. You did not do so, nor he did.
    A. You did not do so, he nor did.
    B. You did not do so, nor did he.
    C. You did not do so, he did nor.
    D. None of these.
24. Hardly I had opened the window when a stream of cool breeze started rushing in.
    A. Hardly I had opened the window then.........
    B. Hardly had I opened the window when.........
    C. Hardly had I opened the window then.........
    D. None of these.
25. No sooner he did open the window, when the cool breeze started rushing in.
    A. No sooner did he open the window than ....
    B. No sooner did he open the window when ....
    C. No sooner he did open the window than ....
    D. None of these.
26. Neither she laughed nor I did.
    A. Neither she laughed nor did I.
    B. Neither she laughed did nor I.
    C. Neither she laughed I did nor.
    D. None of these.
27. Deepak alongwith his aunts were present in the party.
    A. Deepak alongwith his aunts were present in the parties.
    B. Deepak alongwith his aunts was present in the party.

C. Deepak alongwith his aunt were present in the party.
D. None of these.

28. Many a girls have gone to see the movie.
    A. Many a girl have gone to see the movie.
    B. Many a girls has went to see the movies.
    C. Many a girl has gone to see the movie.
    D. None of these.

29. Sohan, like Mohan, are good singers.
    A. Sohan, like Mohan, is a good singer.
    B. Sohan, like Mohan, is a good singers.
    C. Sohan, like Mohan, are a good singer.
    D. None of these.

30. The train arrived before I reached the station.
    A. The train arrived before I had reached the station.
    B. The train arrived before I have reached the station.
    C. The train had arrived before I reached the station.
    D. None of these.

31. Either he or she has done his work.
    A. Either he or she has done their works.
    B. Either he or she has done her work.
    C. Either he or she has done their work.
    D. None of these.

32. A hundred miles are a high distance.
    A. A hundred miles are a big distance.
    B. A hundred miles are a long distance.
    C. A hundred miles is a long distance.
    D. None of these.

33. 'A Tale of Two Cities' were written by Charles Dickens.
    A. 'A Tale of Two Cities' was written by Charles Dickens.
    B. 'A Tale of Two Cities' is wrote by Charles Dickens.
    C. 'A Tale of Two Cities' are wrote by Charles Dickens.
    D. None of these.

34. Many a boys were playing in the garden.
    A. Many a boy were playing in the garden.
    B. Many a boys was playing in the garden.
    C. Many a boy was playing in the garden.
    D. None of these.

35. A bandit besides his gangsters were nabbed by the police.
    A. A bandit besides his gangster were nabbed by the police.
    B. A bandit besides his gangsters was nabbed by the police.
    C. A bandits besides his gangsters was nabbed by the police.
    D. None of these.

36. The bell went when I reached the school.
    A. The bell went when I had reached the school.
    B. The bell had gone when I have reached the school.

C. The bell had gone when I reached the school.
D. None of these.

37. My teacher told me that the earth revolved round the sun.
   A. My teacher told me that the earth was revolving round the sun.
   B. My teacher told me that the earth revolves round the sun.
   C. My teacher told me that the earth had revolved round the sun.
   D. None of these.

38. Rice and curry are the favourite food of my brother.
   A. Rice and curry is the favourite food...
   B. Rice and curry are the favourite foods...
   C. Rice and curry is the favourite foods...
   D. None of these.

39. The Principal together with his staff were on a tour to the Himalayas.
   A. The Principal together with his staffs were...
   B. The Principal together with his staffs was...
   C. The Principal together with his staff was...
   D. None of these.

40. Neither Ravi nor his friends was present in the class.
   A. Neither Ravi nor his friend were present in the class.
   B. Neither Ravi nor his friends was present in the classes.
   C. Neither Ravi nor his friends were present in the class.
   D. None of these.

41. None of the ten pens are yours.
   A. None of the ten pen are yours.
   B. None of the ten pens is yours.
   C. None of the ten pens are your.
   D. None of these.

42. The captain with all his players are in the playground.
   A. The captain with all his player are in the playgrounds.
   B. The captain with all his player is in the playgrounds.
   C. The captain with all his players is in the playground.
   D. None of these.

Answers

1	2	3	4	5	6	7	8	9	10
C	B	C	B	B	C	A	C	B	A
11	12	13	14	15	16	17	18	19	20
B	C	B	B	C	B	C	B	B	C
21	22	23	24	25	26	27	28	29	30
C	B	B	B	A	A	B	C	A	C
31	32	33	34	35	36	37	38	39	40
B	C	A	C	B	C	B	A	C	C
41	42								
B	C								

❑ ❑ ❑

MODALS

Directions: *In the following questions choose the correct options to fill in the blanks:*

1. You ...... not bring the child here.
   A. have   B. had
   C. need   D. would

2. ...... you live long!
   A. Will   B. May
   C. Shall D. Can

3. ...... God help you!
   A. Can   B. Will
   C. May   D. Shall

4. ...... that I were a leader!
   A. Would B. Should
   C. Could D. Will

5. It ...... be ten o'clock now.
   A. could B. would
   C. should D. will

6. He ...... have reached the station by now.
   A. shall B. will
   C. would D. should

7. Being a receptionist, she will ...... type a letter.
   A. has to   B. have to
   C. need to D. must

8. The birds ...... fly high in the sky.
   A. may   B. should
   C. can   D. would

9. ...... I open the main gate?
   A. Should B. Would
   C. Could D. Must

10. If you played well, we ...... win the match.
    A. would B. should
    C. must   D. need

11. I think you .... not mind my reciting the poem loudly.
    A. should B. could
    C. may   D. would

12. ..... I sit here for some time?
    A. Can   B. Shall
    C. Will   D. Must

13. You ...... take the child to an intelligent doctor.
    A. shall   B. will
    C. ought to D. would

14. She ...... smoke in those days.
    A. used to B. could
    C. would   D. had to

15. If I were you I ... not attend the meeting.
    A. can   B. would
    C. could D. should

16. You .... submit your file to the authorities within a week.
    A. have   B. had
    C. should D. would

17. ...... I use your phone?
    A. Have   B. Could
    C. Would D. Had

18. ..... you give me your pen?
    A. May   B. Can
    C. Must   D. Dare

19. There ...... be an hospital at this place.
    A. have to B. may
    C. used to D. might

20. He ...... read and write when he was young.
    A. would B. could
    C. should D. can

21. He said that he ..... sing a song at the party.
    A. should   B. would
    C. can   D. will
22. She asked if he ...... help her.
    A. should   B. can
    C. must   D. would
23. We .... respect our elders.
    A. need to   B. have to
    C. ought to   D. had to
24. Nothing .... be done under such circumstances.
    A. can   B. used to
    C. must   D. have to
25. She ..... not ask about it.
    A. has   B. have
    C. had   D. dare
26. ...... that I were an actor!
    A. Would   B. Should
    C. Could   D. Will
27. Had you made one more effort you ...... have won the race.
    A. will   B. may
    C. would   D. shall
28. I ...... solve any sum.
    A. may   B. am
    C. must   D. can
29. ...... I smoke here?
    A. Can   B. Will
    C. Could   D. Must
30. The passengers .... keep watch on their luggage.
    A. has   B. have
    C. should   D. had
31. Work hard lest you .... fail.
    A. should   B. may
    C. can   D. must
32. .... I come in, madam?
    A. Can   B. May
    C. Will   D. Must
33. It ...... rain tonight.
    A. shall   B. will
    C. may   D. can
34. You ...... love your countrymen.
    A. need to   B. have to
    C. had to   D. ought to
35. .... you like some pastries?
    A. Should   B. Would
    C. Could   D. Will
36. You .... smoke here.
    A. shall not   B. will not
    C. should not D. would not
37. .... I say more about it?
    A. Need   B. Ought
    C. Should   D. Dare
38. You .... leave without my permission.
    A. mustn't
    B. ought not to
    C. may not
    D. might not
39. You .... pay full attention to your teacher.
    A. should   B. can
    C. may   D. would
40. .... that I were a billionaire!
    A. Could   B. Should
    C. Would   D. Ought
41. .... you like some biscuits?
    A. Would   B. Should
    C. Could   D. Will
42. .... I open the door?
    A. Would   B. Should
    C. Could   D. Might

43. You .... do some jogging in the morning to maintain your figure.
    A. could   B. might
    C. should   D. would
44. .... I go now or would you like to give me some more instructions?
    A. Should   B. Would
    C. Could   D. Might
45. .... you come across stale bread, you must ring me up. I .... try to ascertain who is not working honestly in my company.
    A. Would, should
    B. Could, should
    C. Could, would
    D. Should, would
46. You .... drive slow because there is a school ahead.

    A. would   B. could
    C. should   D. may
47. I .... like to check your blood pressure and once again I advise you to reduce the intake of salt.
    A. should   B. would
    C. could   D. shall
48. I .... not tell him about it if I were you.
    A. should   B. could
    C. may   D. would
49. .... you mind not drinking here? It is a hospital.
    A. Would   B. Could
    C. Should   D. Wouldn't
50. What .... he say to you if you didn't obey him?
    A. should   B. shall
    C. would   D. will

Answers

1	2	3	4	5	6	7	8	9	10
C	B	C	A	C	B	B	C	A	A
11	12	13	14	15	16	17	18	19	20
D	A	C	A	B	A	B	B	C	B
21	22	23	24	25	26	27	28	29	30
B	D	C	A	D	A	C	D	A	C
31	32	33	34	35	36	37	38	39	40
A	B	C	D	B	C	A	A	A	C
41	42	43	44	45	46	47	48	49	50
A	B	C	A	D	C	B	D	A	C

❑❑❑

TENSES

Directions (Qs. 1 to 25): *Fill in the blanks with correct present tense forms of the verbs given in brackets. Select your answer from the given options.*

1. They .... (live) in Shri Nagar for five years.

    A. are living
    B. were living
    C. has been living
    D. have been living

2. At the moment the child .... (play) in the garden.

   A. playing
   B. plays
   C. is playing
   D. has been playing

3. I .... (tell) you already about it.
   A. told   B. have told
   C. tells   D. am telling

4. If you .... (study) hard, you will secure a first division.
   A. studied   B. study
   C. have studies D. are study

5. She ....(pass) the post office on her way to school every day.
   A. is passing
   B. has been passing
   C. passes
   D. passed

6. He .... (read) since morning.
   A. have been reading
   B. has been reading
   C. is reading
   D. had been reading

7. This pen .... (cost) me ten rupees.
   A. costs   B. costing
   C. has cost   D. costed

8. He .... (wait) for me since morning.
   A. has been waiting
   B. have been waiting
   C. had been waiting
   D. is waiting

9. The sun .... (shine) by day.
   A. shining
   B. has been shining
   C. shines
   D. is shining

10. The bell .... (ring) just now.
   A. rings   B. ringing
   C. rung   D. has rung

11. She .... (attend) college since 4th July.
   A. has been attending
   B. attends
   C. is attending
   D. attended

12. Why .... (you come) late every day?
   A. do you come
   B. did you come
   C. have you come
   D. did you come

13. When he .... (meet) you, he will love you.
   A. will meet   B. is meeting
   C. meets   D. has met

14. It .... (not rain) now.
   A. does not rain
   B. did not rain
   C. has not rained
   D. is not raining

15. I .... (not yet give) up hope.
   A. have not yet given
   B. do not yet given
   C. did not yet give
   D. am not giving

16. If you ..... (be) hungry, you can eat.
   A. being   B. are
   C. have been   D. will be

17. The earth .... (move) round the sun.
   A. is moving
   B. has been moving
   C. moves
   D. moving

18. The sun .... (rise) in the east and .... (set) in the west.
   A. rising, is setting
   B. rises, sets
   C. rising, setting
   D. has been rising, has been setting

19. He .... (suffer) from malaria since day before yesterday.
    A. has been suffering
    B. have been suffering
    C. suffers
    D. is suffering
20. It .... (rain) all the year round here.
    A. has rained
    B. is raining
    C. rains
    D. has been raining
21. He .... (write) to me every month.
    A. is writing
    B. writes
    C. has been writing
    D. has been writing
22. Where .... he .... (go) to play in the evening?
    A. did, go   B. has, gone
    C. does, go   D. does, going
23. This servant .... (work) with us for ten years.
    A. works
    B. has been working
    C. is working
    D. does work
24. What time .... you .... (reach) home in the evening?
    A. do, reach
    B. does, reach
    C. did, reached
    D. have, reached
25. How .... you .... (get) on with your studies?
    A. is, get   B. do, get
    C. is, getting   D. have, got

Directions (Qs. 26 to 45): *Fill in the blanks with correct past tense forms of the verbs given in brackets. Select your answer from the given options.*

26. He ...... (buy) a car one month ago.
    A. bought
    B. has bought
    C. has been buying
    D. had been buying
27. She .... (leave) for Jammu yesterday.
    A. leaves
    B. is leaving
    C. has been leaving
    D. left
28. He .... (teach) in this college for five years.
    A. teaches
    B. is teaching
    C. taught
    D. has been teaching
29. I .... (write) to her last week.
    A. wrote
    B. have been writing
    C. had been writing
    D. written
30. He .... (be) weak in English in the beginning.
    A. being   B. been
    C. was   D. had been
31. People .... (vote) them out in the recent elections.
    A. were voting
    B. have been voting
    C. voted
    D. have voted
32. I .... (have) my breakfast at 8.30 a.m. yesterday.
    A. am having
    B. was having
    C. will be having
    D. have been doing

33. I .... (write) a letter when she knocked at the door.
    A. wrote   B. had writing
    C. have written   D. was writing
34. We .... (bathe) in the river when it was raining.
    A. were bathing
    B. have been bathing
    C. are bathing
    D. did bath
35. He .... (watch) television when I came in.
    A. watched
    B. was watching
    C. had watched
    D. has been watching
36. He .... (tell) me that he had never met you.
    A. is telling   B. did tell
    C. told   D. has told
37. He .... (arrive) before I came.
    A. was arriving
    B. is arriving
    C. had arrived
    D. has been arriving
38. He ...... (arrive) here only last night.
    A. has arrived
    B. arrived
    C. had arrived
    D. was arriving
39. If you .... (work hard), you would have passed.
    A. have worked hard
    B. had worked hard
    C. have been working hard
    D. worked hard
40. She .... (come) to see me yesterday.
    A. came
    B. has came
    C. had came
    D. had been coming
41. When I reached his home, he .... (sleep).
    A. has slept   B. had sleep
    C. was sleeping   D. slept
42. When he left this morning, the sun .... (shine).
    A. shines   B. has shone
    C. had shone   D. was shining
43. Madhu .... (not attend) the office yesterday.
    A. was not attending
    B. did not attend
    C. was not attend
    D. had not attend
44. Last year, it .... (not rain) heavily.
    A. did not rain
    B. had not rain
    C. has not rian
    D. was not rain
45. I .... (write) to him yesterday.
    A. has written
    B. and written
    C. wrote
    D. have been writing

Directions (Qs. 46 to 55): *Fill in the blanks with correct future tense forms of the verbs given in brackets. Select your answer from the given options.*

46. I don't think we .... (meet) again.
    A. are meeting
    B. will be meeting
    C. will meet
    D. can meet
47. He .... (be) here early next month.
    A. was   B. has been
    C. had been   D. will be

48. If I go to school late, the teacher .... (punish) me.
    A. is punishing
    B. punishing
    C. will punish
    D. shall punish
49. If you study hard, you .... (get) a first class.
    A. are getting
    B. will get
    C. will be getting
    D. shall get
50. He .... (leave) for Shri Nagar next week.
    A. will leave
    B. shall leave
    C. going to leave
    D. will be leaving
51. The child .... (arrange) his books in the bag.
    A. will arranging
    B. shall be arranging
    C. will be arranging
    D. have been arranging
52. Tony .... (wait) for you.
    A. will waiting
    B. shall be waiting
    C. will be waiting
    D. have been waiting
53. The peon .... (ring) the bell by 10 o'clock.
    A. shall ringing
    B. will ringing
    C. shall have rung
    D. will have rung
54. It .... (rain) for three hours.
    A. shall raining
    B. will raining
    C. shall have been raining
    D. will have been raining
55. Teena .... (sing) songs since morning.
    A. shall singing
    B. will singing
    C. will have been singing
    D. shall have been singing

Answers

1	2	3	4	5	6	7	8	9	10
D	C	B	B	C	B	C	A	C	D
11	12	13	14	15	16	17	18	19	20
A	A	C	D	A	B	C	B	A	A
21	22	23	24	25	26	27	28	29	30
B	C	B	A	B	A	D	C	A	C
31	32	33	34	35	36	37	38	39	40
C	B	D	A	B	C	C	B	B	A
41	42	43	44	45	46	47	48	49	50
C	D	B	A	C	C	D	C	B	A
51	52	53	54	55					
C	C	D	D	C					

Sentence Corrections 3

The most common errors in English are of spellings, grammar and usage of words. By learning the rules and regular practice, the errors can be easily spotted and corrected.

Directions (Qs. 1 to 150): *Read each sentence to find out whether there is any grammatical error in it. The error, if any will be in one part of the sentence. The letter of that part is the answer. If there is no error, the answer will be 'E'. (Avoid the errors of punctuation, if any).*

1. (A) He fixed a metal ladder/(B) for the wall below his window/ (C) so as to be able to/(D) escape if there was a fire./(E) No error.

2. (A) Scarcely had I/(B) finished washing the car/(C) than the master came/(D) and asked me to clean the floor of the house./(E) No error.

3. (A) Students/(B) as well as the teacher/(C) was/(D) playing./(E) No error.

4. (A) Neither Ram/(B) nor Shyam/ (C) are/(D) at fault./(E) No error.

5. (A) Neither women/(B) nor/(C) children/(D) was admitted./(E) No error.

6. (A) If I shall /(B) go to Calcutta/(C) I shall bring/(D) a beautiful watch for you./(E) No error.

7. (A) I told him that/(B) he could/ (C) go home/(D) by all mean./(E) No error.

8. (A) After the death/(B) of their father/(C) the two brothers are/ (D) having their hand at the daggers./(E) No error.

9. (A) He added insult/(B) to his wounds/(C) by making/(D) sarcastic comments./(E) No error.

10. (A) He has achieved/(B) success in life/(C) from dint of/(D) hard work./(E) No error.

11. (A) He burnt a fire/(B) and started/(C) roasting/(D) the chicken./(E) No error.

12. (A) I have written/(B) a letter/(C) at him to his Delhi address/(D) today./(E) No error.

13. (A) His favourite maxim/(B) is − cut your shirt/(C) according/(D) to the cloth./(E) No error.

14. (A) His brother/(B) Dharmender is/(C) an excellent cook/(D) is it not?/(E) No error.

15. (A) I have/(B) brought a/(C) he-duck and a she-duck/(D) for my friend./(E) No error.
16. (A) Later on he/(B) became a monk/(C) and she became/(D) a monkess./(E) No error.
17. (A) By arresting the local criminals/(B) and encouraging good people/(C) we can end/(D) hostilities of that area./(E) No error.
18. (A) The apparently obvious solutions/(B) to most of his problems/(C) were overlook by/(D) many of his friends./(E) No error.
19. (A) We decided not tell to/(B) the patient about/(C) the disease he was/(D) suffering from./(E) No error.
20. (A) The principals of equal justice/(B) for all is one of/(C) the cornerstones of our/(D) democratic way of life./(E) No error.
21. (A) The Trust has succeeded/(B) admirably in raising/(C) money for/(D) its future progra-mmes./(E) No error.
22. (A) Honesty, integrity and being intelligent/(B) are the qualities which/(C) we look for when/(D) we interview applicants./(E) No error.
23. (A) In order to save petrol,/(B) motorists must have to/(C) be very cautious/(D) while driving along the highways./(E) No error.
24. (A) The war of/(B) Panipat was/(C) won by/(D) Babar in 1526./(E) No error.
25. (A) He applied the break/(B) to stop the scooter/(C) and averted/(D) the accident./(E) No error.
26. (A) He has recruited/(B) many persons/(C) to canvas for him/(D) during the forth coming elections./(E) No error.
27. (A) His father is/(B) suffering from/(C) a serious heart attack/(D) and his death is eminent./(E) No error.
28. (A) Ram and Ramesh are/(B) fast friends/(C) the farmer is a merchant/(D) and the latter is an officer./(E) No error.
29. (A) It is a fact/(B) that Ferozepore is/(C) further than/(D) Faridkot from Delhi./(E) No error.
30. (A) I feel that/(B) I have given you/(C) very trouble/(D) in this matter./(E) No error.
31. (A) These two brothers/(B) cannot live without/(C) one another/(D) for a long time./(E) No error.
32. (A) I shall/(B) do your work/(C) in these holidays/(D) without fail./(E) No error.
33. (A) Hindustan Times/(B) of Delhi/(C) is the best/(D) newspaper in India./(E) No error.
34. (A) Gold of South Africa/(B) is exported to/(C) many/(D) countries./(E) No error.
35. (A) The chairman/(B) as well as six other/(C) members of the committee/(D) were present./(E) No error.

36. (A) Whether he will be/(B) able to come/(C) or may not/(D) depends on the train service./(E) No error.
37. (A) He requested/(B) the director/(C) to admit his son/(D) in his institution./(E) No error.
38. (A) On his way back/(B) he was absorbed with/(C) his own/(D) thoughts./(E) No error.
39. (A) She had no sooner/(B) arrived than/(C) she was asked/(D) to leave again./(E) No error.
40. (A) He counted the books/(B) to make sure that/(C) none of them/(D) were missing./(E) No error.
41. (A) Buses run along this road/(B) but today/(C) they didn't run/(D) because of a strike./(E) No error.
42. (A) This book is/(B) well printed and attractively bound/(C) making altogether/(D) an attractive volume./(E) No error.
43. (A) I/(B) am thinking/(C) you are/(D) over reacting./(E) No error.
44. (A) Tushar was trying for admission/(B) in the Medical College/(C) even though his parents wanted him/(D) to take up computers./(E) No error.
45. (A) The weather being cold and stormy/(B) we decided not to go out/(C) for the whole day and/(D) stayed indoors./(E) No error.
46. (A) The old man was leading/(B) a happy and leisurely/(C) life after his retirement/(D) from service./(E) No error.
47. (A) Normally I don't wear spectacles/(B) but today/(C) I wear one /(D) because of the sun./(E) No error.
48. (A) A little elder/(B) to myself me,/(C) both were devoted /(D) to tennis and football./(E) No error.
49. (A) You can get/(B) all the informations/(C) you want/(D) in this book./(E) No error.
50. (A) He was/(B) such a fast writer that/(C) he used to write a story/(D) during two hours./(E) No error.
51. (A) He took/(B) computer/(C) coaching for three full/(D) academic years./(E) No error.
52. (A) The government has shown /(B) a lukewarm attitude /(C) to the sufferings of /(D) the aged./(E) No error.
53. (A) It is the duty of the government /(B) of taking up measures/(C) for providing social care welfare/(D) to the old people./(E) No error.
54. (A) He is possessing/(B) this apartment/(C) for the last /(D) five years./(E) No error.
55. (A) This company/(B) manufactures/(C) many/ (D) cold drinks./(E) No error.
56. (A) Next summer/(B) there is a chance/(C) of my visiting /(D) a hill station./(E) No error.
57. (A) The boy sitting /(B)at the corner of the classroom /(C) is constantly/(D) watching at the window./(E) No error.

58. (A) Our laxity/(B) in duty increases /(C) with our dislike /(D) for work./(E) No error.
59. (A) His /(B) knowledge /(C) of English are /(D) very limited./(E) No error.
60. (A) How to solve the financial crisis /(B) is the main concern/(C) of the government/(D) at the moment./(E) No error.
61. (A) Everyone of the survivors /(B) of the train accident /(C) have told/(D) the same story./(E) No error.
62. (A) Each cigarette/(B) which /(C) a person smokes/(D) does some harm to him./(E) No error.
63. (A) As soon as the Managing Director/(B) entered the factory/(C) all the workers approached him and /(D) report the matter./(E) No error.
64. (A) He studied /(B) at /(C) the Medical College/(D) during three years./(E) No error.
65. (A) This is /(B) the painting/(C) I was /(D) telling you./(E) No error.
66. (A) The mother as well as /(B) the daughters were/(C) mysteriously missing /(D) from the house./(E) No error.
67. (A) It is/(B) extremely important /(C) for an engineer /(D) to know to use a computer./(E) No error.
68. (A) The Director has asked that/(B) each clerk and supervisor/(C) sign their name on the attendance register/(D) before leaving the office./(E) No error.
69. (A) In India/(B) as early as the nineteenth century, /(C) young boys enjoyed/(D) to play cricket./(E) No error.
70. (A) She is /(B) more clever /(C) than/(D) I thought she was./(E) No error.
71. (A) A body of volunteers/(B) have been/(C) orgnised to assist the committee/(D) in their attempt to collect funds./(E) No error.
72. (A) The blue curtain/(B) on the window/(C) provides an appropriate contrast/(D) with the pink wall./(E) No error.
73. (A) Her ability to/(B) interact and communicate with strangers/(C) is one of her/(D) stronger points./(E) No error.
74. (A) If he will follow/(B) his teacher's instructions/ (C) he will secure good marks/(D) in his examination./(E) No error.
75. (A) Sooner than she had arrived /(B) her friends arranged a dinner /(C) in her honour in the/(D) best restaurant in town./(E) No error.
76. (A) Ever since this child/(B) was taught by/(C) its new tutor/(D) it has done in exams./(E) No error.
77. (A) Children ran/(B) into the school building/(C)when/(D) the bell started ringing./(E) No error.
78. (A) To the volunteers/(B) who worked so hard/ (C) on campaigning, the election result was profound/(D) disappointing. /(E) No error.

79. (A) It is essential that/(B) AIDS is diagnosed and treated /(C) as early as possible in order/(D) to achieve a successful cure./(E) No error.
80. (A) There has been/(B) little change in the patient's condition /(C) until he was/(D) shifted to the intensive care unit./(E) No error.
81. (A) We have heard his speech/(B) many a time/(C) but today he was/ (D) best./(E) No error.
82. (A) The people gathered there / (B) were very much surprised /(C) at hearing the news of a child surviving /(D) under the debris./ (E) No error.
83. (A) Each of the candidates whom/ (B) I have chosen to contest election /(C) have indicated that/ (D) he will be happy to do so./(E) No error.
84. (A) The alarmed report of/(B) earthquake in Ahmedabad /(C) frightened everyone of /(D) the adjoining region./(E) No error.
85. (A) While interrogating, he disclosed/(B) that he used to snatch chains/(C) along with his accomplice/(D) who was recently killed in a road accident./(E) No error.
86. (A) The burning of leaves/(B) have been/(C) declared illegal in Delhi /(D) due to the pollution it causes./(E) No error.
87. (A) The decomposed body of a 13-year old boy /(B) who was / (C) suspected to have been kidnapped,/(D) was find lying./(E) No error.
88. (A) On hearing/(B) Gurmeet's screams, Surjeet/(C) came rushing /(D) and he too was stabbed./(E) No error.
89. (A) The value of the rupee/(B) declines/(C) as the rate of inflation /(D) raises./(E) No error.
90. (A) Before T.V., the common man haven't got/ (B) the opportunity /(C) to see his leaders /(D) express their views./(E) No error.
91. (A) The new model of the washing machine/(B) costs/(C) twice as much as/(D) last year's model./(E) No error.
92. (A) He hoped to finish/(B) the assignment /(C) in the last month/ (D) but in fact he could not./(E) No error.
93. (A) Everybody/(B) was in the lawn/ (C) enjoying/ (D) themselves./(E) No error.
94. (A) Nobody offered to give up / (B) their seat /(C) to the blind man /(D) holding his stick in his palm./ (E) No error.
95. (A) Subhash Chandra Bose/(B) was a great nationalist/(C) and a/ (D) great scholar./(E) No error.
96. (A) If you would have seen/(B) yesterday's cultural programme,/ (C) I am sure you /(D) would have enjoyed watching the little ones dance./(E) No error.
97. (A) In evaluating your progress/(B) I have taken/ (C) into account your classroom performance, your attendance, your sincerity and / (D) how you have improved./(E) No error.

98. (A) Although the marks/(B) obtained in written examination by both the candidates/(C) are same yet the/(D) differences among them are considerable in the marks obtained in interview./(E) No error.

99. (A) Aristotle systematically /(B) set out the various forms of the syllogism/(C) that has remained /(D) an essential reference for logic./(E) No error.

100. (A) The lucky number will be announced/(B) just one time; therefore,/(C) you must listen /(D) very careful in order to tally your own number./(E) No error.

101. (A) Every citizen /(B) should cast vote /(C) for the candidate /(D) of their choice./(E) No error.

102. (A) I don't even/(B) let anyone know/(C) about what /(D) all I am dealing with./(E) No error.

103. (A) Today, while standing/(B) at the crossroads of life, and /(C) nowhere to go,/(D) I see life to be meaningless./(E) No error.

104. (A) Travelling deep down the memory lane, I find it /(B) fairly difficult/(C) to reach out to the early days /(D) when I was still a toddler./(E) No error.

105. (A) What we do,/(B) has some effect on others and /(C) so has their actions /(D) upon us./(E) No error.

106. (A) Very few persons march/(B) straight to succeed,/(C) without going through/(D) periods of temporary failure and discouragement./(E) No error.

107. (A) You can find many persons/(B) who have made fortunes because /(C) their mind /(D) were well focussed on success./(E) No error.

108. (A) The unexpected increased demand of this newspaper everyday /(B) from all over India/ (C) is a matter of great satisfaction and motivation/(D) for the editor./(E) No error.

109. (A) I believe /(B) you to have read/ (C) the latest issue /(D) of this magazine./(E) No error.

110. (A) Was it her/(B) who got injured/(C) when the stove/(D) bursted?/(E) No error.

111. (A) I doubt/(B) if Vineet/(C) has few /(D) than twenty tatoos./(E) No error.

112. (A) As long as/(B) the rain/(C) continued/(D) I stayed at home./ (E) No error.

113. (A) I have cooked/(B) for two hours /(C) and I am /(D) now tired./(E) No error.

114. (A) At the moment Sachin /(B) play/ (C) in /(D) the garden./(E) No error.

115. (A) The song sang/(B) by her/(C) was appreciated /(D) by everyone. /(E) No error.

116. (A) He said/(B) he would go/(C) to see a movie/ (D) this evening./(E) No error.

117. (A) Will you/(B) kindly/(C) wait / (D) for his return./(E) No error.

118. (A) He was/(B) so serious/(C) when /(D) he died./(E) No error.

119. (A) You will/(B) not succeed/(C) if you won't/ (D) try./(E) No error.

120. He is (A) the most intelligent student/(B) of the class/(C) yet he/(D) failed./(E) No error.

121. (A) The day is gone/(B) when one had /(C) to run from pillar to post to borrow money /(D) to study abroad./(E) No error.

122. (A) I follow/(B) your magazine/(C) for the/(D) the past two years./(E) No error.

123. (A) Have you ever/(B) came acrossed a painting by Picasso and/(C) found yourself engulfed in a brightly coloured canvas which your senses/(D) cannot interpret./(E) No error.

124. (A) I agree /(B) in part with/(C) many of these arguments and/(D) even at one time endorsed them./(E) No error.

125. (A) With /(B) our every acts,/(C) the world reveals to us/(D) a new face./(E) No error.

126. (A) Very early/(B) we are/(C) going to /(D) advertise it./(E) No error.

127. (A) Our arena is /(B) not only India/(C) but we want our presence/(D) to be felt internationally as a centre of excellence./(E) No error.

128. (A) There is a review of/(B) each and every /(C) articles being published /(D) in our journal./(E) No error.

129. (A) By the advent of cable television,/(B) at the beginning of /(C) this decade, the entertain-ment industry/(D) took a giant stride forward in our country./(E) No error.

130. (A) Only you know/(B) what is best for you, so be strong and bold and/(C) have to take decisions and be prepared /(D) to live with them forever./(E) No error.

131. Group involvement/(A) will be entertaining/(B) but expensive,/(C) ultimately if you/(D) don't stop spending on others./(E) No error.

132. (A) Being vengeful/(B) will not bring any result,/(C) instead /(D) you should keep a cool head./(E) No error.

133. (A) You are advised to/(B) not to nag/(C) anyone or /(D) criticise their actions./(E) No error.

134. (A) Handling the situation/(B) patiently and diplomatically/(C) is the only way/(D) to favourable results./(E) No error.

135. (A) Your earnings although for/(B) the moment/(C) will be more or less the same, /(D) your future looks more promising./(E) No error.

136. He is (A) one of those persons/(B) who I am sure,/(C) always do his best /(D) even in most difficult circumstances./(E) No error.

137. (A) Do you insist/(B) that we meet/(C) at least once to discuss/(D) on the subject./(E) No error.

138. (A) I must have fallen several times before I could stand walk and then run./(B) Having learnt that,/(C) I surely do remember how frantically /(D) I am running all my life./(E) No error.

139. (A) Renowned Japanese Attorney at Law and visiting Professor/(B) at both Harvard and Yale law schools Mr./(C) Yasuharu Nagashima pondered on corporate governance and structural/(D) changes in Asian society./(E) No Error.

140. (A) The IOC has also submitted a proposal/(B) to the government to/(C) spread the capacity of the six million tonnes refinery to/(D) nine million tonnes at an estimated cost of ₹ 1605 crore./(E) No Error.

141. (A) The Minister asked the Deputy Commissioner to arrange/(B) exact water supply in the complex/(C) and arrangement for the construction/(D) of judicial lock-up in the district courts./(E) No Error.

142. (A) Congress workers in Delhi looked enthusiastic for the first time in a decade/(B) and half as Mrs. Sonia Gandhi gave a boost to their party's campaign for/(C) the Delhi Assembly elections by launching an all-out, no-holds-barred/(D) broadside against the BJP government./(E) No Error.

143. (A) With the arrest of two persons,/(B) the police claims to have busted an inter-state gang of/(C) cheat, according to Mr P. Shukla/(D) district police chief./(E) No Error.

144. (A) At least 50 persons were feared dead/(B) in flooding and landslides in South Korea/(C) as Typhoon Olga walked into the country packing more/(D) heavy rain and strong winds./(E) No Error.

145. (A) After years of investigating Hillary Rodham Clinton,/(B) Whitewater prosecutors laid out/(C) their case in an indictment that/(D) does not charge her with wrongdoing but accuses her former law partner of 15 felonies./(E) No Error.

146. (A) A week after they sentenced to/(B) death for assassination Bangladesh's founding father Sheikh Mujibur Rahaman/(C) four out of the 15 convicts/(D) have moved the High Court against the trial court order./(E) No Error.

147. (A) A spies racket involved in passing on/(B) sensitive defence documents to/(C) Pakistani intelligence officials here/(D) was busted today with the arrest of a man from Bengal./(E) No Error.

148. (A) Russian security forces and/(B) a band of attackers waged two furious/(C) gun battles near breakway Chechnya,/(D) leaving four officers and at least 10 militants dead./(E) No Error.

149. (A) At least 15 persons were/(B) feared drowned/(C) when a boat capsized/(D) midstream in Ganga./(E) No Error.

150. (A) Hectic construction activities/(B) that had been taking place/(C) here for the past two decades had/(D) rotten the town's natural drainage./(E) No Error.

Answers

1	2	3	4	5	6	7	8	9	10
B	C	C	C	D	A	D	D	B	C
11	12	13	14	15	16	17	18	19	20
A	C	B	D	C	D	C	C	A	A
21	22	23	24	25	26	27	28	29	30
E	A	B	A	A	C	D	C	C	C
31	32	33	34	35	36	37	38	39	40
C	C	A	A	D	C	D	B	A	D
41	42	43	44	45	46	47	48	49	50
C	C	B	B	D	A	C	B	D	D
51	52	53	54	55	56	57	58	59	60
A	E	B	A	C	E	D	D	C	E
61	62	63	64	65	66	67	68	69	70
C	B	D	D	D	B	D	C	D	C
71	72	73	74	75	76	77	78	79	80
B	D	D	A	A	B	E	D	B	C
81	82	83	84	858	6	87	88	89	90
D	C	C	A	A	B	D	A	D	A
91	92	93	94	95	96	97	98	99	100
E	A	D	B	D	A	D	D	C	D
101	102	103	104	105	106	107	108	109	110
D	C	A	B	A	B	B	A	E	A
111	112	113	114	115	116	117	118	119	120
C	A	A	B	A	E	D	C	C	C
121	122	123	124	125	126	127	128	129	130
A	A	B	D	B	A	B	C	A	C
131	132	133	134	135	136	137	138	139	140
C	C	A	D	A	C	D	D	C	C
141	142	143	144	145	146	147	148	149	150
B	B	C	C	E	B	A	E	D	D

❏ ❏ ❏

Sentence Improvement 4

One may use the same words in many ways but the best way is only one that makes the perfect usage of the words and conveys the proper meaning of the expression. Try it yourself in the following questions.

Directions: *In these questions, a part of the sentence is bold. Below are given alternatives to the bold part at A, B and C which may improve the sentence. Choose the correct alternative. In case no improvement is needed, your answer is D.*

1. For most people who exercise **at the** morning, there is no getting around the question: Eat and run? Or run and eat later?
   A. in the
   B. in
   C. at the time of
   D. No Improvement

2. Are ad agencies even attempting to peer into the keyhole of this indulgence sanctum to garner consumer insights **ahead of** the curve?
   A. above
   B. over
   C. within
   D. No Improvement

3. Too many people rush into the world of credit and don't stop to think about how **their actions could affect their** credit score and ability to qualify for credit in the future.
   A. their actions may affect their
   B. their actions might affect their
   C. their actions will affect their
   D. No Improvement

4. According to the report, **number of deal with** vaccines were energized by concerns around avian flu, SARS, and biodefense products, while looming patent expirations led to more deals in generics.
   A. number of deals in
   B. number of deal in
   C. number of deals with
   D. No Improvement

5. This is how the Bombay High Court responded to the state government's purported **moral stand which** dance bars were causing grave harm to society.
   A. moral stand in
   B. moral stand at
   C. moral stand that
   D. No Improvement

6. If you have a high credit limit, use **at least a** third of it.
   A. atleast a
   B. at last a
   C. utmost a
   D. No Improvement

7. Fitness experts will say that **first eating provides** fuel for a proper workout.
   A. eating in the beginning provides
   B. first eat provides
   C. eating first provides
   D. No Improvement

8. One study that examined the claim directly found that a group of people did **burned much calories from fat on days** when they exercised on an empty stomach than on days when they had a small breakfast first.
   A. burn more calories from fat on days
   B. burn more calorie from fat on days
   C. burnt more calories from fat on days
   D. No Improvement

9. Carefree children spent their afternoons **to run about barefoot,** their clothes dusty, and telltale twigs of the neighbour's mango tree in their hair.
   A. running barefoot in the sun
   B. run about barefoot in the sun
   C. running about barefoot in the sun
   D. No Improvement

10. A year ago, a 13-year-old girl attempted suicide because her mother **refuses to pay his** mobile bills.
    A. refuses to pay her
    B. refused to pay her
    C. refused to pay his
    D. No Improvement

11. Discreet salience **is extremely important** to create that 'irresistible-yet-unattainable' image for brands that want to take India seriously
    A. was extremely important
    B. is mainly important
    C. was important extremely
    D. No Improvement

12. This, over a designer outfit that he wanted for a friend's party and **that his sensitive** parents refused him.
    A. which his sensitive
    B. which his insensitive
    C. that his insensitive
    D. No Improvement

13. Goa was full of non-Goa property hunters **rushing about buying up the place** like tomorrow was an expired lease.
    A. rushing in buying up the place
    B. rushed about buying up the place
    C. rushing about to buy up the place
    D. No Improvement

14. Property hunting is a **tired and hungry** making business.
    A. is a tiresome and hungry
    B. is a tiring and hungry
    C. is a tiring and waste
    D. No Improvement

15. Cultural differences aside, **till luxury need speaks** in a manner that befits.
    A. luxury still needs to speak
    B. luxury still need to speak
    C. luxury till need to speak
    D. No Improvement

16. Indian food—the culinary avatar of the subcontinent's social history presented on a platter—**is without doubt the best food** in the world.
    A. is undoubtly the greatest food
    B. is without doubt greatest food
    C. is best food without doubt
    D. No Improvement

17. It must retain the language of poetry. **It needed to create** stories, and not statements.
    A. It needed creating
    B. It needs creating
    C. It needs to create
    D. No Improvement

18. Asia-Pacific has become the first region **to reach aggregate profiting** in biotech.
    A. to reach aggregated profitability
    B. to reach aggregate profitability
    C. to reach aggregate of profit
    D. No Improvement

19. India is deviating to embrace the West. If Western luxury brands deviate a little, **albeit selectively**, they will find rich Indian arms open far and wide.
    A. though selectively
    B. however selectively
    C. albeit selectedly
    D. No Improvement

20. China and India continued to attract attention and deals, motivated by the desire to increase access to these **largest and growing** drug markets and by the need to lower the costs of drug development.
    A. larger and growing
    B. large and growing
    C. larger and grown
    D. No Improvement

21. Luxury brands are **still above of the** clover curve here, with their elite (small) audiences.
    A. still ahead of the
    B. still in the
    C. still far of the
    D. No Improvement

22. Agencies **hence needed to be** sure of returns before investing, say ad men.
    A. hence needs to be
    B. so needs to be
    C. hence need to be
    D. No Improvement

23. India is still a nascent market and that's the spirit everyone's **looking at it**.
    A. looking for it
    B. looking in it
    C. looking with it
    D. No Improvement

24. Questioning the state's move to allow women to serve liquor but not dance in bars **of the ground that** dancing aroused physical lust.
    A. on the grounds that
    B. of the grounds that
    C. over the grounds that
    D. No Improvement

25. For England the positives from their crushing series lose come in the shape of James Anderson and Kevin Pietersen, **both of which** have made significant strides up the rankings.
    A. both of which
    B. both of whom
    C. both of who
    D. No Improvement

26. International campaigns can work well for luxury here, **but context cannot be** ignored.
    A. so context cannot be
    B. but context cannot
    C. but context couldn't
    D. No Improvement

27. For one, the Indian luxury context, **while evolved rapidly**, still has its own meaning, and its own implications.
    A. while evolved rapid
    B. which evolving rapidly
    C. while evolving rapidly
    D. No Improvement

28. But too much of availability can compromise a luxury brand or **made it lose** its lustre.
    A. make her lose
    B. make him lose
    C. make it lose
    D. No Improvement

29. Still, it's under-the-upper **layers themselves who** are aspiring for slivers of luxury.
    A. layers themselves which
    B. layer itself who
    C. layers themself which
    D. No Improvement

30. It is like saying Hindi movies, with skimpily dressed dancers, would **effect public** order.
    A. effect your
    B. affect public
    C. affected public
    D. No Improvement

31. The court held that a few women being involved in prostitution was no **justice to deny other** bar girls the right to livelihood.
    A. justification to declare other
    B. justification to deny other
    C. justice to let other
    D. No Improvement

32. All-rounder Irfan Pathan has also made some progress **over the** player rankings.
    A. above the
    B. at the
    C. up the
    D. No Improvement

33. A former PM **joined hands** with a suspended Lok Sabha member to float a new political outfit.
    A. folded hands
    B. walked hand in hand
    C. shaked hands
    D. No Improvement

34. Pakistan's two former PMs had met in London **to ask** a strategy to return home from exile.
    A. to chalk out
    B. to negotiate
    C. to create
    D. No Improvement

35. It's a family potboiler, medical thriller and political drama **all in**

one—except that it's all too real and all too grim.
A. all 3 in one
B. all coupled into one
C. all rolled into one
D. No Improvement

36. India's efforts to get international support for its civil nuclear energy programme got **a go ahead on** Sunday as Germany indicated it would not come in the way of the India-US nuclear deal.
A. a life in
B. a boost on
C. a boost at
D. No Improvement

37. Is it time for old bungalows to **bite the dust**?
A. go down
B. get down
C. come down
D. No Improvement

38. The bungalows was an outward manifestation of a certain **way in life**, and with that era gone.
A. way for life
B. way of life
C. way at life
D. No Improvement

39. The builder Mittals will reportedly **raise their money**-raking high-rise behind it.
A. highten their money
B. rise their money
C. raise there money
D. No Improvement

40. The impatient present has usually demolished **more of the** past before we wake up to the irretrievable loss.
A. much of
B. much of their
C. much of the
D. No Improvement

41. Preservation is a romantic notion; demolition **quiet** more practical reasons.
A. has many
B. had many
C. have many
D. No Improvement

42. You must get back to your **charming self** and impress the audience with your social skills.
A. own self
B. main self
C. own uniqueness
D. No Improvement

43. Stay focused on your goals and don't **get disturbed by** non-materialistic possessions.
A. get involved by
B. get betrayed by
C. get distracted by
D. No Improvement

44. You may appear more optimistic than your detractors **may want it to be**.
A. want you to be
B. wish yourself to be
C. seek you be
D. No Improvement

45. There are a number of mineral springs in the Czech territory, which **has been used** for medicinal purposes since the early 15th century.
A. have been used
B. had been used
C. has being used
D. No Improvement

46. The picturesque mountains **offers** excellent bungee jumping spots.
    A. shows
    B. provides
    C. offer
    D. No Improvement

47. Begin your **meal with** traditional faves like potato soup, beef soup with liver dumplings or dill soup made from sour milk.
    A. meals with
    B. meal in
    C. meals of
    D. No Improvement

48. You can also **go to the** National Museum building and the famous Prague State Opera.
    A. went to
    B. visit the
    C. saw
    D. No Improvement

49. If they close the Gulf for a **length of time** to shipping, then certainly we could look at $150, probably higher.
    A. larger amount of time
    B. larger duration of time
    C. larger amount of hours
    D. No Improvement

50. **More of them** are owned by the state and even the privately-owned ones are open to the public.
    A. Most of which
    B. Most of them
    C. Most of all
    D. No Improvement

51. Constructed in the ninth century by the Prince Booivoj, the castle has transformed **oneself** from a wooden fortress surrounded by earthen bulwarks to the imposing form it has today.
    A. himself
    B. herself
    C. itself
    D. No Improvement

52. Apart from frequent art exhibitions, **their are also** permanent collections devoted to archaeology, anthropology, mineralogy, natural history and numismatics.
    A. there is also
    B. there are also
    C. their are also
    D. No Improvement

53. You can visit the Czech Museum of Fine Arts, **at a** permanent exhibition on Czech Kubism.
    A. with a
    B. for a
    C. in a
    D. No Improvement

54. Tensions **above** Iran come at a time of strong demand for energy.
    A. under
    B. inside
    C. over
    D. No Improvement

55. Because its shores line the narrow Straits of Hormuz, Iran **could quickly hit** both military and commercial shipping.
    A. will quickly hit
    B. shall quickly hit
    C. will be quick hitting
    D. No Improvement

56. US **can launch** strikes at uranium enrichment facilities in Iran.
    A. might launch
    B. could launch
    C. might launched
    D. No Improvement

57. Trust your instincts and **see** all hurdles.
    A. get freedom from
    B. visualize
    C. overcome
    D. No Improvement

58. You may lose the war, but with calm, poise and serenity you will win the big battle **that may be following**.
    A. that may follows
    B. that may follow
    C. that might be following
    D. No Improvement

59. **There is times** when your best efforts could prove fruitless because of wrong timing.
    A. There are time
    B. There are times
    C. There is time
    D. No Improvement

60. You'll be a little more romantic and may want to **go away** from the hustle-bustle around you.
    A. get away
    B. have get away
    C. got away
    D. No Improvement

61. All you want are a few more hugs of affection, which will not be too difficult **to come**.
    A. to come by
    B. to came
    C. to come in
    D. No Improvement

62. People **around you** could get too sensitive, but try to respect them for that perhaps it will help you during pay-back time.
    A. by you
    B. about you
    C. near you
    D. No Improvement

63. Success **is a made up of** good fortune and hard work.
    A. is
    B. is a
    C. is a blend of
    D. No Improvement

64. The flower style and placement can completely change **the feel of** a room.
    A. the feeling of
    B. the feeling for
    C. a feel of
    D. No Improvement

65. The material (of artificial flower), style of arrangement and location should **complementing each other**.
    A. complement one another
    B. complement each other
    C. complement other
    D. No Improvement

66. Houses with **more of** carvings in their interiors, can go for gerberas.
    A. many
    B. lots of
    C. lot of
    D. No Improvement

67. For an artistic look, have lots of cherry blossoms **put together** in a vase.
    A. together

B. jumbled together
C. made together
D. No Improvement

68. If you **have heavy carving** furniture, go for an arrangement in a container with an antique touch.
    A. have heavy carved
    B. had heavy carved
    C. had heavy carving
    D. No Improvement

69. For a traditional party, such as Diwali or Holi, traditional marigold and jasmine are **a best option**.
    A. the better option
    B. the best option
    C. the best options
    D. No Improvement

70. Don't expose to direct sun or keep them **under fan and near an AC**.
    A. under fan or near an AC
    B. beside fan or near an AC
    C. under fan or under an AC
    D. No Improvement

71. Use of disprin and aspirin **help the** buds to bloom faster.
    A. helped the
    B. helps in the
    C. helps the
    D. No Improvement

72. If you prefer the lived-in comfy look, clear glass flower vases **make for** cheerful addition.
    A. makes for
    B. make for a
    C. makes for a
    D. No Improvement

73. Cut the stem of the flower every other day. This helps it to consume water and last for a **longer duration of time**.
    A. longer span of time
    B. longer period of time
    C. larger period of time
    D. No Improvement

74. The ability to trust others, and understand the needs of others, is **directly relates** to touching.
    A. directly relating
    B. directly related
    C. direct relation
    D. No Improvement

75. Touch and positive attitudes **has been proven** to go together.
    A. have been proven
    B. have been proved
    C. have been prove
    D. No Improvement

76. New Delhi **was watching the** political thriller unfold in the hilly kingdom with apparent nervousness.
    A. was watching the
    B. is watching the
    C. was watching a
    D. No Improvement

77. Anti-monarch agitators cheer **on top of a** bus in Kathmandu on Tuesday.
    A. above a
    B. at the top of a
    C. above the
    D. No Improvement

78. Indian Railway Catering and Tourism Corporation an autonomous body under the railways ministry, **has drawing up** a plan to open 2000 such stalls which would serve standard food.

    A. has drawed up
    B. have drawn up
    C. has drawn up
    D. No Improvement

79. The stalls are **to come** up at "A" and "B" grade station.
    A. likely to be coming
    B. likely to come
    C. like to come
    D. No Improvement

80. To avoid controversies, IRCTC also **plans to continue** samosa-chai stalls which currently dot stations.
    A. plan to continue
    B. plan's to continue
    C. plan to continuing
    D. No Improvement

81. Airbus has been quietly pitching the standing-room only option to Asian carriers, though **none had agreed** to it yet.
    A. none have been agreed
    B. none have being agreed
    C. none have agreed
    D. No Improvement

82. High fuel costs, for example, are **making it difficult for** carriers to turn a profit.
    A. making difficult for
    B. making difficulty for
    C. making it as difficult as
    D. No Improvement

83. The new seat technology alone, **when used in** add more places for passengers, can add millions in additional annual revenue.
    A. used to
    B. when used to
    C. when using to
    D. No Improvement

84. While you may never win the lottery, **able to** get cash for paper assets is a sure bet.
    A. being able to
    B. getting able to
    C. in being able to
    D. No Improvement

85. At Chattarpur Enclave, **the first thing** that hits you is a massive under construction illegal building where work has been stopped.
    A. a first thing
    B. one of the first thing
    C. the first best thing
    D. No Improvement

86. Multi-storeyed housing units would be constructed through public private partnership **at the land** occupied by slum-dwellers.
    A. in the land
    B. on the land
    C. over the land
    D. No Improvement

87. In view of the **few availability of** land, the ministry has decided to take up rehabilitation work on a self-sustaining basis.
    A. little availability of
    B. some availability of
    C. scarce availability of
    D. No Improvement

88. A new notification by the urban development ministry now **makes land available to school** only through auction.
    A. makes land available to schools
    B. making land available to schools
    C. making land available to school
    D. No Improvement

89. One of the first **lesson that a** young MNC manager learns is that "God is in the details."

A. lesson which a
B. lessons that a
C. lessons which a
D. No Improvement

90. Likewise, investors are more interested in crunching numbers than **they are for** fielding calls from potential sellers.
A. they are in
B. they are at
C. they are in favour of
D. No Improvement

91. With each passing day your memories **grow deep**, your loving nature will always be cherished.
A. grew deep
B. grew deeper
C. grow deeper
D. No Improvement

92. It may not beat winning the lottery, **but money** you can take to the bank.
A. but it's money
B. so it's money
C. but it's money that
D. No Improvement

93. Wisdom, Vision, Ideals & Thought **continue to guide** us every moment in our Journey ahead.
A. continue to guiding
B. continuously guide
C. continuing at guiding
D. No Improvement

94. Delhi government **are now blaming** DDA for stalling big infrastructure projects in the Capital.
A. is now putting blaming on
B. is now blaming
C. is now blaming the
D. No Improvement

95. Be happy with the status quo and **preserve it by** conciliating others.

A. preserve that by
B. it is preserved
C. preserving it by
D. No Improvement

96. Have graceful movements, liquid eyes, and a gliding walk, **although** overweight.
A. though
B. even if
C. even
D. No Improvement

97. But people resent that most of the poverty funds **are lost for** corruption and administrative expenses.
A. are lost in
B. are lost at
C. is lost in
D. No Improvement

98. It is **very difficult** to store and save almost everything—money, possessions, energy words food, fat.
A. most difficult
B. very much difficult
C. highly difficult
D. No Improvement

99. Now pause Live TV & watch **with your convenience** and also record your favourite TV programme.
A. at your convenient
B. your convenience
C. at your convenience
D. No Improvement

100. To avoid **last hour rushing,** please immediately deposit VAT and file your Monthly and Quarterly DVAT return.
A. last rush
B. last minute rush
C. last minute rushing
D. No Improvement

Answers

1	2	3	4	5	6	7	8	9	10
A	D	C	A	C	D	C	A	C	C
11	12	13	14	15	16	17	18	19	20
D	C	D	B	A	D	C	C	D	B
21	22	23	24	25	26	27	28	29	30
C	C	D	A	C	D	C	C	C	C
31	32	33	34	35	36	37	38	39	40
B	C	C	A	C	B	D	B	D	C
41	42	43	44	45	46	47	48	49	50
A	D	C	A	D	C	A	B	D	B
51	52	53	54	55	56	57	58	59	60
C	B	A	C	D	A	C	B	B	A
61	62	63	64	65	66	67	68	69	70
A	C	C	D	B	B	D	A	B	A
71	72	73	74	75	76	77	78	79	80
C	D	B	B	A	A	D	C	B	C
81	82	83	84	85	86	87	88	89	90
C	D	B	A	D	B	C	A	B	A
91	92	93	94	95	96	97	98	99	100
C	A	A	B	D	B	A	D	C	B

❏ ❏ ❏

Jumbled Words 5

The words form a sentence and convey their true meaning only when they are arranged in a proper order. One must study and practise it regularly.

Directions: *In the following questions, some parts of the sentence have been jumbled up. You are required to rearrange these parts which are labelled P, Q, R and S to produce the correct sentence. Choose the option with proper sequence.*

1. We are doing
   P : to the people
   Q : to give relief
   R : all we can
   S : but more funds are needed
   The correct sequence should be
   A. P Q R S   B. R Q P S
   C. Q P R S   D. S P Q R

2. The man
   P : when he was
   Q : in the office last evening
   R : could not finish
   S : all his work
   The correct sequence should be
   A. P Q R S   B. Q R S P
   C. R Q P S   D. R S P Q

3. The people decided
   P : they were going
   Q : how much
   R : to spend

   S : on the construction of the school building
   The correct sequence should be
   A. Q P R S   B. P Q R S
   C. P R Q S   D. S Q P R

4. The man said that
   P : those workers
   Q : would be given a raise
   R : who did not go on
   S : strike last month
   The correct sequence should be
   A. P Q R S   B. P R S Q
   C. Q P R S   D. R S P Q

5. I think
   P : the members
   Q : are basically in agreement
   R : of the group
   S : on the following points.
   The correct sequence should be
   A. R Q P S   B. S Q R P
   C. P R Q S   D. P Q S R

6. While it was true that
   P : I had
   Q : to invest in industry
   R : some lands and houses
   S : I did not have ready cash

The correct sequence should be
A. P Q R S   B. P R S Q
C. S Q P R   D. Q P R S

7. P : But your help
   Q : to finish this work
   R : it would not have been possible
   S : in time
   The correct sequence should be
   A. P R Q S   B. S P Q R
   C. R P Q S   D. P Q R S

8. The boy
   P : in the competition
   Q : who was wearing spectacles
   R : won many prizes
   S : held in our college
   The correct sequence should be
   A. P Q R S   B. R P S Q
   C. Q R P S   D. Q P S R

9. About 200 years ago,
   P : in the south of India
   Q : an old king
   R : ruled over a kingdom
   S : called Rajavarman.
   The correct sequence should be
   A. Q S R P   B. P Q R S
   C. Q P S R   D. Q S P R

10. P : his land
    Q : a wooden plough
    R : the Indian peasant still uses
    S : to cultivate.
    The correct sequence should be
    A. R Q P S   B. Q P S R
    C. S R Q P   D. R Q S P

11. He was a man,
    P : even if he had to starve
    Q : who would not beg
    R : borrow or steal
    S : from anyone.
    The correct sequence should be
    A. P Q R S   B. P R Q S
    C. Q R S P   D. Q P R S

12. P : in the progress of
    Q : universities play a crucial role
    R : our civilization
    S : in the present age.
    The correct sequence should be
    A. S Q P R   B. Q R S P
    C. Q R P S   D. S Q R P

13. P : far out into the sea
    Q : for the next two weeks there were further explosions
    R : which hurled
    S : ashes and debris.
    The correct sequence should be
    A. Q R P S   B. R S P Q
    C. Q R S P   D. S R P Q

14. William Shakespeare,
    P : in his lifetime
    Q : the great English dramatist
    R : wrote thirty-five plays
    S : and several poems.
    The correct sequence should be
    A. P Q R S   B. R S P Q
    C. Q S R P   D. Q R S P

15. Whenever I am,
    P : with an old friend of mine
    Q : in New Delhi
    R : to have dinner
    S : I always try.
    The correct sequence should be
    A. S Q P R   B. Q S R P
    C. R P S Q   D. P R Q S

16. P : I don't know
    Q : must have thought
    R : what people sitting next to me
    S : but I came away.
    The correct sequence should be
    A. R S Q P   B. R Q S P
    C. P Q R S   D. P R Q S

17. P : in estimating the size of the earth
    Q : but they were hampered by the lack of instruments of precision
    R : ancient astronomers
    S : used methods which were theoretically valid
    The correct sequence should be
    A. R P Q S   B. P R Q S
    C. R S Q P   D. R P S Q

18. P : It is a pity that
    Q : by offering a handsome dowry
    R : a number of parents think that
    S : they will be able to ensure the happiness of their daughters
    The correct sequence should be
    A. S Q R P   B. P R S Q
    C. P S R Q   D. P R Q S

19. The common man
    P : in nurturing
    Q : a more active role
    R : communal harmony
    S : should play
    The correct sequence should be
    A. P R S Q   B. S Q P R
    C. S Q R P   D. P R Q S

20. The doctor
    P : able to find out
    Q : what has caused
    R : the food poisoning
    S : has not been
    The correct sequence should be
    A. S P R Q   B. P R Q S
    C. P R S Q   D. S P Q R

21. P : was suspended
    Q : the officer being corrupt
    R : before his dismissal
    S : from service
    The correct sequence should be
    A. Q P S R   B. Q P R S
    C. R S Q P   D. R S P Q

22. With an unsteady hand
    P : on my desk
    Q : from his pocket
    R : he took an envelope
    S : and threw it
    The correct sequence should be
    A. Q R P S   B. Q R S P
    C. R Q P S   D. R Q S P

23. P : she gave her old coat
    Q : to a beggar
    R : the one with the brown fur on it
    S : shivering with cold
    The correct sequence should be
    A. S Q R P   B. S P R Q
    C. P R Q S   D. P S Q R

24. It is a privilege
    P : to pay tax
    Q : of every citizen
    R : as well as the duty
    S : who is well-placed
    The correct sequence should be
    A. R P S Q   B. S P R Q
    C. R Q S P   D. S Q R P

25. It is not good
    P : of the wicked persons
    Q : to overthrow
    R : to accept the help
    S : the righteous persons
    The correct sequence should be
    A. R S Q P   B. Q S R P
    C. R P Q S   D. Q P R S

26. Life is judged
    P : and not by
    Q : of work done
    R : the longevity of years
    S : by the quality
    The correct sequence should be
    A. QSPR B. SQRP
    C. QSRP D. SQPR

27. P : When he learns that
    Q : you have passed the examination
    R : in the first division
    S : your father will be delighted
    The correct sequence should be
    A. QPSR B. SPQR
    C. QRSP D. SRQP

28. P : The journalist
    Q : saw
    R : countless number of the dead
    S : driving across the field of battle
    The correct sequence should be
    A. PQSR B. PQRS
    C. PSQR D. SRQP

29. P : Jane planned
    Q : some stamps
    R : to buy
    S : this afternoon
    The correct sequence should be
    A. PRQS B. PSQR
    C. QRPS D. QSPR

30. Her mother
    P : when she was
    Q : hardly four years old
    R : began to teach Neha
    S : English
    The correct sequence should be
    A. RSQP B. SRPQ
    C. RSPQ D. SRQP

31. P : Bill had
    Q : a friend
    R : an appointment
    S : to meet
    The correct sequence should be
    A. PSRQ B. PRSQ
    C. QSRP D. QRSP

32. For fear
    P : that may or may not affect them perhaps at first
    Q : of upsetting young people
    R : only healthy people over 80 should be sequenced
    S : about their genetic propensities
    The correct sequence should be
    A. SQPR B. QSRP
    C. SQRP D. QSPR

33. While traditional
    P : under made-up Americans aliases pretending familiarity with a culture and climate
    Q : India sleeps a dynamic young cohort of highly skilled articulate professionals
    R : they've never actually experienced earning salaries that were undreamt of by their elders
    S : work through the night in the call centres functioning on US time
    The correct sequence should be
    A. PRQS B. QSPR
    C. PSQR D. QRPS

34. IITs are
    P : of great self-confidence and competitive advantage for India today
    Q : in science and technology which has become a source

R : as they epitomize his creation of an infrastructure for excellence
S : perhaps Jawaharlal Nehru's most consequential legacy

The correct sequence should be
A. Q P S R   B. S R Q P
C. Q R S P   D. S P Q R

35. As India
P : from nearly 250 years of the British rule in India
Q : first major struggle for independence from the British rule
R : celebrates the Diamond Jubilee of its independence
S : it also observes simultaneously the 150th Anniversary of the Great Indian Mutiny

The correct sequence should be
A. R S P Q   B. Q P S R
C. R P S Q   D. Q S P R

36. There have been
P : a day after high intensity violence left at least 50 persons
Q : sporadic clashes between
R : dead in the northern city of Tripoli
S : the Lebanese army and militants

The correct sequence should be
A. Q S R P   B. S Q R P
C. Q S P R   D. S Q P R

37. Although
P : of non-owner managers came to be widely appreciated
Q : political freedom from the British masters
R : came to us in 1947 it was not until

S : well into the following decade that the role

The correct sequence should be
A. S P Q R   B. Q R S P
C. S R Q P   D. Q P S R

38. Conditions
P : for marketing in the U.S. and Canada
Q : Mexico as a manufacturing base
R : that Indian companies aspiring to tap
S : would have to fulfil include the complex rules of origin

The correct sequence should be
A. R Q P S   B. S P Q R
C. R P Q S   D. S Q P R

39. Aside
P : of the same three-storey building in the military academy
Q : from eating in the same dining hall
R : half to the north of the entrance half to the south
S : the 206 troops live side by side on the ground floor

The correct sequence should be
A. R P S Q   B. Q S P R
C. R S P Q   D. Q P S R

40. Russia's test firing
P : to US steps that have sparked an arms race
Q : of an intercontinental ballistic missile on
R : and undermined world security
S : Tuesday was in response

The correct sequence should be
A. S Q P R   B. Q S R P
B. S Q R P   D. Q S P R

41. Marks, cities, civilization—
    P : on the verge of globalization; poised to
    Q : the slow ascent to where he is today, poised
    R : it is in this order that primitive man made
    S : achieve universal prosperity and abundance
    The correct sequence should be
    A. R Q P S   B. P S R Q
    B. R S P Q   D. P Q R S

42. I bow my head
    P : for their sense of the beautiful in
    Q : nature and for their foresight in investing beautiful
    R : manifestations of nature with a religious significance
    S : in reverence to our ancestors
    The correct sequence should be
    A. Q R S P   B. S P Q R
    B. Q P S R   D. S R Q P

43. With all the crime and sleaze
    P : I am not sure how many parents will be able to
    Q : how many will have the courage to satisfy the child's uncomfortable queries
    R : that dominates the front page of the newspapers today
    S : read out the headlines to their children and if they do so
    The correct sequence should be
    A. R P S Q   B. S Q R P
    C. R Q S P   D. P R S Q

44. The way
    P : processes that govern their actions
    Q : nutrients become integral parts
    R : depends on the physiological and biochemical
    S : of the body and contribute to its functions
    The correct sequence should be
    A. Q R S P   B. P S R Q
    C. Q S R P   D. S P R Q

45. Thus,
    P : international surveys would henceforth record
    Q : if dirt-poor people in the developing world
    R : their wealth of happiness alongside their material poverty
    S : display a general sense of well-being
    The correct sequence should be
    A. S Q R P   B. Q S P R
    C. S Q P R   D. Q S R P

46. It's
    P : someone who's grieving but
    Q : natural to feel uncomfortable
    R : that prevent you from being there
    S : or awkward when you have to help
    The correct sequence should be
    A. Q P S R   B. R S P Q
    C. Q S P R   D. R P S Q

47. Developing countries
    P : along the equator, which
    Q : could become leaders in energy production
    R : are expected to face the brunt of global warming
    S : with a solar energy breakthrough
    The correct sequence should be
    A. Q S P R   B. P R Q S
    C. Q R P S   D. P S Q R

48. A diversified
    P : use as a heating or power generation fuel by converting gas into
    Q : adding a new dimension to the traditional use of gas
    R : of natural gas is emerging
    S : amongst other products, high quality diesel transportation fuel virtually free of sulphur
    The correct sequence should be
    A. R P Q S   B. S Q P R
    C. R Q P S   D. S P Q R

49. As things stand
    P : but a majority still does not have access to English
    Q : linguistic edge they are equipped with
    R : after globally because of the
    S : Indian professionals are much sought
    The correct sequence should be
    A. R S P Q   B. S R Q P
    C. R S Q P   D. S R P Q

50. While advocates
    P : of its provisions with the
    Q : there is some misguided concern about a possible clash of some
    R : of social reform have generally hailed the new legislation
    S : religious and customary practices in vogue in the country
    The correct sequence should be
    A. R Q P S   B. Q R S P
    C. R Q S P   D. Q R P S

51. He has
    P : while he was in a reverie
    Q : found the book
    R : at the bus-stop
    S : he lost
    The proper sequence should be:
    A. Q R S P   B. P R Q S
    C. Q S R P   D. P Q S R

52. Then the women
    P : lamenting their evil desire
    Q : that had brought
    R : wept loudly
    S : this sorrow upon them
    The proper sequence should be:
    A. R P Q S   B. R Q P S
    C. P Q S R   D. P R Q S

53. It is easy to excuse
    P : but it is hard
    Q : in a boy of fourteen
    R : the mischief of early childhood
    S : to tolerate even unavoidable faults
    The proper sequence should be:
    A. R P Q S   B. Q R S P
    C. Q R P S   D. R P S Q

54. I don't remember
    P : I saw a man dying in front of a hospital
    Q : but when I left Lucknow in 2014
    R : hit apparently by a fast moving car
    S : the exact date
    The proper sequence should be:
    A. S Q R P   B. S Q P R
    C. Q R P S   D. S P R Q

55. Since the beginning of history
    P : have managed to catch
    Q : the Eskimos and Red Indians
    R : by a very difficult method
    S : a few specimens of this acquatic mammal
    The proper sequence should be:
    A. Q P R S   B. S Q P R
    C. S Q R P   D. Q P S R

56. I saw that
    P : but seeing my host in this mood
    Q : I deemed it proper to take leave
    R : as I had frequently done before
    S : it had been my intention to pass the night there

    The proper sequence should be:
    A. Q P S R   B. Q R P S
    C. S P Q R   D. S R P Q

57. It was to be
    P : before their school examination
    Q : which was due to start
    R : the last expedition
    S : in a month's time

    The proper sequence should be:
    A. S R Q P   B. R Q S P
    C. R P Q S   D. S P R Q

58. They felt safer
    P : to watch the mountain
    Q : of more than five miles
    R : as they settled down
    S : from a distance

    The proper sequence should be:
    A. R P S Q   B. R S Q P
    C. P Q S R   D. P R S Q

59. If you need help
    P : promptly and politely
    Q : ask for attendants
    R : to help our customers
    S : who have instructions

    The proper sequence should be:
    A. S Q P R   B. Q P S R
    C. Q S R P   D. S Q R P

60. He was so kind and generous that
    P : he not only
    Q : made others do so
    R : but also
    S : helped them himself

    The proper sequence should be:
    A. P S R Q   B. S P Q R
    C. P R S Q   D. Q P R S

61. People
    P : at his dispensary
    Q : went to him
    R : of all professions
    S : for medicine and treatment

    The proper sequence should be:
    A. Q P R S   B. R P Q S
    C. R Q S P   D. Q R P S

62. When it began to rain suddenly on the first of January
    P : to celebrate the new year
    Q : we ran for shelter
    R : to the neighbouring house
    S : where many people had gathered

    The proper sequence should be:
    A. Q R P S   B. P S Q R
    C. P R S Q   D. Q R S P

63. The master
    P : who was very loyal to him
    Q : punished the servant
    R : without giving any valid reason
    S : when he left the work unfinished

    The proper sequence should be:
    A. R Q P S   B. R Q S P
    C. Q P S R   D. Q R P S

64. The appearance
    P : this dinosaurs were at their peak
    Q : of the first mammals on the earth
    R : at the time when
    S : went almost unnoticed

    The proper sequence should be:
    A. S R P Q   B. Q S R P
    C. Q R P S   D. R P Q S

65. It is easier
    P : to venture into space
    Q : for men
    R : beneath their feet
    S : than to explore
    The proper sequence should be:
    A. Q R P S   B. Q P S R
    C. P S R Q   D. P Q S R

66. It is very easy
    P : a great deal more than one realises
    Q : may mean
    R : that a phrase that one does not quite understand
    S : to persuade oneself
    The proper sequence should be:
    A. R S Q P   B. S P Q R
    C. S R Q P   D. R Q P S

67. The national unity of a free people
    P : to make it impracticable
    Q : for there to be an arbitrary administration
    R : depends upon a sufficiently even balance of political power
    S : against a revolutionary opposition that is irreconciably opposed to it.
    The proper sequence should be:
    A. Q R P S   B. Q R S P
    C. R P Q S   D. R S P Q

68. He told us that
    P : and enjoyed it immensely
    Q : in a prose translation
    R : he had read Milton
    S : which he had borrowed from his teacher
    The proper sequence should be:
    A. R S Q P   B. Q R P S
    C. R Q S P   D. R Q P S

69. This time
    P : exactly what he had been told
    Q : the young man did
    R : beyond his dreams
    S : and the plan succeeded
    The proper sequence should be:
    A. Q P R S   B. Q P S R
    C. P Q S R   D. Q S R P

70. As a disease
    P : and breaks up marriages
    Q : accidents and suicides
    R : alcoholism leads to
    S : affecting all ages
    The proper sequence should be:
    A. S R P Q   B. R P S Q
    C. S R Q P   D. R Q P S

71. This majestic mahogany table
    P : belongs to an old prince
    Q : which has one leg missing
    R : who is no impoverished
    S : but not without some pride
    The proper sequence should be:
    A. P Q S R   B. Q R S P
    C. P R S Q   D. Q P R S

72. We have to
    P : as we see it
    Q : speak the truth
    R : there is falsehood and darkness
    S : even if all around us
    The proper sequence should be:
    A. R Q S P   B. Q R P S
    C. R S Q P   D. Q P S R

73. He sat
    P : through the Town Hall Park
    Q : which flanked a path running
    R : under the boughs
    S : of a spreading tamarind tree
    The proper sequence should be:
    A. P Q S R   B. R S Q P
    C. R S P Q   D. P R S Q

74. We went
    P : along the railway line
    Q : and had a right to
    R : where other people were not allowed to go
    S : but daddy belonged to the railway

    The proper sequence should be:
    A. R P Q S   B. P R S Q
    C. R S Q P   D. P R Q S

75. In the darkness
    P : the long, narrow beard
    Q : was clearly visible with
    R : the tall stooping figure of the doctor
    S : and the aquiline nose

    The proper sequence should be:
    A. R Q P S   B. P S Q R
    C. R S Q P   D. Q P R S

76. It is foolish
    P : of those who possess them
    Q : to believe that
    R : will result in victory
    S : the use of nuclear weapons

    The correct sequence should be:
    A. R S P Q   B. Q S R P
    C. P R Q S   D. S Q P R

77. A distressing fact is that
    P : social accountability
    Q : are dominated only by greed
    R : many people today
    S : and there is hardly any

    The correct sequence should be:
    A. S R P Q   B. Q S R P
    C. P R Q S   D. R Q S P

78. I once had
    P : every morning
    Q : a client who swore
    R : for the past four years
    S : she had a headache

    The correct sequence should be:
    A. P R S Q   B. Q S P R
    C. R P Q S   D. S Q R P

79. People know
    P : not only of the smokers themselves,
    Q : that smoking tobacco
    R : but also of their companions
    S : is injurious to the health

    The correct sequence should be:
    A. P S Q R   B. R P S Q
    C. Q P R S   D. Q S P R

80. He had
    P : finished his lunch
    Q : hardly
    R : at the door
    S : when someone knocked

    The correct sequence should be:
    A. Q P R S   B. P Q R S
    C. Q P S R   D. R P Q S

81. Mr. Sexena was a profound scholar who
    P : was held in high esteem by all those
    Q : who read his books and visited him regularly
    R : till his untimely death
    S : though not popular with the general public

    The correct sequence should be:
    A. P Q R S   B. R P Q S
    C. S R Q P   D. S P Q R

82. The Government wants that
    P : by the veterinary surgeons
    Q : by the butchers
    R : all the goats slaughtered
    S : must be medically examined

    The correct sequence should be:
    A. R P S Q   B. Q S R P
    C. R Q S P   D. P R S Q

83. The general line about television
    P : is that it is very exciting,
    Q : but also potentially very dangerous
    R : immensely powerful
    S : that I took myself
    The correct sequence should be:
    A. P Q R S   B. S P R Q
    C. P R Q S   D. R P Q S

84. The second test of good government is that
    P : to every man and woman
    Q : and act only with their consent
    R : it should give a lot of freedom
    S : and should treat their personalities with respect and sympathy
    The correct sequence should be:
    A. Q S P R   B. S R Q P
    C. R P S Q   D. P Q R S

85. The teacher warned that
    P : he would not let
    Q : go home
    R : those students
    S : who do not finish the class-work
    The correct sequence should be:
    A. P Q R S   B. P R Q S
    C. P R S Q   D. R S P Q

86. Towards the end of the eighteenth century, quite a number of economists
    P : in the near future
    Q : at the possibility of
    R : were seriously perturbed
    S : the world facing starvation
    The correct sequence should be:
    A. P R Q S   B. R Q S P
    C. Q S P R   D. R P Q S

87. The best way of understanding our own civilization
    P : is to examine
    Q : an ordinary man
    R : in the life of
    S : an ordinary day
    The correct sequence should be:
    A. P Q R S   B. R Q P S
    C. P S R Q   D. R S P Q

88. What greater thing is there
    P : for two human souls to feel
    Q : to rest on each other in all sorrow,
    R : that they are joined for life,
    S : to strengthen each other in all labour
    The correct sequence should be:
    A. S Q R P   B. R P Q S
    C. Q R S P   D. P R S Q

89. Fame
    P : by showing off
    Q : to the best advantage
    R : one's ability and virtue
    S : is earned
    The correct sequence should be:
    A. P Q R S   B. S P R Q
    C. P R S Q   D. P Q S R

90. When he was a child
    P : passed his happiest hours
    Q : the boy who was to become Britain's Baron Haden
    R : staring out of his apartment window
    S : living in New York
    The correct sequence should be:
    A. Q S P R   B. P R Q S
    C. S Q P R   D. R S Q P

91. P : The teacher had to be specially careful

Q : because he enjoyed the confidence
R : about how he faced up to this problem
S : of all the boys
The correct sequence should be:
A. P R Q S
B. Q P S R
C. S P R Q
D. P S R Q

92. Movies made in
P : all around the globle
Q : Hollywood in America
R : by people
S : are seen at the same time
The correct sequence should be:
A. Q S R P
B. Q R P S
C. P S R Q
D. Q P S R

93. P : The foundations of the prosperity of a state
Q : primary health and education but also
R : involves the creation of job oppotunities
S : does not merely rest on
The correct sequence should be:
A. P S Q R
B. P Q R S
C. P R Q S
D. P S R Q

94. I am pure
P : and will be happy
Q : sooner or later
R : a day will come
S : when all will be equal
The correct sequence should be:
A. Q P R S
B. Q S R P
C. R Q S P
D. R S Q P

95. P : To do his/her work properly
Q : it should be the pride and honour
R : without anybody forcing him/her
S : of every citizen in India
The correct sequence should be:

A. Q S R P
B. P R Q S
C. Q S P R
D. P Q R S

96. The person who can state
P : correct than the person who cannot
Q : is more likely to be
R : his antagonist's point of view
S : to the satisfaction of the antagonist
The correct sequence should be:
A. R S Q P
B. R Q P S
C. P Q R S
D. S Q R P

97. The time has come
P : for future generations to come
Q : that the ideal of peace is a distant ideal
R : or one which can be postponed
S : when man must no longer think
The correct sequence should be:
A. P Q R S
B. S Q R P
C. Q R S P
D. R S P Q

98. I had been staying with
P : at his cottage among the Yorkshire falls
Q : a friend of mine
R : a delightfully lazy fellow
S : some ten miles away from the railway station
The correct sequence should be:
A. P Q R S
B. Q R P S
C. Q R S P
D. R Q P S

99. All the evil in this world is brought about by person
P : when they ought to be up
Q : but do not know
R : nor what they ought to be doing
S : who are always up and doing

The correct sequence should be:
A. P Q S R   B. Q P R S
C. S Q P R   D. P Q R S

100. If all the countries
P : of mankind and agree to obey
Q : work together for the common good
R : with each other and there will be no more war
S : the laws, then they will never fight

The correct sequence should be:
A. P Q R S   B. Q S P R
C. Q P S R   D. R Q P S

Answers

1	2	3	4	5	6	7	8	9	10
B	D	A	B	C	C	A	C	A	D
11	12	13	14	15	16	17	18	19	20
C	A	C	D	B	D	C	B	B	D
21	22	23	24	25	26	27	28	29	30
B	D	C	C	B	D	B	C	A	B
31	32	33	34	35	36	37	38	39	40
B	D	B	B	C	C	C	A	B	D
41	42	43	44	45	46	47	48	49	50
A	B	A	C	B	C	B	A	B	A
51	52	53	54	55	56	57	58	59	60
C	A	D	B	D	D	C	A	C	A
61	62	63	64	65	66	67	68	69	70
C	D	C	C	B	B	D	C	B	C
71	72	73	74	75	76	77	78	79	80
D	D	B	B	A	B	D	B	D	C
81	82	83	84	85	86	87	88	89	90
D	C	B	C	B	B	C	D	B	C
91	92	93	94	95	96	97	98	99	100
A	A	A	C	C	A	B	B	C	C

Jumbled Sentences 6

A paragraph is formed from sentences, it will convey its true meaning and purpose only when the sentences are arranged in a proper manner. Try and practise it.

Directions: *In these questions, each passage consists of six sentences. The first and the sixth sentences are given in the beginning. The middle four sentences in each passage have been removed and jumbled up. These jumbled sentences are labelled P, Q, R and S. Choose the proper sequence of the four sentences P, Q, R, and S from the alternatives A, B, C and D.*

1. S_1: She said on the phone that she would report for duty next day.
   S_6: Eventually we reported to the police.
   P : We waited for a few days, then we decided to go to her place.
   Q : But she did not.
   R : We found it locked.
   S : Even after that we waited for her for quite a few days.
   The proper sequence should be:
   A. P R S Q   B. Q P S R
   C. Q P R S   D. S Q P R

2. S_1: A force of attraction exists between everybody in the universe.
   S_6: The greater the mass, the greater is the earth's force of attraction on it—we call this force of attraction gravity.
   P : Normally it is very small but when one of the bodies is a planet, like the earth, the force is considerable.
   Q : It has been investigated by many scientists including Galileo and Newton.
   R : Everything on or near the surface of the earth is attracted by the mass of the earth.
   S : This gravitational force depends on the mass of the bodies involved.
   The proper sequence should be:
   A. P R Q S   B. P R S Q
   C. Q S R P   D. Q S P R

3. S_1: Metals are today being replaced by polymers in many applications.
   S_6: Many Indian Institutes of Science and Technology run special programmes on polymer science.

P : Above all, they are cheaper and easier to process, making them a viable alternative to metals.
Q : Polymers are essentially long chains of hydrocarbon molecules.
R : Today polymers as strong as metals have been developed.
S : These have replaced the traditional chromium-plated metallic bumpers in cars.
The proper sequence should be:
A. Q R S P   B. R S Q P
C. R Q S P   D. Q R P S

4. S_1: It is regrettable that there is widespread corruption in the country at all levels.
S_6: This is indeed a tragedy of great magnitude.
P : So there is hardly anything that the government can do about it now.
Q : And there are graft and other malpractices too.
R : The impression that corruption is a universal phenomenon persists and the people do not cooperate in checking this evil.
S : Recently several offenders were brought to book, but they were not given deterrent punishment.
The proper sequence should be:
A. Q S R P   B. S Q R P
C. R S Q P   D. P Q S R

5. S_1: It was a dark moonless night.
S_6: They all seemed to him to be poor and ordinary—mere childish words.
P : He turned over the pages, reading passages here and there.
Q : He heard them on the floor.
R : The poet took down his books of poems from his shelves.
S : Some of them contained his earliest writings which he had almost forgotten.
The proper sequence should be:
A. R P Q S   B. R Q S P
C. R S P Q   D. R P S Q

6. S_1: A noise started above their heads.
S_6: Nearly two hundred lives were lost on the fateful day.
P : But people did not take it seriously.
Q : That was to show everyone that there was something wrong.
R : It was a dangerous thing to do.
S : For, within minutes the ship began to sink.
The proper sequence should be:
A. P Q S R   B. P R Q S
C. Q P R S   D. Q P S R

7. S_1: The cooperative system of doing business is a good way of encouraging ordinary workers to work hard.
S_6: The main object is to maintain the interest of every member of the society and to ensure that the members participate actively in the projects of the society.
P : If the society is to be well run, it is necessary to prevent insincere officials being elected to the committee

which is solely responsible for the running of the business.
Q: They get this from experienced and professional workers who are not only familiar with the cooperative system, but also with efficient methods of doing business.
R: To a large extent, many cooperative societies need advice and guidance.
S: The capital necessary to start a business venture is obtai-ned by the workers' contri-butions.
The proper sequence should be:
A. S Q P R   B. P Q S R
C. S R Q P   D. P S R Q

8. S_1: American private lives may seem shallow.
S_6: This would not happen in China, he said.
P: Students would walk away with books they had not paid for.
Q: A Chinese journalist commented on a curious institution: the library.
R: Their public morality, however, impressed visitors.
S: But in general they returned them.
The proper sequence should be:
A. P S Q R   B. Q P S R
C. R Q P S   D. R P S Q

9. S_1: The *Bhagavadgita* recognises the nature of man and the needs of man.
S_6: A man who does not harmonise them, is not truly human.
P: All these three aspects constitute the nature of man.
Q: It shows how the human being is a rational one, an ethical one and a spiritual one.
R: More than all, it must be a spiritual experience.
S: Nothing can give him fulfilment unless it satisfies his reason, his ethical conscience.
The proper sequence should be:
A. P S R Q   B. R S P Q
C. Q P S R   D. P S Q R

10. S_1: I usually sleep quite well in the train, but this time I slept only a little.
S_6: It was shut all night, as usual.
P: Most people wanted it shut and I wanted it open.
Q: As usual, I got angry about the window.
R: The quarrel left me completely upset.
S: There were too many people and too much luggage all around.
The proper sequence should be:
A. R S Q P   B. S Q P R
C. S Q R P   D. R S P Q

11. S_1: For decades, American society has been called a melting pot.
S_6: In recent years, such differences—accentuated by the arrival of immigrants from Asia and other parts of the world in the United States—have become something to celebrate and to nurture.
P: Differences remained—in appearance, mannerisms, customs, speech, religion and more.
Q: The term has long been a cliche, and a half-truth.

R : But homogenisation was never achieved.
S : Yes, immigrants from diverse cultures and traditions did cast off vestiges of their native lands and become almost imperceptibly woven into the American fabric.
The proper sequence should be:
A. Q R S P B. S Q R P
C. S Q P R D. Q S R P

12. S_1: While talking to a group, one should feel self-confident and courageous.
S_6: Any man can develop his capacity if he has the desire to do so.
P : Nor is it a gift bestowed by Providence on only a few.
Q : One should also learn how to think calmly and clearly.
R : It is like the ability to play golf.
S : It is not as difficult as most men imagine.
The proper sequence should be:
A. S Q P R B. Q S P R
C. Q R S P D. R S Q P

13. S_1: In 1934, William Golding published a small volume of poems.
S_6: But *Lord of the Flies* which came out in 1954 was welcomed as "a most absorbing and instructive tale".
P : During the World War II (1939-45) he joined the Royal Navy and was present at the sinking of the *Bismarck*.
Q : He returned to teaching in 1945 and gave it up in 1962, and is now a full-time writer.
R : In 1939, he married and started teaching at Bishop Wordsworth's School in Salisbury
S : At first his novels were not accepted.
The proper sequence should be:
A. R P Q S B. R P S Q
C. S R P Q D. S Q P R

14. S_1: Our ancestors thought that anything which moved itself was alive.
S_6: Therefore some scientists think that life is just a very complicated mechanism.
P : The philosopher Descartes thought that both men and animals were machines.
Q : But a machine such as a motorcar or a steamship moves itself, and as soon as machines which moved themselves had been made, people asked, "Is man a machine?"
R : And before the days of machinery that was a good definition.
S : He also thought that the human machine was partly controlled by the soul action on a certain part of the brain, while animals had no souls
The proper sequence should be:
A. P R S Q B. R P Q S
C. P S Q R D. R Q P S

15. S_1: But how does a new word get into the dictionary?
S_6: He sorts them according to their grammatical function, and carefully writes a definition.

P : When a new dictionary is being edited, a lexicographer collects all the alphabetically arranged citation slips for a particular word.
Q : The dictionary makers notice it and make a note of it on a citation slip.
R : The moment a new word is coined, it usually enters the spoken language.
S : The word then passes from the realm of hearing to the realm of writing.
The proper sequence should be:
A. P Q R S   B. P R S Q
C. R Q P S   D. R S Q P

16. S_1: The heart is the pump of life.
S_6: All this was made possible by the invention of the heart-lung machine.
P : They have even succeeded in heart transplants.
Q : Nowadays surgeons are able to stop a patient's heart and carry out complicated operations.
R : A few years ago it was impossible to operate on a patient whose heart was not working properly.
S : If the heart stops we die in about five minutes.
The proper sequence should be:
A. S R Q P   B. S P R Q
C. S Q P R   D. S R P Q

17. S_1: Throughout history man has used energy from the sun.
S_6: This energy comes from inside atoms.
P : Today, when we burn wood or use electric current we are drawing on energy.
Q : However, we now have a new supply of energy.
R : All our ordinary life depends on the sun.
S : This has come from the sun.
The proper sequence should be:
A. S Q P R   B. R Q P S
C. Q S R P   D. P S R Q

18. S_1: In India marriages are usually arranged by parents.
S_6: She felt she was a modern girl and not a subject for bargaining
P : Sometimes girls and boys do not like the idea of arranged marriages.
Q : Most young people accept this state of affairs.
R : Shanta was like that.
S : They assume their parents can make good choices.
The proper sequence should be:
A. S P R Q   B. P S R Q
C. Q S P R   D. R Q P S

19. S_1: I had halted on the road.
S_6: I decided to watch him for a while and then go home.
P : As soon as I saw the elephant I knew I should not shoot him.
Q : It is a serious matter to shoot a working elephant.
R : I knew that his 'mast' was already passing off.
S : The elephant was standing eighty yards from the road.
The proper sequence should be:
A. S P Q R   B. P Q S R
C. R Q P S   D. S R P Q

20. S_1: A man can be physically confined within stone walls.
    S_6: No tyranny can intimidate a lover of liberty.
    P : But his mind and spirit will still be free.
    Q : Thus his freedom of action may be restricted.
    R : His hopes and aspirations still remain with him.
    S : Hence, he will be free spiritually if not physically.
    The proper sequence should be:
    A. P Q R S   B. S R Q P
    C. Q P R S   D. Q P S R

21. S_1: The dictionary is the best friend for your task.
    S_6: Soon you will realize that this is an exciting task
    P : That may not be possible always.
    Q : It is wise to look it up immediately.
    R : Then it must be firmly written on the memory and traced at the first opportunity.
    S : Never allow a strange word to pass unchallenged.
    The proper sequence should be:
    A. P Q R S   B. S P Q R
    C. Q R P S   D. S Q P R

22. S_1: Far away in a little street there is a poor house.
    S_6: His mother has nothing to give but water, so he is crying
    P : Her face is thin and worn and her hands are coarse, pricked by a needle, for she is a seamstress.
    Q : One of the windows is open and through it I can see a poor woman.
    R : He has fever and he is asking for oranges.
    S : In a bed in a corner of the room her little boy is lying ill.
    The proper sequence should be:
    A. S R Q P   B. P Q S R
    C. Q P S R   D. R S P Q

23. S_1: Kolkata unlike other cities, has kept its trams.
    S_6: The foundation stone was laid in 1972.
    P : As a result, there is horrendous congestion.
    Q : It was going to be the first in South Asia.
    R : They run down the centre of the road.
    S : To ease in the city decided to build an underground railway line.
    The proper sequence should be:
    A. P R S Q   B. P S Q R
    C. S Q R P   D. R P S Q

24. S_1: We now know that oceans are very deep.
    S_6: This reaches from India to the Antarctic.
    P : For example, the Indian Ocean has a range called the Indian Ridge.
    Q : Much of it is fairly flat.
    R : However, there are great mountain ranges as well.
    S : On average the bottom is two and a half to three and a half miles down.
    The proper sequence should be:
    A. S Q P R   B. P Q S R
    C. R S Q P   D. Q P R S

25. S_1: As he passed beneath her he heard the swish of her wings.

S_6: The next moment he felt her wings spread outwards.
P : He was not falling head long now.
Q : Then monstrous terror seized him.
R : But it only lasted a minute.
S : He could hear nothing.
The proper sequence should be:
A. P S Q R B. Q S P R
C. Q S R P D. P R Q S

26. S_1: When a satellite is launched, the rocket begins by going slowly upwards through the air.
S_6: Consequently, the rocket still does not become too hot.
P : However, the higher it goes, the less air it meets.
Q : As the rocket goes higher, it travels faster.
R : For the atmosphere becomes thinner.
S : As a result there is less friction.
The proper sequence should be:
A. Q P R S B. Q S P R
C. P Q R S D. P Q S R

27. S_1: Sunbirds are among the smallest of Indian birds.
S_6: Our common sunbirds are the purple sunbird, the glossy black species and purple-rumped sunbird, the yellow and maroon species
P : Though they are functionally similar to the hummingbirds of the New World, they are totally unrelated.
Q : They do eat small insects too.
R : They are also some of the most brilliantly-coloured birds.
S : Sunbirds feed on nectar mostly and help in pollination.
The proper sequence should be:
A. S Q P R B. R P S Q
C. Q P R S D. P S R Q

28. S_1: Venice is a strange and beautiful city in the north of Italy.
S_6: This is because Venice has no streets.
P : There are about four hundred old stone bridges joining the island of Venice.
Q : In this city there are no motor cars, no horses and no buses.
R : These small islands are near one another.
S : It is not an island but a hundred and seventeen islands.
The proper sequence should be:
A. P Q R S B. P R Q S
C. S R P Q D. P Q S R

29. S_1: A ceiling on urban property.
S_6: Since their value would exceed the ceiling fixed by the Government.
P : No mill-owner could own factories or mills or plants.
Q : And mass circulation papers.
R : Would mean that.
S : No press magnate could own printing presses.
The proper sequence should be:
A. Q S R P B. R P S Q
C. S R P Q D. Q P S R

30. S_1: The weather-vane often tops a church spire, tower or high building.
S_6: The weather-vane can, however, give us some indication of the weather.
P : They are only wind-vanes.
Q : Neither alone can tell us what the weather will be.

R : They are designed to point to the direction from which the wind is coming.
S : Just as the barometer only tells us the pressure of the air, the weather-vane tells us the direction of the wind.
The proper sequence should be:
A. P Q R S   B. P S R Q
C. P R S Q   D. S P Q R

31. S_1: Most of the universities in the country are now facing financial crisis.
S_6: The Government should realise this before it is too late.
P : Cost benefit yardstick thus should not be applied in the case of the universities.
Q : The current state of affairs cannot be allowed to continue for long.
R : Universities cannot be equated with commercial enterprises.
S : Proper development of universities and colleges must be ensured
The proper sequence should be:
A. Q R P S   B. Q S P R
C. Q R S P   D. Q P R S

32. S_1: I keep on flapping my big ears all day.
S_6: Am I not a smart, intelligent elephant?
P : They also fear that I will flap them all away.
Q : But children wonder why I flap them so.
R : I flap them so to make sure they are safely there on either side of my head.
S : But I know what I am doing.

The proper sequence should be:
A. S R Q P   B. Q P S R
C. Q P R S   D. P S R Q

33. S_1: Urban problems differ from State to State and city to city.
S_6: There is no underground drainage system in most cities, and the narrow historical roads are already congested.
P : Most of the cities have neither water nor the required pipelines.
Q : The population in these cities has grown beyond the planners' imagination.
R : However, certain basic problems are common to all cities.
S : Only broad macro-planning was done for such cities, without envisaging the future growth, and this has failed to meet the requirements.
The proper sequence should be:
A. P Q S R   B. Q P S R
C. R Q P S   D. R S Q P

34. S_1: A gentleman who lived alone always had two plates placed on the table at dinner time.
S_6: In this way the cat showed her gratitude to her master.
P : One day just as he sat down to dine, the cat rushed into the room.
Q : One plate was for himself and the other was for his cat.
R : She dropped a mouse into her own plate and another into her master's plate.
S : He used to give the cat a piece of meat from his own plate.
The proper sequence should be:
A. Q S P R   B. P S R Q
C. Q R S P   D. R P Q S

35. S_1: I took cigarettes from my case.
S_6: Then he continued to draw on it.
P : But when the fit of coughing was over, he replaced it between his lips.
Q : I lit one of them and placed it between the lips.
R : Then with a feeble hand he removed the cigarette.
S : Slowly he took a pull at it and coughed violently.
The proper sequence should be:
A. P S Q R   B. Q P S R
C. Q S R P   D. S R P Q

36. S_1: Forcasting the weather has always been a difficult business.
S_6: He made his forecasts by watching flights of the birds or the way smoke rose from fire.
P : During a period of drought, streams and rivers dried up, the cattle died from thirst and the crops were ruined.
Q : Many different things affect the weather and we have to study them carefully to make an accurate forecast.
R : Ancient Egyptians had no need of this weather in the Nile valley hardly ever changes.
S : In early times, when there were no instruments, such as thermometer or the barometer, man looked for tell-tale signs in the sky.
The proper sequence should be:
A. P R Q S   B. Q P R S
C. Q R P S   D. S P Q R

37. S_1: Once upon a time there lived three young men in a certain town of Hindustan.
S_6: All of them set out in search of their foe called Death.
P : All the people of the neighbourhood were mortally afraid of them.
Q : They were so powerful that they could catch growling lions and tear them to pieces.
R : Someone told them that they would become immortal if they killed Death.
S : The young men believed themselves to be very good friends.
The proper sequence should be:
A. Q P R S   B. S Q P R
C. R S Q P   D. S R P Q

38. S_1: Duryodhana was a wicked prince.
S_6: This enraged Duryodhana so much that he began to think of removing Bhima from his way.
P : One day Bhima made Duryodhana fall from a tree from which Duryodhana was stealing fruits.
Q : He did not like that Pandavas should be loved and respected by the people of Hastinapur.
R : Duryodhana specially hated Bhima.
S : Among the Pandavas, Bhima was extraordinarily strong and powerful.
The proper sequence should be:
A. P S Q R   B. Q P R S
C. Q S R P   D. P S R Q

39. S₁: You know my wife, Madhavi, always urged me to give up smoking.
S₆: Poor girl!
P : I really gave it up.
Q : And so when I went to jail I said to myself I really must give it up, if for no other reason than of being self-reliant.
R : When I emerged from jail, I wanted to tell her of my great triumph!
S : But when I met her, there she was with a packet of cigarettes.
The proper sequence should be:
A. P S R Q   B. S P Q R
C. Q P R S   D. R S P Q

40. S₁: A black-haired, young woman came tripping along.
S₆: Both disappeared from view.
P : She was leading a young man wearing a hat.
Q : The woman swept it off and tossed it in the air.
R : The child jumped up to catch the hat.
S : The young man tossed his head to shake the hat back.
The proper sequence should be:
A. P S Q R   B. R P S Q
C. Q R P S   D. S Q R P

41. S₁: Jawaharlal Nehru was born in Allahabad on 14 Nov., 1889.
S₆: He died on 27 May, 1964.
P : Nehru met Mahatma Gandhi in February, 1920.
Q : In 1905 he was sent to London to study at a school called Harrow.
R : He became the first Prime Minister of Independent India on 15 August, 1947.
S : He married Kamla Kaul in 1915.
The proper sequence should be:
A. Q R P S   B. Q S P R
C. R P Q S   D. S Q R P

42. S₁: An elderly lady suddenly became blind.
S₆: The lady said that she had not been properly cured because she could not see all her furniture.
P : The doctor called daily and every time he took away some of her furniture he liked.
Q : At last, she was cured and the doctor demanded his fee.
R : She agreed to pay a large fee to the doctor who would cure her.
S : On being refused, the doctor wanted to know the reason.
The proper sequence should be:
A. P Q R S   B. R P Q S
C. R S P Q   D. R Q P S

43. S₁: The path of Venus lies inside the path of the Earth.
S₆: When at its brightest, it is easily seen with the naked eye in broad daylight.
P : When at its farthest from the Earth, Venus is 160 million miles away.
Q : With such a wide range between its greatest and least distances it is natural that at sometimes Venus appears much brighter than at others.
R : No other body ever comes so near the Earth, with the exception of the Moon and an occasional comet or asteroid.

S : When Venus is at its nearest to the earth it is only 26 million miles away.
The proper sequence should be:
A. S R P Q B. S Q R P
C. P S Q R D. Q P R S

44. S_1: Religion is not a matter of mere dogmatic conformity.
S_6: A man of that character is free from fear, free from hatred.
P : It is not merely going through the ritual prescribed to us.
Q : It is not a question of ceremonial piety.
R : Unless that kind of transformation occurs, you are not an authentically religious man.
S : It is the remaking of your own self, the transformation of your nature.
The proper sequence should be:
A. S P R Q B. Q P S R
C. P S R Q D. S P Q R

45. S_1: For some time in his youth, Abraham Lincoln was manager of a shop.
S_6: Never before had Lincoln had so much time for reading as he had then.
P : Then a chance customer would come.
Q : Young Lincoln's way of keeping shop was entirely unlike anyone else's.
R : Lincoln would jump up and attend to his needs and then revert to his reading.
S : He used to lie full length on the counter of the shop eagerly reading a book.

The proper sequence should be:
A. S R Q P B. Q S P R
C. S Q R P D. Q P S R

46. S_1: Minnie went shopping one morning.
S_6: She drove home with an empty shopping basket.
P : Disappointed she turned around and returned to the parking lot.
Q : She got out and walked to the nearest shop.
R : She drove her car into the parking lot and stopped.
S : It was there that she realised that she'd forgotten her purse at home.
The proper sequence should be:
A. R S Q P B. R Q S P
C. P Q R S D. Q P R S

47. S_1: Several sub-cities have been planned around the capital.
S_6: Hopefully the housing problem will not be as acute as at present after these sub-cities are built.
P : Dwarka is the first among them.
Q : They are expected to alleviate the problem of housing.
R : It is coming up in the south-west of the capital.
S : It will cater to over one million people when completed.
The proper sequence should be:
A. Q P R S B. P R S Q
C. P Q R S D. Q R S P

48. S_1: Just as some men like to play football or tennis, so some men like to climb mountains.
S_6: You look down and see the whole country below you.

P : This is often very difficult to do, for mountains are not just big hills.
Q : Paths are usually very steep, and some mountain-sides are straight up and down, so that it may take many hours to climb as little as one hundred feet.
R : There is always the danger that you may fall off and be killed or injured.
S : Men talk about conquering a mountain, and the wonderful feeling it is to reach the top of a mountain after climbing for hours and may be, even for days.
The proper sequence should be:
A. P Q R S   B. Q P S R
C. R Q P S   D. S R Q P

49. S_1: Ms. Paras started a petrol pump in Madras.
S_6: Thus she has shown the way for many others.
P : A total of twelve girls now work at the pump.
Q : She advertised in newspapers for women staff.
R : They operate in two shifts.
S : The response was good.
The proper sequence should be:
A. P Q S R   B. S Q P R
C. Q S P R   D. P Q R S

50. S_1: Your letter was a big relief.
S_6: But don't forget to bring chocolate for Geeta.
P : How did your exams go?
Q : After your result, you must come here for a week.
R : You hadn't written for over a month.
S : I am sure you will come out with flying colours.
The proper sequence should be:
A. P S R Q   B. Q R P S
C. R P S Q   D. R S P Q

Answers

1	2	3	4	5	6	7	8	9	10
C	D	A	A	D	C	A	B	B	B
11	12	13	14	15	16	17	18	19	20
B	B	A	C	A	A	D	C	B	A
21	22	23	24	25	26	27	28	29	30
D	C	D	A	C	A	A	C	B	D
31	32	33	34	35	36	37	38	39	40
A	B	D	A	C	B	B	C	C	A
41	42	43	44	45	46	47	48	49	50
B	B	A	B	B	B	A	A	C	C

Fill in the Blanks 7

Filling the blanks is such an exercise that begins with the primary schools and continues at the highest level of competitive examinations. One must practise it regularly to score well.

Directions: *Pick out the most effective word(s) from the given options to fill in the blanks and make each sentence meaningfully complete.*

1. You must ensure the correctness of the information before ....
   A. drawing B. enabling
   C. learning D. jumping

2. The rocket .... the target and did not cause any casualty.
   A. sensed B. reached
   C. missed D. exploded

3. It is desirable to take .... in any business if you want to make profit.
   A. advice B. risk
   C. loan D. recourse

4. They wasted all the money on purchase of some .... items.
   A. excellent B. important
   C. significant D. trivial

5. When he found the wallet his face glowed but soon it faded as the wallet was ....
   A. empty B. vacant
   C. recovered D. stolen

6. He has served the country by .... many significant positions.
   A. appointing B. creating
   C. developing D. holding

7. The frequent errors are a result of the student's ....
   A. talent B. smartness
   C. carelessness D. perception

8. The robbers eventually .... in breaking into the house.
   A. succeeded B. decided
   C. caught D. trained

9. I finally .... her to stay another day.
   A. advised B. persuaded
   C. suggested D. called

10. Most of the people who .... the book exhibition were teachers.
    A. witnessed B. presented
    C. conducted D. attended

11. One requires great .... to teach and handle little children who are restless.
    A. patience B. attitude
    C. determination D. knowledge

12. The researchers will .... some of the causes of increasing poverty in the state.
    A. fund　　　　B. investigate
    C. promote　　D. circulate

13. I usually perform .... when nobody is watching me.
    A. alone　　　B. good
    C. better　　　D. hard

14. It was .... to everyone that the minister had been drinking.
    A. observed　　B. known
    C. discovered　D. realised

15. I would rather stay indoors .... the rain stops.
    A. so　　　　B. waiting
    C. until　　　D. usually

16. The process should be completed as far as possible within a week, ... which the matter should be brought to notice of the officer concerned.
    A. following　　B. failing
    C. realizing　　D. referring

17. The officers are .... to regular transfers.
    A. free　　　B. open
    C. subject　D. available

18. All letters received from Government should .... be acknowledged.
    A. suddenly
    B. obviously
    C. immediately
    D. occasionally

19. Mumbai office .... a meeting of senior officials to discuss the high incidence of frauds.
    A. attended　　B. convened
    C. reported　　D. registered

20. The note should be .... to all the concerned departments for their consideration.
    A. regulated　B. requested
    C. carried　　D. forwarded

21. Your present statement does not .... what you said last week.
    A. accord to　B. accord in
    C. accord with　D. accord for

22. I had a vague .... that the lady originally belonged to Scotland.
    A. notion　　　B. expression
    C. imagination　D. theory

23. The prisoner showed no .... for his crimes.
    A. hatred　　　B. obstinacy
    C. remorse　　D. anger

24. It is inconceivable that in many schools children are subjected to physical .... in the name of discipline.
    A. violation　B. exercise
    C. violence　D. security

25. We have not yet fully realised the .... consequences of the war.
    A. happy　　B. pleasing
    C. grim　　　D. exciting

26. Happiness consists in being .... what we have.
    A. contented to
    B. contented with
    C. contented for
    D. contented in

27. His rude behaviour is a .... his organization.
    A. disgrace for
    B. disgrace on
    C. disgrace upon
    D. disgrace to

28. No child is .... understanding. One has to wait and provide proper guidance.
    A. dull to   B. dull in
    C. dull of   D. dull for
29. I am fully .... the problems facing the industry.
    A. alive with B. alive to
    C. alive for   D. alive on
30. The Romans were .... science.
    A. bad in   B. bad to
    C. bad for   D. bad at
31. Although I was .... of his plans, I encouraged him, because there was no one else who was willing to help.
    A. sceptical   B. remorseful
    C. fearful   D. excited
32. You have no business to .... pain on a weak and poor person.
    A. inflict   B. put
    C. direct   D. force
33. Her uncle died in a car accident. He was quite rich. She suddenly .... all her uncle's money.
    A. succeeded   B. caught
    C. gave   D. inherited
34. There was a major accident. The plane crashed. The pilot .... did not see the tower.
    A. likely   B. probably
    C. scarcely   D. hurriedly
35. The car we were travelling in .... a mile from home.
    A. broke off
    B. broke down
    C. broke into
    D. broke up
36. What are you .... in the kitchen cupboard?
    A. looking in B. looking on
    C. looking to D. looking for
37. I did not see the point of .... waiting for them, so I went home.
    A. hanging around
    B. hang on
    C. hang together
    D. hanging up
38. He lost confidence and .... of the deal at the last minute.
    A. backed out
    B. backed on
    C. backed down
    D. backed onto
39. To the dismay of all the students, the class monitor was .... berated by the Principal at a school assembly.
    A. critically
    B. ignominiously
    C. prudently
    D. fortuitously
40. All attempts to revive the fishing industry were .... failure.
    A. foredoomed to
    B. heading at
    C. predicted for
    D. estimated to
41. There are .... parked outside than yesterday.
    A. fewer cars
    B. few cars
    C. less cars
    D. a small number of cars
42. The minister had to .... some awkward questions from reporters.
    A. fend   B. fend at
    C. fend out   D. fend off

43. The .... of evidence was on the side of the plaintiff since all but one of the witnesses testified that his story was correct.
    A. propensity
    B. force
    C. preponderance
    D. brunt

44. Attention to detail is .... of a fine craftsman.
    A. hallmark
    B. stamp
    C. seal of authority
    D. authenticity

45. Behaving in a .... and serious way, even in a .... situation, makes people respect you.
    A. Calm, difficult
    B. steady, angry
    C. flamboyant, tricky
    D. cool astounding

46. Along with a sharp rise in ...., a recession would eventually result in more men, women, and children living in ....
    A. crime, apathy
    B. fatalities, poor
    C. deaths, slums
    D. unemployment, poverty

47. The government has .... to provide financial aid to the ones .... by severe floods in the city.
    A. desired, troubled
    B. promised, havoc
    C. failed, affected
    D. wanted, struck

48. An airplane with .... passengers on board made an unscheduled .... as the airport to which it was heading was covered with thick fog.
    A. imitable, slip
    B. faulty, stop
    C. variety, halt
    D. numerous, landing

49. Deemed universities .... huge fees, but have not been successful in providing .... education to our students.
    A. collect, maintaining
    B. pay, better
    C. ask, good
    D. charge, quality

50. If the banks desire to .... profit, they should get rid of .... measures.
    A. lose, concentrate
    B. increase, populist
    C. earn, unhealthy
    D. maximise, traditional

51. Leadership defines what the future should look like and .... people with that vision.
    A. aligns   B. develops
    C. trains   D. encourages

52. We upset ourselves by responding in an .... manner to someone else's actions.
    A. unabashed   B. irrational
    C. arduous   D. arguable

53. All the people involved in that issue feel a great .... to his suggestion.
    A. contradiction
    B. adherence
    C. indifference
    D. repugnance

54. These elections will be remembered as much for its antiincumbency mood as for its .... mandate
    A. invincible

B. rational
C. unprecedented
D. deliberate

55. How do you expect us to stay in such a .... building even if it can be hired on a nominal rent?
A. scruffy   B. disperate
C. fragmented   D. robust

56. .... efforts from all concerned are required to raise the social and economic conditions of our countrymen.
A. Perpetual   B. Dynamic
C. Massive   D. Exploring

57. Many companies see technology as a .... for a whole host of business problems.
A. consideration B. preference
C. linking   D. panacea

58. Known as devout and serious person, she also has .... sense of humour
A. better   B. plentiful
C. quick   D. good

59. The matter would have become serious if .... action had not been taken
A. hasty   B. fast
C. timely   D. unusual

60. The .... with which he is able to yield the paint brush is really remarkable.
A. ease   B. practice
C. majesty   D. sweep

61. The speaker did not properly use the time as he went on .... on one point alone.
A. devoting
B. deliberating
C. diluting
D. dilating

62. They decided to .... down their original plans for the bigger house and make it smaller.
A. climb   B. turn
C. scale   D. play

63. Usha was badly .... by the news which she got in the letter
A. electrified B. petrified
C. deranged   D. shaken

64. In spite of her other .... she still managed to find time for her hobbies
A. occupations
B. preoccupations
C. predilections
D. business

65. Success comes to those who are vigilant not to permit .... from the chosen path
A. distraction B. deviation
C. alienation   D. diversion

66. It is advisable to .... on this issue rather than create unnecessary problem by taking a rigid stand
A. lose
B. promise
C. evade
D. compromise

67. After a short holiday she came back totally ....
A. rejuvenated B. reborn
C. refurbished D. revamped

68. The victim tried to tell us what had happened but his .... were not audible.
A. assailants   B. sounds
C. letters   D. words

69. The .... between the twins is so slight that it is very difficult to identify one from the other.
    A. similarity   B. distance
    C. resemblance   D. difference
70. The members were .... of the date of the meeting well in advance.
    A. communicated
    B. conveyed
    C. ignorant
    D. informed
71. A .... of ships was kept ready to scour the sea in case of an emergency.
    A. group   B. pack
    C. unit   D. fleet
72. I had not expected to meet him; it was quite an .... meeting.
    A. organised   B. intentional
    C. undesirable   D. accidental
73. The window of our room .... the rear.
    A. overlooks   B. opens
    C. opposes   D. adjoins
74. I could .... see the sight since it was dark.
    A. clearly   B. barely
    C. obviously   D. aptly
75. The top-ranking manager .... his success in the profession to his Managing Director's guidance.
    A. account   B. agrees
    C. attributes   D. claims
76. Does your pride keep you .... making the decision you know you should?
    A. away   B. alert
    C. from   D. quiet
77. Their .... to scale the mountain peak was an absolute failure.
    A. attempt   B. desire
    C. anxiety   D. proposal
78. The writer, like a spider .... a web; the creatures caught in the web have no substance, no reality.
    A. spins   B. catches
    C. writes   D. compiles
79. In a .... move the Chief Minister today dropped two ministers from the cabinet.
    A. secret   B. delicate
    C. continuous   D. surprise
80. In his address to the teachers, the Vice-Chancellor .... certain measures being taken for improving the quality of college education.
    A. declined   B. directed
    C. advised   D. highlighted
81. Change the legal system are inevitable for we are not working for a .... society.
    A. backward   B. dynamic
    C. stagnant   D. modern
82. Modern science began .... the influence of Copernicus, Kepler, Galileo and Newton.
    A. by   B. under
    C. from   D. upon
83. A meeting of senior police officers was held to .... the law and order situation of the town.
    A. review   B. curb
    C. cover   D. support
84. The problems that India's economic development faces are ....
    A. myopic   B. dubious
    C. enormous   D. strong

85. In our zeal for progress we should not .... the executive with more powers.
    A. avoid   B. arm
    C. give   D. enhance

86. At present, all over the world, moral standards, ... to have fallen.
    A. look   B. wish
    C. started   D. appear

87. He was one of the .... spirits behind the successful agitation of the citizens for keeping the city clean.
    A. revolving B. moving
    C. evolving   D. amazing

88. You've never .... me about your experiences in Scotland.
    A. described B. explained
    C. told   D. said

89. The student .... that book from the library to study at home.
    A. issued   B. borrowed
    C. hired   D. lent

90. I wish I .... a king.
    A. was   B. am
    C. should be D. were

91. He .... to listen to my arguments and walked away.
    A. denied   B. disliked
    C. objected   D. refused

92. The flow of blood was so .... that the patient died.
    A. intense   B. adequate
    C. profuse   D. extensive

93. When I met her yesterday, it was the first time I .... her since Christmas.
    A. saw
    B. have seen
    C. had seen
    D. have been seing

94. Can you pay .... all these articles?
    A. for   B. of
    C. off   D. out

95. He .... the role of the organisation in creating environmental awareness among the people.
    A. commanded
    B. commended
    C. commented
    D. commemorated

96. I .... you to be at the party this evening.
    A. expect
    B. hope
    C. look forward to
    D. desire

97. The consequence of economic growth has now .... to the lowest level.
    A. flowed   B. percolated
    C. gone   D. crept

98. The employees were unhappy because their salary was not increased ....
    A. marginally
    B. abruptly
    C. substantially
    D. superflously

99. .... the being a handicapped person, he is very co-operative and self-reliant.
    A. Because   B. Although
    C. Since   D. Despite

100. The child broke .... from his mother and ran towards the painting.
    A. away   B. after
    C. down   D. with

101. With his .... income, he finds it difficult to live a comfortable life.
    A. brief
    B. sufficient
    C. meagre
    D. huge

102. He could .... a lot of money in such a short time by using his intelligence and working hard.
    A. spend
    B. spoil
    C. exchange
    D. accumulate

103. Though the brothers are twins, they look ....
    A. alike
    B. handsome
    C. indifferent
    D. different

104. Unfavourable weather conditions can .... illness.
    A. cure
    B. detect
    C. treat
    D. enhance

105. No sooner did the bell ring, ... the actor started singing.
    A. when
    B. than
    C. after
    D. before

106. If I .... realised it, I would not have acted on his advice.
    A. was
    B. had
    C. were
    D. have

107. Why don't you .... your work in advance before commencing it.
    A. start
    B. complete
    C. finish
    D. plan

108. Contemporary economic development differs .... from the Industrial Revolution of the 19th century.
    A. usually
    B. specially
    C. literally
    D. markedly

109. Mounting unemployment is the most serous and .... problem faced by India today.
    A. profound
    B. intractable
    C. unpopular
    D. dubious

110. Unemployment is not only .... throughout the emerging world, but is growing worse, especially in urban areas.
    A. endemic
    B. peripheral
    C. absorbing
    D. prolific

111. Manpower is the .... means of converting other resources to mankind's use and benefit.
    A. inimitable
    B. indivisible
    C. indispensable
    D. inequitable

112. This article tries to .... us with problems of poor nations so that we help them more effectively.
    A. enable
    B. convince
    C. allow
    D. acquaint

113. Among human beings, language is the principal .... of communication.
    A. methodology
    B. instrument
    C. accomplishment
    D. theory

114. These essays are intellectually .... are represent various levels of complexity.
    A. persistent
    B. superior
    C. modern
    D. demanding

115. .... the doctor's advice he started taking some daily exercise.
    A. In
    B. To
    C. On
    D. Towards

116. Do you .... giving that book to me for a few days?
    A. desires
    B. mind
    C. call
    D. observe

117. Our volunteers will .... your donations either in cash or kind and give you a receipt.
    A. lend   B. gave
    C. return   D. collect

118. If you need some money, I will .... the amount from my bank and give you.
    A. deposit   B. return
    C. withdraw   D. require

119. .... he wanted to attend his friend's party, he could not attend it.
    A. As   B. But
    C. Since   D. Although

120. The boss considered the situation and .... only three days leave to him.
    A. granted   B. submitted
    C. sanction   D. asked

121. If you want to do well, you must follow a strict .... in your studies.
    A. discipline   B. belief
    C. view   D. report

122. It was very difficult to dig as the ground was very ....
    A. thin   B. soft
    C. rigid   D. hard

123. He was .... with a serious crime.
    A. condemned   B. charged
    C. accused   D. convicted

124. The oil crisis highlighted the need to develop new .... of energy and to conserve those which are already in use.
    A. means   B. preserves
    C. methods   D. sources

125. The wood always .... on water.
    A. floated   B. floats
    C. was floating   D. float

126. He finds it difficult to .... between blue and green as he is colour blind.
    A. recognise   B. see
    C. distinguish   D. study

127. The bright colour of this shirt has .... away.
    A. faded   B. paled
    C. disappeared   D. gone

128. The .... animal was on the look out for food.
    A. savage   B. uncivilised
    C. primitive   D. wild

129. The bank clerk tried to .... money from his friend's account.
    A. embezzle   B. embroil
    C. embellish   D. empower

130. The movement of the train was so .... that all the passengers slept very well.
    A. noisy   B. fast
    C. soothing   D. distracting

131. That rule is applicable .... everyone.
    A. to   B. for
    C. about   D. with

132. Besides other provisions, that shopkeeper deals .... cosmetics too.
    A. with   B. in
    C. at   D. for

133. The music for event was .... by A.R. Rahman.
    A. made
    B. composed
    C. demonstrated
    D. displayed

134. The reward is a .... of her service to mankind.
    A. recognition   B. witness
    C. memorial   D. memento

135. The most important task of the Air Force is to .... the country against an air attack by an enemy.
    A. secure   B. save
    C. defend   D. protect
136. The ruling party will have to put its own house .... order.
    A. in   B. on
    C. to   D. into
137. As a general rule, politicians do not .... centre stage.
    A. forward   B. forbid
    C. forgive   D. forsake
138. Shivam .... classical music. He always prefers Bhimsen Joshi to Asha Bhonsale, and Pandit Jasraj to Kumar Sanu.
    A. adores
    B. apprehends
    C. encompasses
    D. cultivates
139. Indications are that the Government is .... to the prospect of granting bonus to the striking employees.
    A. aligned   B. obliged
    C. reconciled   D. relieved
140. The .... study on import of natural gas from Iran through a pipeline would be completed shortly.
    A. natural   B. calculated
    C. economic   D. feasibility
141. His party is solely to be blamed for the political .... in the country.
    A. devaluation   B. revival
    C. advocacy   D. stalemate
142. We still have not given our .... to conduct the survey of natural resources in our State.
    A. projection
    B. consent
    C. request
    D. compliance
143. He is the best man for this job. He has mental .... to carry it out.
    A. predilection   B. durability
    C. adroitness   D. persuasion
144. Man is ....; however, he is more in need of mental companionship than of physical companionship.
    A. egoistic   B. biological
    C. emotional   D. gregarious
145. We cannot go on strike every year. Now that we have gone on strike we must .... this issue.
    A. clinch   B. culminate
    C. cross   D. canvass
146. I was totally .... by his line of thinking and could not put forth any argument.
    A. demolished
    B. nonplussed
    C. exhausted
    D. refuted
147. Any problem to be .... needs to be broken down to small pieces.
    A. chosen   B. taught
    C. tackled   D. posed
148. He has .... people visiting him at his house because he fears it will cause discomfort to neighbours.
    A. forbidden   B. warned
    C. stopped   D. request
149. Nowadays, why .... people so scared of each other?
    A. were   B. is
    C. had   D. are
150. If the perceptions of two individuals do not .... there is bound to be problems.
    A. reflect   B. differ
    C. match   D. express

Answers

1	2	3	4	5	6	7	8	9	10
A	C	B	D	A	D	C	A	B	D
11	12	13	14	15	16	17	18	19	20
A	B	C	A	C	B	C	C	B	D
21	22	23	24	25	26	27	28	29	30
C	A	C	C	C	B	D	B	B	D
31	32	33	34	35	36	37	38	39	40
B	C	C	B	C	C	D	A	B	A
41	42	43	44	45	46	47	48	49	50
A	D	D	A	A	D	C	D	C	B
51	52	53	54	55	56	57	58	59	60
A	A	D	C	A	A	D	D	C	A
61	62	63	64	65	66	67	68	69	70
D	C	D	B	A	D	A	D	D	D
71	72	73	74	75	76	77	78	79	80
D	D	A	B	C	C	A	A	D	D
81	82	83	84	85	86	87	88	89	90
C	B	A	C	B	D	B	C	B	D
91	92	93	94	95	96	97	98	99	100
D	C	C	A	B	A	B	C	D	A
101	102	103	104	105	106	107	108	109	110
C	D	D	D	B	B	D	D	B	A
111	112	113	114	115	116	117	118	119	120
C	D	B	D	C	B	D	C	D	A
121	122	123	124	125	126	127	128	129	130
A	D	B	D	B	C	A	D	A	C
131	132	133	134	135	136	137	138	139	140
A	B	B	A	C	A	D	A	C	D
141	142	143	144	145	146	147	148	149	150
D	B	C	D	A	B	C	C	D	C

❑ ❑ ❑

Cloze Test 8

A cloze test is a procedure in which a person is asked to supply words that have been removed from a passage as a test of his ability to comprehend text. Practice it regularly to score well.

Directions: *In each of the following passages some numbered blank spaces are given. For each numbered blank space four answer choices are given. Pick out the one which is the most appropriate for that blank space, keeping the trend of the passage in mind.*

PASSAGE-1

Every action we perform ....(1).... a result. And, naturally, we lay claim ....(2).... the results or fruits ....(3).... from that action in the ....(4).... that it is we who perform the action. This is .....(5).... ignorance because ....(6).... is it the Lord who ....(7).... the result of any action, it is by His will ....(8).... that even the action is accomplished. The will of the Lord ....(9).... whether we cooperate with His will or strive ....(10).... . If God wills that an action takes place, he arranges for the ....(11).... for it to happen. It is ....(12).... experience that sometimes despite our best efforts we ....(13).... achieve the results we desire, and at other times the seemingly most ....(14).... situations mysteriously get ....(15).... . ....(16).... way man chooses to act, both the act and the outcome of the cost are dependent ...(17)... on the will of the Lord.

Questions

1. A. produce   B. produces
    C. causes   D. undergoes
2. A. on   B. at
    C. to   D. for
3. A. occuring   B. obtaining
    C. deriving   D. falling
4. A. belief   B. hope
    C. fantasy   D. folly
5. A. sheen   B. keen
    C. sheer   D. sheathe
6. A. alone   B. only that
    C. not only   D. for only
7. A. declares   B. decides
    C. ordains   D. ornate
8. A. completely   B. entirely
    C. only   D. alone
9. A. prevails always
    B. prevails everywhere
    C. is prevalent
    D. always prevails
10. A. alone
    B. always
    C. constantly
    D. independently

11. A. wherewithal B. whereabouts
    C. whatsoever   D. wherefore
12. A. usual   B. general
    C. universal   D. common
13. A. does not   B. may not
    C. do not   D. might not
14. A. intractable B. intangible
    C. internecine D. intricate
15. A. subsided   B. resolved
    C. solved   D. converted
16. A. Whatever   B. All the
    C. All those   D. Whichever
17. A. mainly   B. actually
    C. entirely   D. generally

PASSAGE-2

For centuries, women not only in India but all over the world ....(1).... treated as ....(2).... secondary position to men. ....(3).... human history men ....(4).... far greater power then women to name, classify, and order the worlds in which they both live. ....(5).... studies in various parts of the world point out to a wide ....(6).... in male and female roles ....(7).... cultures and demonstrate the possibility of change in these sex-determined roles. The 20th century in particular ....(8).... the cause of gender justice by internationalizing struggles for equality ....(9).... women and other oppressed people. Women's struggles against their ....(10).... were intertwined in ....(11).... degrees with ideologies and movements based on the values of freedom, self-determination, equality, democracy and justice.

Questions

1. A. has been   B. have been
   C. had been   D. were
2. A. occupying   B. taking
   C. possessing D. serving
3. A. All through B. Throughout
   C. Since   D. From
4. A. have   B. had
   C. have had   D. enjoy
5. A. Sociological
   B. Anthropological
   C. General
   D. Practical
6. A. concord   B. repulsion
   C. disagreement D. variation
7. A. among   B. across
   C. between   D. of
8. A. developed   B. envolved
   C. promoted   D. entertained
9. A. for   B. to
   C. among   D. by
10. A. subsidiary
    B. subsequent
    C. subservience
    D. subordination
11. A. various   B. varying
    C changing   D. differing

PASSAGE-3

What is required today in our country is ....(1).... of a new political culture based on full respect for human liberty, on pluralism and on a better social deal for all. The major ....(2).... facing us today is to carry out democratic transformation in all the ....(3)...., social, cultural, economic and political. The events of the 20th century ....(4).... one thing absolutely clear that human ....(5)...., everywhere, specially in countries whose political structures were ....(6).... to reflect the revolutionary aspirations of the people ....(7).... not only under stress and strain but are ....(8).... vast upheavals because of the ....(9).... of democracy. At the same time it has also to be understood that democracy cannot be ....(10).... into a static mould.

Questions

1. A. growing   B. developing
   C. creating   D. creation
2. A. development B. crisis
   C. challenge   D. drawback
3. A. corners   B. context
   C. realm   D. spheres
4. A. have made B. has made
   C. had made   D. made
5. A. travails   B. traverse
   C. traps   D. transverse
6. A. supposed   B. meant
   C. caused   D. forced
7. A. were   B. was
   C. are   D. have been
8. A. developing B. evolving
   C. experiencing D. faced with
9. A. denial   B. rebuff
   C. rebuttal   D. absence
10. A. shaped   B. flex
    C. frozen   D. caused

PASSAGE-4

We are living in very exciting ....(1).... . The ....(2).... change is dizzying and the impact this progress is having on our present and – more importantly – on our future is difficult to ....(3).... in its ...(4).... . This is the age of ....(5).... micro processors, sophisticated software, new hardware technology and high bandwith, high-speed networks. The PC gave us a new way to work, play and ....(6).... . In fact, it brought ....(7).... our desktops computing power, which until a few years ....(8).... had only been available to corporates. With the ....(9).... of the internet, the PC ....(10).... us the most convenient and flexible way to head on to the Net.

Questions

1. A. periods   B. days
   C. phase   D. times
2. A. phase   B. pace
   C. sphere   D. drastic
3. A. guess   B. forecast
   C. comprehend D. approximate
4. A. whole   B. entirety
   C. fruition   D. fullness
5. A. strong   B. changing
   C. powerful   D. sonorous
6. A. convey
   B. communicate
   C. entertain
   D. enjoy
7. A. onto   B. to
   C. on   D. at
8. A. back   B. earlier
   C. behind   D. before
9. A. addendum   B. adherence
   C. afoot   D. advent
10. A. allowed   B. privileged
    C. brought   D. offered

PASSAGE-5

The development of an area depends on the resources ....(1).... in the area, the needs and ....(2).... of the people living there and the technological skill ....(3).... by them. Humans play an important and decisive role in the ....(4).... of development of an area. We choose the ....(5).... of resources which could be developed to our ....(6)..... . The natural ....(7).... available in an area ....(8).... value as a resource only when people find a use for them. There are ....(9).... where large potential resources are available, but they ....(10).... developed for economic reasons. Lack of capital for investments, roads and railway lines, and other ....(11).... facilities may stand in the way of resource development.

Questions

1. A. present B. prevalent
   C. available D. exist
2. A. inspirations B. aspirations
   C. ambitions D. curiosity
3. A. handled B. practised
   C. availed D. possessed
4. A. system B. design
   C. pattern D. style
5. A. class B. group
   C. variety D. types
6. A. good B. advantage
   C. approach D. favour
7. A. secrets
   B. phenomenon
   C. products
   D. endowments
8. A. get B. acquire
   C. possess D. takes
9. A. instances B. events
   C. circumstances D. happenings
10. A. have not yet been
    B. haven't been
    C. are not yet
    D. yet have not been
11. A. common B. general
    C. infrastructural D. structural

PASSAGE-6

The Naxal problem in India is basically socio-economic in ....(1).... . The main reasons ....(2).... the Naxal movement in India are the ....(3).... of peasants and their weak social and economic position. ....(4).... of the peasants are landless labourers whose lands have been ....(5).... occupied by the landlords. Moreover, the landlords give ....(6).... wages to the peasants. Their ....(7).... suffering at the hands of the landlords thus encourage many peasants to take law ....(8).... their own hands. Due to their poor economic condition the peasants easily ....(9).... the trap of the naxal leaders who have their ....(10).... interests. Illeteracy, unemployment, police excessess, corruption and ....(11).... administration furthur ....(12).... this complex problem.

Questions

1. A. form B. shape
   C. behaviour D. nature
2. A. for B. of
   C. in D. behind
3. A. complaisance B. exploitation
   C. domination D. excultation
4. A. Many B. Much
   C. Most D. All
5. A. imperiously B. imperatively
   C. forcefully D. forcibly
6. A. improper B. small
   C. inadequate D. insufficient
7. A. long B. brutal
   C. pathetic D. great
8. A. in B. into
   C. on D. by

9.	A. fall into	B. fall in	
	C. fell in	D. fell into	
10.	A. selfish	B. vested	
	C. vicious	D. vindictive	
11.	A. failed	B. improper	
	C. inefficient	D. bureaucratic	
12.	A. heighten	B. deepen	
	C. add	D. worsen	

PASSAGE-7

Visualisation is a strong ....(1).... to memory. Those persons who ......(2)..... a powerful memory cannot do so without taking the help of visualisation. Such persons have developed the skills to ....(3).... visualisation even in such ....(4).... tasks as remembering names and numbers. These persons have the names and numbers ....(5).... in their brain even after hearing those names and figures only once. On the other hand those who take the help of revising to memorise ....(6).... to forget it once they have ....(7).... the practice of revising ....(8).... the ones who have applied visualisation to memorise. Psychologists ....(9).... in visualisation a powerful tool for personality development. The more you visualise, the more you are ....(10).... your attitude and behaviour to the blue prints of your vision and ....(11).... more you are inching towards success.

Questions

1. A. way   B. path
   C. aid   D. symptom
2. A. command   B. master
   C. rule   D. enjoy
3. A. use   B. apply
   C. put   D. place

4. A. trivial   B. difficult
   C. mundane   D. unscrupulous
5. A. impress   B. imprinted
   C. impinge   D. store
6. A. bent   B. incline
   C. prone   d. tend
7. A. dropped   B. left
   C. gave up   D. given up
8. A. unlike   B. opposite
   C. contrary   D. not like
9. A. found   B. have found
   C. sees   D. finds
10. A. shaping   B. moulding
    C. making   D. attuning
11. A. actually
    B. factually
    C. subsequently
    D. consequently

PASSAGE-8

No doubt various ....(1).... and Acts are there to eliminate the ....(2).... practice of child labour. But the ....(3).... is that, these are not being implemented in both letter and spirit, for which the ....(4).... of the problem remains as it was. Therefore a judicious, pragmatic, integrated and time-bound ....(5).... supplemented by ....(6).... follow-up action is essential to ....(7).... the problem that ....(8).... deep root in our Society. It is true that child labour can't be ....(9)... with a magic wand. If we ....(10).... time-bound goals and follow, of course, with the ....(11).... assistance of ILO and UNICEF, it is possible to eliminate the problem of child labour. With strong political will power and people's backing nothing is ....(12).... . Rather ....(13).... the bud we should let it blossom and spread its fragrance all around. ....(14).... lies the progress and prosperity of the society.

Questions

1. A. means B. methods
   C. source D. provisions
2. A. unjust B. inhuman
   C. mal D. illegal
3. A. anxiety B. abrasion
   C. tragedy D. conclusion
4. A. magnitude B. depth
   C. gravity D. soaring
5. A. approach B. analysis
   C. survey D. scheme
6. A. continuous B. thorough
   C. throughout D. regular
7. A. outroot B. uproot
   C. downroot D. grassroot
8. A. have B. has
   C. had D. has taken
9. A. wipe out B. wipe off
   C. wipe up D. wiped
10. A. keep B. put
    C. put up D. set
11. A. ongoing B. continuing
    C. unending D. frequent
12. A. insurmountable B. intangible
    C. inscrutable D. incorrigible
13. A. killing B. hurting
    C. destroying D. nipping
14. A. Here B. There
    C. Therein D. Herein

PASSAGE-9

Though the government has tried to ....(1).... Naxalism with all its might, much more needs to be done to totally root out the ....(2).... of Naxalism. The roots of Naxalism ....(3).... economic backwardness and social exploitation of the peasants and the weaker classes. Thus, the best way to ....(4).... Naxalism is to bring the naxals ....(5).... the mainstream. ....(6).... policies and schemes should be implemented effectively ....(7).... the Naxals economically stable. They should be ....(8).... to participate in democratic processes. The government has to ....(9).... the social upliftment of the Naxals. Use of force in ....(10).... Naxalism will yield little success.

Questions

1. A. crush B. handle
   C. tackle D. suppress
2. A. menace B. whole
   C. gamut D. stems
3. A. lies in B. are in
   C. abound in D. exist in
4. A. crash B. crush
   C. break D. defy
5. A. in B. on
   C. into D. within
6. A. Current B. Latest
   C. Occuring D. Existing
7. A. so that
   B. so as to make
   C. such that
   D. to make
8. A. insisted B. brought
   C. encouraged D. forced
9. A. assure B. insure
   C. guarantee D. ensure
10. A. countering B. defying
    C. banishing D. desecrating

PASSAGE-10

Mankind's most ....(1).... treasure of thoughts is carefully preserved in the golden casket of books. The ....(2).... of books is as vast as the universe, for there is no corner of it which they have left ....(3).... . There is no ....(4).... of books on any topic, be it as simple as the composition of sodium nitrate or as ....(5).... as the mechanism of a spacecraft rocketing towards mars. The ....(6).... of books is not only most easily available but is enlightened, dependable and lifelong. In times of distress they make us stoically ....(7).... of the object that causes uneasiness and we learn to ....(8).... with the sting of adversity.

Questions _____

1. A. costly   B. important
    C. valuable   D. vast
2. A. area   B. scope
    C. storage   D. kingdom
3. A. unexplored
    B. unseen
    C. untouched
    D. unapproached
4. A. lack
    B. dearth
    C. shortage
    D. insufficiency
5. A. extriate   B. intricate
    C. intrinsic   D. internecine
6. A. company
    B. assistance
    C. friendship
    D. companionship
7. A. defiant   B. defendant
    C. defensible   D. delusive
8. A. adapt   B. adopt
    C. exist   D. co-exist

PASSAGE-11

The common ....(1).... deeply embedded in all holy scriptures is to know one's real self. This message serves as a warning as well as ....(2).... to humankind to rise above body-mind consciousness. Living in this world just for ....(3).... of carnal desires and thinking it to be-all of life is a great ....(4).... . It is very important to know that we will ....(5).... to suffer till we ....(6).... to identify ourselves with gross body and mind. Thus, ...(7).... of our true divine nature is of ....(8).... importance.

Questions _____

1. A. inscriptions   B. belief
    C. message   D. notions
2. A. an exhortation
    B. emendation
    C. exegesis
    D. entrenchment
3. A. satiation   B. satiety
    C. content   D. sensuality
4. A. sin   B. curse
    C. fallacy   D. farcial
5. A. go on   B. continue
    C. subject   D. cause
6. A. end   B. stop
    C. cease   D. leave
7. A. knowledge   B. realisation
    C. appreciation   D. recognition
8. A. spiritual   B. worldly
    C. general   D. paramount

PASSAGE-12

We are all ....(1).... of the communal riots in Godhra and its ....(2).... . There are many who believe that the events in the rest of Gujarat were a ....(3).... to Godhra. We can understand a common man's reaction on seeing a close relative or friend being ....(4).... . ....(5)..., on such occasions, may be ......(6).... as a natural emotional reaction. But people in authority cannot ....(7).... to make such a comment. The Government cannot allow anyone to take the law ....(8).... his hands and it is duty bound to maintain law and order. ....(9)...., we are not a vigilante society yet. The violence in Gujarat is an ....(10).... . It is the ....(11).... of undesirable elements that are fortunately not ....(12).... in number. The majority of our people will get over this ....(13).... so that India can continue its march towards becoming a just society and an internationally competitive and ....(14).... economy.

Questions

1. A. conscious B. knowing
   C. aware D. sensitive
2. A. follows
   B. consequences
   C. subsequence
   D. aftermath
3. A. reaction B. reply
   C. response D. restitution
4. A. humiliated B. assaulted
   C. affronted D. annihilated
5. A. Retrogression B. Revengeful
   C. Retrocede D. Retaliation
6. A. understood
   B. understandable
   C. pardonable
   D. thought
7. A. expect B. think
   C. dare D. afford
8. A. in B. on
   C. into D. at
9. A. Since B. After all
   C. Above all D. As
10. A. aberration B. abysmal
    C. apotheosis D. aversion
11. A. cause B. built-up
    C. planning D. creation
12. A. great B. much
    C. large D. big
13. A. catharsis B. catastrophe
    C. crisis D. castigation
14. A. self-developed
    B. self-realised
    C. self-recognised
    D. self-reliant

PASSAGE-13

This book is ....(1).... of the disquiet that ....(2).... in the minds and hearts of the women of the region. The objective of this work is to ....(3).... attention to the tragedy of Kashmir. The fact that while ....(4).... of the secular and mixed tradition of Kashmir is all gone, its breathtaking beauty is ....(5).... by the harsh realities of the terror and brutality, the ....(6).... violence that people, especially the women, have to ....(7).... . The writer hopes that the book can ....(8).... a move towards peace and ....(9).... . It is a ....(10).... objective. This is a book which ....(11).... to be read for its honest ....(12).... to capture the voices, the images, the very spirit, sometimes crushed sometimes ....(13)..., of the women of the region called Kashmir.

Questions

1. A. an exploration
   B. chronicle
   C. record
   D. an exploitation

2. A. stays   B. lies
    C. rages   D. exist
3. A. focus   B. draw
    C. pull   D. direct
4. A. most   B. many
    C. each   D. much
5. A. belied   B. removed
    C. destructed   D. influenced
6. A. prevailing   B. growing
    C. continuing   D. regular
7. A. go through   B. live through
    C. succumb   D. face
8. A. effect   B. affect
    C. influence   D. invigorate
9. A. retreat
    B. tranquility
    C. negotiation
    D. reconciliation
10. A. superb   B. fruitful
    C. wise   D. brave
11. A. meant   B. supposed
    C. needs   D. deserves
12. A. endeavour   B. effusion
    C. endurance   D. empathy
13. A. yielding   B. indomitable
    C. indiscernible   D. ineffable

PASSAGE-14

....(1).... has been said about a new global effort to ....(2).... sustainable development. ....(3).... were adopted and declarations were issued on a new ....(4).... between rich and poor countries that would ....(5).... the world to the Millennium Development Goals on poverty, health, education and gender .....(6).... . The global fight against hunger is in ....(7).... need of a much stronger ....(8).... . If a ....(9).... in the spread of undernourishment is proving hard to ....(10)...., elimination of hunger must be a goal that keeps getting ....(11).... further and further ....(12).... the future. In the vast majority of developing countries there is a ....(13).... in the efforts to reduce malnutrition.

Questions

1. A. Lot   B. Much
    C. Large   D. More
2. A. accentuate   B. accelerate
    C. adjurate   D. actuate
3. A. Agreement
    B. Arrangement
    C. Plans
    D. Agendas
4. A. coalition
    B. friendship
    C. partnership
    D. combination
5. A. bring   B. get
    C. take   D. place
6. A. equality   B. liberty
    C. prosperity   D. partiality
7. A. absolute   B. acute
    C. urgent   D. substantial
8. A. thrust   B. thump
    C. bolt   D. thrash
9. A. minimisation   B. diminish
    C. reduction   D. reduce
10. A. bring   B. bring about
    C. achieve   D. attain
11. A. pulled   B. pushed
    C. motion   D. acuteness
12. A. towards   B. to
    C. in   D. into
13. A. sickness   B. slackening
    C. inactiveness   D. inception

PASSAGE-15

....(1).... people today remember the war that was fought after China invaded India in 1962. Not because the war was never really ....(2).... . Nor because it was ....(3).... almost before it began. The reason is ....(4).... that most of us were yet to be born. The main reason for the Chinese attack seems to ....(5).... to establish the ....(6).... order, expose our ....(7)...., put us in our place. The official reason, ...(8)...., was the territorial dispute, ...(9).... more than 100,000 square kilometres. ....(10).... speaking, India borders Tibet, not China. The McMohan Line ....(11).... the border with Tibet in what is now Arunachal Pradesh was the result of a 1914 treaty ....(12).... British India and Tibet. This was not ....(13).... to the Chinese the result was a .....(14)..... nose. The Chinese attack was ....(15).... fast and furious. ....(16).... brave soldiers ....(17).... down their lives, but India was simply unable to halt the ....(17).... . Panic quickly ....(18)....

Questions

1. A. A few   B. Few
   C. Fewer   D. A little
2. A. joined   B. combined
   C. acted   D. approved
3. A. finished   B. ceased
   C. over   D. stopped
4. A. simple   B. simply
   C. common   D. commonly
5. A. had been   B. have
   C. had   D. have been
6. A. pecking
   B. unavoiding
   C. powerful
   D. selfish
7. A. projections
   B. pretensions
   C. presumption
   D. pretending
8. A. more over   B. probably
   C. perhaps   D. however
9. A. effecting   B. causing
   C. affecting   D. influencing
10. A. Formally   B. Informally
    C. Broadly   D. Technically
11. A. relating   B. dividing
    C. defining   D. laying
12. A. among   B. between
    C. of   D. by
13. A. favourable B. favoured
    C. acceptable D. accepting
14. A. angry   B. bloody
    C. honed   D. blitz
15. A. quick   B. prick
    C. sudden   D. unassuming
16. A. Some   B. Few
    C. Many   D. A lot of
17. A. onrush   B. onset
    C. omnipotence D. omen
18. A. come in   B. gone in
    C. set in   D. set out

PASSAGE-16

Man has always been ....(1).... with flying because it ....(2).... a sense of freedom, of romance and thrill-something too ....(3).... to resist. It is the task of the ....(4).... of the skies to safeguard Indian air-space from unwelcome ....(5)..... . The Indian Air Force ....(6).... a chequered and glorious history. From its ....(7).... days of single-engine aeroplanes like Tempests and Spitfires to the state of the art multi-engine, supersonic MIG and Sukhoi fighters, the Indian Air Force ....(8).... a long way. In addition to the already existing ....(9).... of aircraft and weapon systems, plans are ....(10).... to enhance its air defence power and ....(11).... capability through upgradation and ....(12).... .

Questions

1. A. fascinated   B. moved
   C. inspired   D. fancied
2. A. generates   B. cultivates
   C. reaps   D. evokes
3. A. envisaging   B. impressing
   C. enchanting   D. laudable
4. A. sentinels   B. sedulous
   C. venturous   D. fervid
5. A. emigrants   B. intruders
   C. foreigners   D. tourists
6. A. had   B. have
   C. have had   D. has had
7. A. early
   B. undeveloped
   C. growing
   D. embryonic
8. A. had come   B. has come
   C. have come   D. came
9. A. invention
   B. inventory
   C. mechanism
   D. technique
10. A. progressive B. afresh
    C. afoot   D. affluent
11. A. combat   B. increase
    C. intensify   D. ensure
12. A. acquisition
    B. acknowledgement
    C. acquiescence
    D. accumulation

PASSAGE-17

Libraries were never ....(1).... the place to ....(2).... . They never will be. But those who've visited libraries for the ....(3).... pleasure of it will testify to the feeling of ....(4).... on entering the labyrinth ....(5).... high with books. Suddenly, a ....(6).... spent reading seems the ideal. It's a similar experience to ....(7).... in a bookshop. The difference : in the second situation, despair ....(8).... you as your eyes zoom ....(9).... on the price; in the first there is the ....(10).... that all these books are yours for the asking. Today, ...(11)...., library use is almost ....(12).... necessity-based. The reading room is ....(13).... full with students poring ....(14).... their books..

Questions

1. A. realised   B. seen
   C. recognised   D. considered
2. A. hung out
   B. hang out
   C. hang out in
   D. hung out in
3. A. mere   B. sheer
   C. trivial   D. trifle
4. A. exhilaration
   B. exhaustion
   C. expedition
   D. extrapolation
5. A. going   B. moving
   C. pile   D. towering
6. A. long time   B. whole life
   C. life time   D. life long
7. A. browsing
   B. move about
   C. move
   D. stroll

8. A. swamps   B. swab
   C. swoon   D. swoop
9. A. at   B. on
   C. in   D. upon
10. A. idea   B. surity
    C. certainty D. knowledge
11. A. although B. however
    C. in fact   D. moreover
12. A. wholly   B. partially
    C. outwardly D. purely
13. A. tight   B. completely
    C. over crowded D. cramped
14. A. into   B. onto
    C. over   D. upon

3. A. without   B. scarcely
   C. not   D. hardly
4. A. foolish   B. absurd
   C. mean   D. unmindful
5. A. does not B. do not
   C. don't   D. won't
6. A. part   B. step
   C. enthusiasm D. measures
7. A. has been B. have been
   C. are   D. had been
8. A. are not being told
   B. are not told
   C. have not been told
   D. had not been told
9. A. by   B. under
   C. in   D. into

PASSAGE-18

The ridge is on the ....(1).... of collapse. The stems of trees are being slaughtered without any ....(2).... or reason. The nearby residents cut plants just for cooking purpose ....(3).... realising that their ....(4).... act will spoil the environment. Though the forest department must have foreign guards in the area yet they ....(5).... seem to have the will and strength to take ....(6).... to stop the felling of trees. Everyday one can see wood and fresh cut stems which ....(7)... taken away by those living in the neighbourhood. It is not clear as to why they ....(8).... about the crime of felling of trees which is punishable ....(9).... the law.

Questions

1. A. verge   B. limit
   C. border   D. boundary
2. A. sense   B. rhyme
   C. rhythm   D. ultimatum

PASSAGE-19

The ....(1).... of a country does not depend on the abundance of its revenue but more ....(2).... by its citizens; its men of education, enlightenment and character. It is for the ....(3).... of higher learning to ....(4).... an academic environment of equity, justice and fair play where those ....(5).... in the ....(6).... task of nation building can ....(7).... their responsibilities in a spirit of sincerity, dedication and commitment. Higher education in India ....(8).... great strides after independence. The ideal of education is to ....(9).... for self-preservation but which also prepares us to recognise and ....(10).... the rights of others and to shoulder our ....(11).... as responsible citizens.

Questions

1. A. prospects B. fortune
   C. protrusion D. gaiety

2. A. illustrated
   B. emancipated
   C. defined
   D. apprehended
3. A. institute   B. centre
   C. college   D. university
4. A. encourage   B. embark
   C. promote   D. polish
5. A. employed   B. recruited
   C. held   D. engaged
6. A. paramount   B. arduous
   C. lucrative   D. laudable
7. A. dispense   B. disburse
   C. carry   D. discharge
8. A. have taken B. had taken
   C. has taken   D. is taking
9. A. evoke   B. prepare
   C. encourage   D. cultivate
10. A. concede   B. preserve
    C. coddle   D. clung
11. A. obligations
    B. obduracy
    C. obsequiousness
    D. portfolio

PASSAGE-20

A people's relation to their culture ....(1).... the same as the relation of a child to its mother's breast. There is ....(2).... any doubt that religious belief is part of the culture of people. ....(3).... it is their religious faith which ....(4)... their lives in many ways, ...(5).... not only which god they worship and how, but also helping them ....(6).... an internal value system, making social living ....(7)...., and impacting the most important events in ordinary lives by ....(8).... the do's and don'ts and the rituals that ....(9).... birth, death and marriage. Whenever a religious conversion ....(10)...., indeed it must be painful, as painful as it is for a child being ....(11).... away from its mother's breast.

Questions

1. A. is   B. has been
   C. have been D. are
2. A. never   B. hardly
   C. improbably D. implicitly
3. A. Probably   B. Perhaps
   C. Incidently D. Often
4. A. protect   B. shield
   C. sustain   D. defend
5. A. determining
   B. deciding
   C. suggesting
   D. laying
6. A. create   B. construct
   C. invent   D. develop
7. A. coherent   B. co-existing
   C. cohesive   D. coerce
8. A. laying down
   B. putting up
   C. determining
   D. formulating
9. A. circle
   B. cycle
   C. encircle
   D. surround
10. A. takes place
    B. took place
    C. had taken place
    D. has taken place
11. A. removed
    B. snatched
    C. weaned
    D. took

Answers

Passage-1

1	2	3	4	5	6
B	C	B	A	C	C
7	8	9	10	11	12
C	D	D	D	A	D
13	14	15	16	17	
C	A	B	D	C	

Passage-2

1	2	3	4	5	6
B	A	B	C	B	D
7	8	9	10	11	
B	C	D	D	B	

Passage-3

1	2	3	4	5	6
D	C	D	A	A	B
7	8	9	10		
C	C	A	C		

Passage-4

1	2	3	4	5	6
D	B	C	B	C	B
7	8	9	10		
A	D	D	D		

Passage-5

1	2	3	4	5	6
C	B	D	C	D	B
7	8	9	10	11	
D	B	A	A	C	

Passage-6

1	2	3	4	5	6
D	A	B	C	D	C
7	8	9	10	11	12
A	B	A	B	C	D

Passage-7

1	2	3	4	5	6
C	A	B	C	B	D
7	8	9	10	11	
A	A	B	D	D	

Passage-8

1	2	3	4	5	6
D	B	C	A	A	D
7	8	9	10	11	12
B	D	B	D	B	A
13	14				
D	C				

Passage-9

1	2	3	4	5	6
C	A	A	B	C	D
7	8	9	10		
B	C	D	A		

Passage-10

1	2	3	4	5	6
C	D	A	B	B	D
7	8				
A	D				

Passage-11

1	2	3	4	5	6
C	A	A	C	B	C
7	8				
B	D				

Passage-12

1	2	3	4	5	6
C	D	A	B	D	B
7	8	9	10	11	12
D	C	B	A	D	C
13	14				
B	D				

Passage-13

1	2	3	4	5	6
A	C	B	A	A	C
7	8	9	10	11	12
B	B	D	D	C	A
13					
B					

Passage-14

1	2	3	4	5	6
B	B	D	C	C	D
7	8	9	10	11	12
C	A	C	B	B	D
13					
B					

Passage-15

1	2	3	4	5	6
B	A	C	B	A	A
7	8	9	10	11	12
B	D	C	A	C	B
13	14	15	16	17	18
C	B	C	C	A	C

Passage-16

1	2	3	4	5	6
A	D	C	A	B	D
7	8	9	10	11	12
D	B	B	C	A	A

Passage-17

1	2	3	4	5	6
D	C	B	A	D	C
7	8	9	10	11	12
A	A	C	D	B	D
13	14				
D	A				

Passage-18

1	2	3	4	5	6
A	B	D	D	B	D
7	8	9			
C	A	B			

Passage-19

1	2	3	4	5	6
A	C	B	C	D	B
7	8	9	10	11	
D	C	B	A	A	

Passage-20

1	2	3	4	5	6
A	B	D	C	B	B
7	8	9	10	11	
C	A	D	A	C	

Comprehension Passages 9

Comprehension means the act of comprehending or the capacity of the mind to understand. In the examination papers, questions on comprehension test are included to judge the ability of the examinees to understand the given passage.

Directions: *Read the following passages and answer the questions given below each passage in the context of the passage.*

PASSAGE-1

Cyber crime is the branded stigma defacing the culture and magnanimity of computer technology. It is up keeping the flag with indomitable triumph against developing computer technology worldwide.

Modern age is striding with marching steps of technology revolution beating the past decade of ancestral belief with ultimate care. Computer invention has unfolded the mystery of quick access with the objective of minimum manpower and cutting the time consumption parameters.

As each coin has dual face of its portrait, likewise computer technology is sick of creeping virus. Synthetic manmade dilemma of site hackers activation is causing setback to the expanding anchor of revolutionary device with great loss of time, economy and data profile as suffered by consumers. A recent report from Internet security firm Websense estimates that 85.6 per cent of all the unwanted e-mails contained links to spam sites. The company's data suggests that the number of malicious sites grew 233 per cent in the last six months and saw 671 per cent growth in the number of malicious sites during the last year. In June alone, the total number of e-mails detected as containing viruses increased by 600 per cent compared to May.

Chat rooms, blogs and message boards where the users post comments have been identified as the top targets of hackers and spammers due to the high traffic these attract. According to Websense, 95 per cent of user-generated comments to blogs, chat rooms and message boards during the first half of the year were malicious.

It is advisable not to click on spurious links and stay away from keying in passwords at unknown sites as they are most likely to be spammed. Hackers can steal your passwords and log in to your account and access critical information like account numbers and contact details among other things.

1. The above passage is:
   A. an advisory for the computer users
   B. an advisory for the Internet users
   C. a warning against possible threat to the Internet users
   D. related to chat rooms, blogs and message boards

2. People who use chat rooms and blogs:
   A. are safe and have no threats from spam
   B. are more prone to malicious e-mails
   C. create virus and hack the accounts of others
   D. are unsafe

3. According to the writer, it is not safe to:
   A. log on to spurious links
   B. access one's own account frequently
   C. have essential information stored in a computer
   D. include data-stealing code

4. Hackers and spammers, according to the writer, are:
   A. a new threat to the Internet users and the economy
   B. only pranksters and not serious threat to the system.
   C. trained, professional technocrats who are an asset
   D. not expert professionals

5. Which word in the passage is synonym of **weblog**?
   A. blog   B. password
   C. site   D. e-mail

6. Which agency has assessed the data record with spam sites?
   A. Microsoft
   B. Internet security from Google
   C. Websense
   D. Spammers

7. Which month dominates the e-mails detection data record?
   A. May
   B. June
   C. Last six months
   D. Last year

PASSAGE-2

Personal sentiments exposure portray in sober class of distinct feature with fair and pleasant expression. As the cruelty can be overpowered by the amicable terms likewise, impossible review let with expression can be publically announced by either electronic device or diary writing habit. On line conversation such as chatting, message convey are the rampant tool of the time to manage in communication congestion.

Blogs, online versions of personal diaries, have been a craze for quite some time now. Some of us, before the Internet age, used to maintain a small diary to jot down random thoughts, reflections, sayings, poems and other such stuff. Their online versions, however, are much more than that. The biggest difference between a blog and a personal diary is while the latter was a very private affair accessible not even to family members, a blog is a public account. In fact the whole world connected to the internet gets to read its contents if they come across it.

What a blogger should keep in mind while blogging is that by displaying our thoughts, emotions, opinions and personal life in full public glory, we are revealing a part of our private life. We are giving outsiders, strangers, friends, colleagues and relatives a full view of what's happening inside us and with our lives, something we would hesitate to do in real life. Once blogging begins, it's difficult to control, and we end up sharing our personal thoughts and emotions that we would otherwise have kept to ourselves. The blog entices us, and we fall to be bait.

Blogs don't preserve our **anonymity**. They let us publish our pictures, professional and personal details, physical address and locations, etc. The biggest precaution to be observed therefore is to think twice before publishing anything, and ask oneself if one would like to make such matters public. The blog readers try to judge us, understand us, get information about us and take pleasure while peeping into our private lives without realising it.

1. Blogs are:
   A. diaries
   B. personal diaries
   C. online diaries
   D. official diaries

2. Earlier the personal diaries were not available even to family members but blog can be read by:
   A. family and friends
   B. friends only
   C. anyone who connects to the Internet
   D. relatives

3. Which one of the following statements is not true?
   A. Blogging does not affect our privacy
   B. Blogging displays our private life in public
   C. Blogging cannot be controlled easily
   D. Blogging allows outsiders to peep into our personal life

4. The writer in the above passage:
   A. favours blogging
   B. criticises the practices
   C. does not want the reader to become a victim of blogging
   D. favours blogging but with some precautions

5. Which word in the passage stands for **'an account from own point of view'**?
   A. version   B. block
   C. affair   D. account

6. The word **'Anonymity'** in the passage refers to:
   A. hostility
   B. friendship
   C. unacknowledged
   D. differences

7. What precaution is stressed by the narrator while releasing personal information?
   A. Suggest comprehensive issue only
   B. Reader friendly blog appreciation
   C. Hiding personal facts
   D. Diary maintenance

PASSAGE-3

South Asian tropical weather reels valuable geographical aesthetic beauty surrounded by wildlife, mountains, steep elevations with dense forest. Human sapiens has been old and innocent victim of natural calamities branded as flood, hurricane, storm, earthquake and tsunami since ages.

Biological data depicts the loss of valuable men and material suffered by mankind owing to the chain reaction by such fatal natural incidents. Global warming has turned an eyesore to the rapid glory of rising civilsation with great mystery yet to be unfolded. UNO data reveals the rate of mortality owed due to natural disaster with great sway of cruel time factor.

Of the 245 natural disasters in the first 11 months of the year, 224 or 91.4 per cent were due to weather, a UN study has found.

Of the 58 million people affected, 55 million were affected by weather-related disasters, which accounted for $15 billion (₹ 7,05,000 crore) spent in coping with these disasters.

A study has found that half of these disasters, mainly storms and floods, have taken place in Asia, Debarati Guha Sapir of Brussels-based CRED said.

And this data does not include the loss due to drought because that takes longer to account for. Guha Sapir said, "We have found that this is due to global warming, weak political systems, urbanisation, weak infrastructure, population increase and deforestation."

"We have to cap the emissions of greenhouse gases because they produce greater risk of disasters," WMO head Michel Jerraud said. Greenhouse gases, mainly carbon dioxide, are causing the climate change that is already affecting farm output, making droughts, floods and storms more frequent and more severe, and raising the sea level.

1. Mark the correct statement(s).
   1. Weather is responsible for most of the natural disasters
   2. There is no need to worry about the climatic changes
   3. All the nations are trying to have a common pact to tackle natural disasters
   A. 1 is correct
   B. Only 2 is correct
   C. Only 3 is correct
   D. 1 and 2 are correct

2. Which one of the following statements is not true?
   A. More than 58 million people have been affected by natural disasters
   B. $15 billion have been spent in coping with these disasters
   C. Most of the natural disasters have taken place in Asia
   D. The report does not include the loss caused by droughts

3. The main cause of natural disasters is:
   A. global warming
   B. weak political system
   C. deforestation
   D. All of these

4. The first priority before the nations and the scientists across the world is:
   A. to cap the emission of greenhouse gases
   B. to reach an agreement on the nuclear weapons
   C. to help one another when natural disasters occur
   D. to find out the causes of natural disasters

5. Which word in the passage means the same as **'serious'**?

A. Reduce   B. Severe
C. Underlined   D. Underscore

6. Which region is mainly affected by these disasters?
   A. United Nation B. Africa
   C. Asia   D. Brussels

7. Which statement is true?
   A. Sea level rise is an alarming incident
   B. Rapid urbanisation is a curse to the global warming
   C. Deforestation with climatic change is responsible for green house gaseous effect
   D. All of these

PASSAGE-4

Time has brought forth different classical and instrumental range of device that serves healing element to the aweful and mentally distressed state of affair. Temperament compatibility matching is a reasonable trend of motion adhered with the concept of body movement termed as dance therapy.

Dance has mobilised different acknowledgement of its noted culture proclaimed by experts and sensational aspirants. Vedas describe the dance origin from aryan culture to the creeping span of modern India. Archaeological Survey of India has claimed the civilsation existence issue owing to excavation of past events traced in the stone idols displayed in dance "mudra".

Dance is an art form that generally refers to movement of the body, usually rhythmic and to music, used as a form of expression, social interaction or presented in a spiritual or performance setting. Gymnastics, figure skating and synchronised swimming are sports that incorporate dance, while martial arts Kata are often compared to dances. Motion in ordinarily inanimate objects may also be described as dances (the leaves dance in the wind). Every dance, no matter what style, has something in common. It not only involves flexibility and body movement, but also physics. If the proper physics is not taken into consideration, injuries may occur. Choreography is the art of creating dances. The person who creates (i.e. choreographs) a dance, is known as the choreographer. Dance has certainly been an important part of ceremony, rituals, celebrations and entertainment since the birth of the earliest human civilisations. Archaeology delivers trace of dance from prehistoric times such as the 9,000 years old Rock Shelters of Bhimbetka painting in India and Egyptian tomb painting depicting dancing figures from circa 3300 BC. One of the earliest structured uses of dance may have been in the performance and in **the telling of myths**. Before the production of written languages, dance was one of the methods of passing these stories down from generation to generation.

1. Dance does not necessarily involve:
   A. movement of the body
   B. face expression
   C. rhythmic movements
   D. costumes

2. According to the passage, which one of the following sports does not incorporate dance?
   A. Figure skating
   B. Gymnastics
   C. Chess
   D. Swimming

3. Which one, according to the passage, is not common in all the dances?
   A. Flexibility
   B. Body movement
   C. Music
   D. Physics

4. Physics in every dance is an important element to:
   A. master the art of dance
   B. to perform it scientifically
   C. to save oneself from injury
   D. to get an award

5. In prehistoric times dance was:
   A. a substitute of written language
   B. a source of entertainment
   C. a necessary ritual
   D. not allowed in royal palaces

6. Choreographer is a term addressed to:
   A. a sports trainer
   B. a gym coach
   C. a painting teacher
   D. a dance teacher

7. What does the term 'the telling of myths' refer to?
   A. Telling the beads
   B. Vedic convention
   C. Spiritual recitation
   D. Protest march

PASSAGE-5

A recent report in New York Times says that in American colleges, students of Asian origin outperform not only the minority group students but the majority Whites as well. Many of these students must be of Indian origin, and their achievement is something we can be proud of. It is unlikely that these talented youngsters will come back to India, and that is the familiar brain drain problem. However, recent statements by the nation's policy makers indicate that the perception of this issue is changing. **Brain bank** and not **brain drain** is the more appropriate idea, they suggest, since the expertise of Indians abroad is only deposited in other places and not lost.

This may be so, but this brain bank, like most of the banks, is one that primarily serves customers in its neighbourhood. The skills of the Asians now excelling in America's colleges will mainly help the USA. No matter how significant, what Non-Resident Indians do for India and what their counterparts do for other Asian counteries is only a by-product. But it is also necessary to ask, or be reminded, why Indians study more fruitfully when abroad. The Asians whose accomplishments New York Times records would have probably had a very different fate if they had studied in India. In America they found elbow room, books and facilities not available and not likely to be available here. The need to prove themselves in their new country and the competition of an international standard they faced there must have cured mental and physical laziness. But other things helping them in America can be obtained here if we achieve a change in social attitudes, especially towards youth.

We need to learn to value individuals and their unique qualities more than conformity and respectability. We need to learn the language of encouragement to add to out skill in flattery. We might also learn to be less liberal with blame and less tight-fisted with appreciation, especially to those showing signs of independence.

1. Among the many groups of students in American colleges, Asian students:
   A. are often written about in newspapers like New York Times
   B. are the most successful academically
   C. have proved that they are as good as the Whites
   D. have only a minority status like the Blacks

2. The students of Asian origin in America include:
   A. a fair number from India
   B. a small group from India
   C. persons from India who are very proud
   D. Indians who are the most hardworking of all

3. In general, the talented young Indians studying in America:
   A. have a reputation for being hardworking
   B. have the opportunity to contribute to India's development
   C. can solve the brain drain problem because of recent changes in policy
   D. will not return to pursue their careers in India

4. There is talk now of the **brain bank**. This idea:
   A. is a solution to the brain drain problem
   B. is a new problem caused partly by the brain drain
   C. is a new way of looking at the role of qualified Indians living abroad
   D. is based on a plan to utilise foreign exchange remittances to stimulate research and development

5. The brain bank has limitations like all banks in the sense that:
   A. a bank's services go mainly to those near it
   B. small neighbourhood banks are not viable in this age of multinationals
   C. only what is deposited can be withdrawn and utilised
   D. no one can be forced to put his assets in a bank

6. The author feels that what Non-Resident Indians do for India:
   A. will have many useful side-effects
   B. will not be their main interest and concern
   C. can benefit other Asian countries, as a by-product
   D. can help American colleges be of service of the world community

PASSAGE-6

Quality dominates the world ahead of its spherical, classical, racial or any undue discrimination ever exercised by any individual. Physical characteristics of a produce differs its structural attribution in quality from substandard produce with richness of prolong usage features declared by the claimant. Talent Hunt initiated by quality seekers have turned the table of established brand on account of innovative additions presented by their hardships.

The simple message that quality matters because it is cheaper to do things right the first time is yet to sink into the thinking of Indian managers and workers who seem quite content to live in their cloistered world where mediocrity reigns supreme. It is only the ignorant who believe that quality consciousness is a cultural trait. Barely half a century back no one associated Japan with high quality, but today 'Made in Japan' is a symbol of assured quality. The daily drill at school is far more important than the seasonal seminar and an obsession with quality at home is the best way of convincing the world that we value good quality. Indian exports will never be recognised for quality unless Indians are known to insist on good quality at home.

Global appreciation surrounds the exceptional brand by keeping up the physical standard neatly and efficiently. It is designed to meet the international standards' numerous logos and certificates to upkeep the label of quality consciousness. It has prime motto of swaying clean chit observation to the sanctioned produce without any objection. Modern age has been proved a turning point to the old established traditional belief. They are using tiring house hold produce to industrial device responsible to deface the status of rapid development. We breath into the cool and fresh air of healthy surrounding devised by mankind monitored by quality management with rigorous span or struggle tackled with due care.

1. The theme of the passage is:
   A. quality consciousness
   B. export promotion
   C. quality management
   D. promoting Indian culture

2. According to the passage, the Indian exports will never be recognised for quality:
   A. unless there is technical advancement
   B. unless there is competition
   C. unless the Indians are known to insist on good quality
   D. unless government supports the exporters

3. Which one of the following statements is true?
   A. Indians are known for their insistence on quality
   B. Indians are not quality conscious
   C. Japan is not known for its quality product
   D. 'Made in Japan' is not a symbol of assured quality

4. The best way to convince the world about quality is:
   A. to conduct seminars on quality control
   B. to advertise the products
   C. to value for quality products at home
   D. All of the above

5. According to the passage, the main fault with the Indian managers is that:
   A. they are not hard-working
   B. they are not quality conscious
   C. they are not well trained in quality control
   D. they lack technical knowledge

6. How quality consciousness is termed as a cultural trait with the ignorant?
   A. The mature opinion of quality
   B. Quality dominates ahead of traditional belief
   C. Cultural trait justifies any quality standard
   D. Quality consciousness leads to management growth

7. Why 'Made in Japan' is a symbol of assured quality?
   A. Traditional belief
   B. Quality consciousness
   C. Age old negligence suffering
   D. High export offer

PASSAGE-7

Creamy outlook with soft speech presentation is a prima facie attraction that brings joy on the withering faces with a mixture of sensational touch. Smile with grace is the ultimate boon to the mankind keeping away any melancholy at bay. Old age is often miscalculated as liability with little attention paid to them. Their talents and learned potential is buried alive with undue care by oblivious approach due to disfigured or deformed physical structure taken over by aged talents of the society.

It happens to us all, however hard we may try to delay the process. We grow old. Cosmetic surgery may remove the wrinkles, skin which has sagged may be tightened by means of a facelift and hair dresser may dye grey hair a more youthful colour, but we cannot remain young forever.

However, what is important is the quality of life. Some people are lucky to be taken care of at home whereas others may have to move to residential homes. The worst part of ageing is that often the mind becomes less alert. As people grow older, they experience short term memory. Later some may **suffer from dementia**, often in the form of Alzheimer's disease.

By no means all people are in this category. Many senior citizens are in the possession of all their faculties and see retirement as a time of freedom. Not only that if they have a generous retirement pension, they are likely to be quite well off with money to be spent on a holiday and other luxuries. Because of this, both businesses and government have a new respect for what is known as grey power.

It is unfortunate that many people regard old people as **geriatrics** who have one foot in the grave. Someone should remind them that they too would be old one day!

They are honoured with senior citizen label granted by the authority with due regard paid from distinct possession of living cadres. One should always bear in mind the old saying "Tit for Tat". Which denotes its symbolic regulation of periodical sufferings. The aforesaid misdoings of emotional disparity, done by striding steps is a curse to the mankind.

1. Cosmetic surgery:
   A. helps in the retention of youth forever
   B. cannot stop the natural process of ageing
   C. is the solution to ageing
   D. is the fancy of the rich
2. While ageing man's greatest worry is:
   A. his growing wrinkles
   B. his short term memory
   C. his quality of life
   D. moving to a residential home
3. The government considers grey power as:

A. a liability
B. an asset
C. neither an asset nor a liability
D. a spent force

4. Retirement is seen as a time of freedom because people:
   A. no longer have to go to office
   B. can enjoy their earnings
   C. can spend time with their families
   D. finally move into residential homes

5. **'Geriatrics'** in the passage refers to:
   A. handicapped people
   B. doctors for the aged
   C. a branch of medicine
   D. aged people

6. What is the theme of the passage?
   A. Old is gold
   B. The grey power
   C. Youth domination in the society
   D. Aged suffering

7. What does the phrase **'suffer from dementia'** refer to?
   A. Harmful
   B. Short term memory loss
   C. Lunacy
   D. Paralysis

PASSAGE-8

The social Darwinist conception of evolution is not that of the biologist but of the propagandist looking for justification for his political theories. The simplistic formulation of ferocious antisocial struggle finds no place in the theories of modern biologists. Even on the animal level the scientific picture is not that of "struggle" and ruthless elimination. If in the tropics a pigmented skin is an advantage, no one is swept to destruction in a fight for blackness. Modifications of that sort, which prove advantageous, gradually establish themselves without trouble. Even living on other animals for food does not imply savagery—fishermen are not unpleasant and aggressive persons; tribes living, as they once did, on shellfish are not haters of their kind; even pig breeders and chicken farmers can be kind to their neighbours and no worse than the rest of us. Lorenz, constantly quoted to defend innate aggression, points out that the predatory carnivores are not angry when bringing down an antelope. It is simply a matter of going to fetch the dinner. A lion can be angry, but not when going out to kill. One might go on and take the whole case to pieces bit by bit, but enough has been said to indicate that the picture of "nature red in tooth and claw" is the poet's view—the phrase was Tennyson's—not the scientist's: it is tendentious, controversial exaggeration, not objective science. Even the notion of the "survival of the fittest" begs the question. If we say that the fittest survive, we only mean that they do survive. It implies no other quality than survival ability. It holds just as well for the oyster or the flourishing flea as for the beautifully adapted camel or flying fox. It does not follow that the survivor is the fittest even in being the finest specimen of its kind, let alone of the kind that we would prefer to see flourish.

1. The instinct to kill in carnivores comes from their:
   A. need to survive

    B. need to prove their might
    C. inherently brutal nature
    D. liking for flesh

2. The writer's attitude towards poets is that of:
    A. awe
    B. scorn
    C. anger
    D. indifference

3. The term **'survival of the fittest'** suggests the survival of the:
    A. mightiest   B. finest
    C. best   D. prepared

4. By citing various examples the writer tries to establish the fact that savagery does not entail:
    A. killing of any kind
    B. killing of lesser animals
    C. killing dispassionately to serve an end
    D. ruthless killing

5. The concept of ferocious antisocial struggle finds credence with:
    A. biologist   B. scientists
    C. Lorenz   D. Darwin

PASSAGE-9

The difficulty in the education of young infants is largely the **delicate balance** required in the parents. Constant watchfulness and much labour are needed to avoid injury to health : these qualities will hardly exist in the necessary degree except where there is strong parental affection. But where this exists, it is very likely not to be wise. To the devoted parents, the child is immensely important. Unless care is taken, the child feels this and judges himself as important as his parents feel but later in life his social environment will not regard him so fondly and the habit of assuming that he is the centre of other people's universe will lead to disappointment. It is, therefore, necessary, not only in the first year, but afterwards also, that parents should be breezy, cheerful and rather matter-of-fact where the child's possible ailments are concerned. In old days, infants were too much patted, sung to, rocked and dandled. This was wrong since it turned them into helpless pampered parasites. The right rule is : encourage spontaneous activities but discourage demands on others. Do not let the child see how much you do for him or how much trouble you take. Let him, wherever possible, taste the joy of success, achieved by his own efforts, not extracted by tyrannising over the grown-ups.

1. **'Delicate balance'** required in parents in sentence one refers to:
    A. cautiousness
    B. possessiveness
    C. indifference
    D. matter-of-factness

2. In the past the excessively fondled children became:
    A. troublesome
    B. mischievous
    C. parasites
    D. abnormal

3. For the possible ailments of the child, the writer advised the parents to be:
    A. indifferent
    B. demanding
    C. unsympathetic
    D. matter-of-fact

4. The author wishes the parents to let the child:
   A. manage his own things
   B. be absolutely free
   C. work under their guidance
   D. seek anybody's help if needed

5. A child pampered by his parents is likely to become:
   A. disappointed
   B. demoralised
   C. dependent
   D. independent

PASSAGE-10

The world dismisses curiosity by calling it idle or mere idle curiosity—even though curious persons are seldom idle. Parents do their best to extinguish curiosity in their children because it makes life difficult to be faced everyday with a string of unanswerable questions about what makes fire hot or why grass grows. Children whose curiosity survives parental discipline are invited to join our university. With the university, they go on asking their questions and trying to find the answers. In the eyes of a scholar, that is what a university is for. Some of the questions which the scholars ask seem to the world to be scarcely worth asking, let alone answering. They asked questions too minute and specialised for you and me to understand without years of explanation. If the world inquires of one of them, why he wants to know the answer to a particular question, he may say, especially if he is a scientist, that the answer will in some obscure way make possible a new machine or weapon or gadget. He talks that way because he knows that the world understands and respects utility.

But to you who are now part of the university, he will say that he wants to know the answer simply because he does not know it, the way the mountain climber wants to climb a mountain, simply because it is there. Similarly, a historian asked by an outsider, why he studies history, may come out with the argument that he has learnt to repeat on such occasions, something about knowledge of the past making it possible to understand the present and mould the future. But if you really want to know why a historian studies the past, the answer is much simpler, something happened and he would like to know what. All this does not mean that the answers which scholars find to their questions have no consequences. They may have enormous consequences but these seldom form the reason for asking the question or pursuing the answers. It is true that scholars can be put to work answering questions for the sake of the consequences as thousands are working now, for example, in search of a cure for cancer. But this is not the primary function of the scholars. The consequences are usually subordinate to the satisfaction of curiosity.

1. The common people consider some of the questions that the scholars ask unimportant:
   A. as they are too lazy and idle
   B. as they are too modest
   C. as it's beyond their comprehension
   D. as it is considered a waste of time

2. According to the passage, parents do their best to discourage curiosity in their children:
   A. because they have no time
   B. because they have no patience to answer them
   C. because they feel that their children ask stupid questions continuously
   D. because they are unable to answer all their questions

3. According to the passage, the children make life difficult for their parents:
   A. by their ceaseless curiosity
   B. by unceasing bombardment of questions
   C. by asking irrelevant questions
   D. by posing profound questions

4. Children whose curiosity survives parental discipline means:
   A. children retaining their curiosity in spite of being discouraged by their parents
   B. children pursuing their mental curiosity
   C. children's curiosity subdued due to parents' intervention
   D. children being disciplined by their parents

5. A historian really studies the past:
   A. to comprehend the present and to reconstruct the future
   B. to explain the present and plan the future
   C. to understand the present and make fortune
   D. to understand the present and mould the future

PASSAGE-11

Shames and delusions are esteemed for soundest truths, while reality is **fabulous**. If men would steadily observe realities only, and not allow themselves to be deluded, life, to compare it with such things as we know, would be like a fairy tale and the Arabian Night's entertainments. If we respect only what is inevitable and has a right to be, music and poetry would resound along the streets. When we are unhurried and wise, we perceive that only great and worthy things have any permanent and absolute existence—that petty fears and petty pleasures are but the shadow of the reality. This is always exhilarating and sublime. By closing the eyes and slumbering and consenting to be deceived by shows, men establish and confirm their daily life of routine and habit everywhere, which still is built on purely illusory foundations. Children, who play life, discern its true law and relations more clearly than men, who fail to live it worthily, but who think that they are wiser by experience; that is by failure.

I have read in a Hindu book that there was a king's son who, being expelled in infancy from his native city, was brought up by a forester and growing up to maturity in that state, imagined himself to belong to the barbarous race with which he lived. One of his father's ministers, having discovered him, revealed to him what he was and the misconception of his character was removed and he knew himself to be a prince, "So soul," continues the Hindu philosopher, "from the circumstances in which it is placed, mistakes its own character, until the truth is revealed to it by some holy teacher and then it knows itself to be Brahma."

We think that is which appears to be. If a man should give us an account of the realities he beheld, we should not recognize the place in his description. Look at a meeting house, or a court house, or a jail, or a shop, or a dwelling house and say what that thing really is before a true gaze and they would all go to pieces in your account of them. Men esteem truth remote, in the outskirts of the system, being the farthest star, before Adam and after the last man. In entirety, there is indeed something true and sublime. But all these times and places and occasions are now and here. God himself culminates in the present moment and will never be more divine in the lapse of all ages. And we are enabled to apprehend at all what is sublime and noble only by the perpetual instilling and drenching of the reality that surrounds us. The universe constantly and obediently answers to our conceptions : Whether we travel fast or slow; the track is laid for us. Let us spend our lives in conceiving, then. The poet or the artist never yet had so fair and noble a design but some of his posterity at least could accomplish it.

1. The author believes that children are often more acute than adults in their appreciation of life's relations because:
   A. children know more than adults
   B. children can use their experience better
   C. children's eyes are unclouded by failure
   D. experience is the best teacher

2. The writer's attitude towards the arts is one of:
   A. indifference   B. suspicion
   C. admiration   D. repulsion

3. The passage implies that human beings:
   A. cannot distinguish the true from the untrue
   B. are immoral if they are lazy
   C. should be bold and fearless
   D. believe in fairytales

4. The author is primarily concerned with urging the reader to:
   A. meditate on the meaninglessness of the present
   B. appraise the present for its true value
   C. look to the future for enlightenment
   D. spend more time in leisure activities

5. The word '**fabulous**' in the passage means:
   A. wonderful   B. delicious
   C. birdlike   D. illusion

PASSAGE-12

The stress-relieving power of humour is well-established. Laughter relieves tension, breaks negative 'holding patterns,' and helps out our problems in perspective. Humour is listed as a major stress-coping mechanism among healthy men. It has been credited with reducing the coronary risk of a high-stress lifestyle. Not only does it help diffuse anxiety and anger, as a heart attack victim points out, it acts as a blocking agent against the ravages of panic. The panic produced by a heart attack can be just as dangerous as the heart attack. It constricts blood vessels and destablises the heart. But through humour, reassurance and positive thinking you can control the panic and thereby enhance your prospects for recovery. Laughter creates an environment for healing. And that goes for all illnesses—not only coronary artery disease. Negative emotions, such as depression, weaken the immune system, making us more susceptible to a host of illnesses ranging from cold to cancer. It stands to reason that positive emotions such as humour and laughter may have the opposite effect, keeping our immune system strong and defending us against sickness. Sick people, especially those who are depressed, take themselves much too seriously. Even though controlled scientific studies for measuring the chemistry of laughter are rare, yet what is there does support the theory that good humour breeds good health.

1. Humour helps fight heart attacks by:
   A. alerting us against pain
   B. beginning a fitness programme
   C. introducing us to high-stress life
   D. removing our worries

2. Panic caused by a heart attack:
   A. makes the blood vessels narrower
   B. builds our confidence
   C. makes us active and self-sufficient
   D. makes us seek medical help

3. It has been proved that humour is:
   A. a negative trait
   B. a solution to all problems
   C. helpful in reducing tensions
   D. present in all healthy men

4. Humour helps us become:
   A. richer   B. healthier
   C. ambitious   D. scientific

5. Negative feelings lead to:
   A. stronger defences
   B. increased opposition
   C. many illnesses
   D. bad reputation

PASSAGE-13

In the technological systems of tomorrow—fast, fluid and self-regulating machines will deal with the flow of physical materials; men with the flow of information and insight. Machines will increasingly perform tasks. Machines and men both, instead of being concentrated in gigantic factories and factory cities, will be scattered across the globe, linked together by amazingly sensitive, **near-instantaneous communications**. Human work will move out of the factory and mass office into the community and the home. Machines will be synchronised, as some already are to the billionth of a second; men will be de-synchronised. The factory whistle will vanish. Even the clock, "the key machine of the modern industrial age," as Lewis Mumford called it a generation ago, will lose some of its power over humans, as distinct from technological affairs. Simultaneously, the organisation needed to control technology will shift from bureaucracy to Ad-hocracy, from permanence to transience and from a concern with the present to a focus on the future.

In such a world, the most valued attributes of the industrial age become handicaps. The technology of tomorrow requires not millions of lightly lettered men, ready to work in unison at endlessly repetitive jobs, it requires not men who take orders in unblinking fashion, aware that **the price of bread is mechanical submission to authority,** but men who can make critical judgments, who can weave their way through novel environments, who are quick to spot new relationships in the rapidly changing reality. It requires men who, in C.R Snow's compelling terms, "have the future in their bones."

1. The future man, according to this passage, must be:
   A. most adaptative and intelligent
   B. most capable of dealing with the changing reality
   C. more concerned with the present than the future
   D. trained and obedient

2. The technological system of tomorrow will be marked by:
   A. dehumanisation
   B. perfection
   C. automation
   D. unpredictability

3. The type of society which the author has mentioned makes a plea for:
   A. a mind assimilative of modern scientific ideas
   B. a critical mind having insight into future
   C. a mind well-versed in cultural heritage
   D. a mind with firm principles of life

4. **'Near-instantaneous communications'** may be regarded as a symbol of:
   A. anachronisation
   B. mischronisation
   C. desynchronisation
   D. synchronisation

5. If a person believes that '**the price of bread is mechanical submission to authority**,' he is:
   A. a believer in devotion to duty
   B. a believer in taking things for granted
   C. a believer in doing what he is told, right or wrong
   D. a believer in the honesty of machines

PASSAGE-14

Foot-racing is a popular activity in the United States. It is seen not only as a competitive sport but also as a way to exercise, to enjoy the **camaraderie** of like-minded people and to donate money for a good cause. Though serious runners may spend months training to compete, other runners and walkers might not train at all. Those not competing might run in an effort to beat their own time or simply to enjoy the fun and exercise. People of all ages, from those less than one year of age (who may be pushed in *strollers*) to those in their eighties, enter into this sport. The races are held in city streets, on college campuses, through parks and in suburban areas and they are commonly 5 to 10 kilometres in length.

The largest foot-race in the world is the 12 kilometre Bay to Breakers race that is held in San Francisco every spring. This race begins on the east side of the city near San Francisco Bay and ends on the west side at the Pacific Ocean. There may be 80,000 or more people running in this race through the streets and hills of San Francisco. In the front are the serious runners who compete to win and who might finish in as little as 34 minutes. Behind them are the thousands who take several hours to finish. In the back of the race are those who dress in costumes and come just for fun. One year, there was a group of men who dressed like Elvis Presley and another group consisted of fire-fighters who were tied together in a long line carrying a fire-hose. There was even a bridal party, in which the bride and the groom threw flowers to bystanders and they were actually married at some point along the route.

1. The word **'camaraderie'** could best be replaced by which of the following words?
   A. Games
   B. Jokes
   C. Companionship
   D. Views

2. The main purpose of the passage is
   A. make fun of runners in costumes
   B. give reasons for the popularity of foot-races
   C. describe a popular activity
   D. encourage people to exercise

3. As used in the passage the word **'strollers'** refers to:
   A. carriages
   B. wheelchairs
   C. wagons
   D. cribs

4. Which of the following is not the reason why people enter foot-races?
   A. To exercise
   B. To enjoy
   C. As a compulsion
   D. For charity

5. Which of the following is not implied by the author?
   A. Foot-races appeal to a variety of people
   B. Running is a good way to strengthen the heart
   C. Workers can compete for prizes
   D. Age and profession is no bar to enter footraces

PASSAGE-15

The conservative is not an extreme individualist. He may be willing to concede numerous arguments of the unqualified individualists, for his own respect for the dignity of the individual is not surpassed by that of any man. Yet he cannot agree to the full implications of individualism, which is based, so he thinks, on an incorrect appraisal of man, society, history, and government. In his own way, the individualist is as much a perfectionist as the socialist, and with perfectionism the conservative can have no **truck**.

In particular, the conservative refuses to go all the way with economic individualism. His distrust of unfettered man, his recognition to groups, his sense of the complexity of the social process, his recognition of the real services that government can perform—all these sentiments make it impossible for him to subscribe to the dogmas and shibboleths of economic individualism : laissez-faire, the negative state, enlightened self-interest, the law of supply and demand, the profit motive. The conservative may occasionally have kind words for each of these nations, but he is careful to qualify his support by stating other, more important social truths. For example, he does not for a moment deny the prominence of the profit motive, but he insists that it be recognised for the selfish thing it is and be kept within socially imposed reasonable limits.

1. Which of the following words can replace the word **'truck'**?
   A. Dealing   B. Bargain
   C. Debate   D. Transport

2. The conservative is:
   A. A perfectionist
   B. An economist
   C. A socialist
   D. None of these

3. Which of the following statements is true?
   A. The socialist and the individualist tend to be broadly similar in their views
   B. The conservative believes that profit motive originates in selfishness
   C. The conservative is also an extreme individualist
   D. None of these

4. The conservative is against economic individualism for all the following reasons except:
   A. he does not trust free men
   B. he believes in the authority of the government
   C. he believes in groups
   D. he feels that social processes are important

5. The author mentions all the following catchwords of economic individualism except:
   A. free trade
   B. the profit motive
   C. balance of trade
   D. the negative state

PASSAGE-16

Every survey ever held has shown that the image of an attractive woman is the most effective advertising gimmick. She may sit astride the mudguard of a new car, or step into it ablaze with jewels, **she may lie at the man's feet stroking his new socks**, she may hold the petrol pump in a challenging pass, or dance through woodland glades in slow motion in all the glory of a new shampoo. Whatever she does, her image sells. The **gynolatry** of our civilization is written large upon its face, upon hoardings, cinema screens, television, newspapers, magazines, tins, packets, cartons, bottles, all consecrated to the reigning deity, the female fetish. Her dominion must not be thought to entail the rule of women, for she is **not a woman**. Her glossy lips and matt complexion, her unfocused eyes and flawless fingers, her extraordinary hair all floating and shining, curling and gleaming, reveal the inhuman triumph of cosmetics, lighting, focussing and printing. She sleeps unruffled, her lips red and juicy and closed, her eyes as crisp and black as if newly painted and her false lashes immaculately curled. Even when she washes her face with a new and creamier toilet soap her expression is as tranquil and vacant, and the paint as flawless as ever. If ever she should appear tousled and troubled, her features are miraculously smoothed to their proper veneer by a new washing powder on a bouillon cube. For, she is a doll : weeping, pouting or sinking, running or reclaiming, she is a **doll**.

1. The author's primary purpose in this passage is:
   A. to ridicule women
   B. to show the dominance of women in advertising
   C. to portray the obsession of women with trivial thing
   D. to depict the emancipation of women

2. What point is the writer trying to make when he says **'she may lie at a man's feet stroking his new socks'**?
   A. Women like being subservient
   B. Women are observed with clothes
   C. This is a typical posture of women in advertising
   D. Women enjoy this kind of intimacy

3. The **'gynolatry'** of one civilization would suggest all the following except that:
   A. women enjoy immense power in modern society
   B. the image of women boost sales as few other things can
   C. women worship is all pervasive in advertising
   D. glamorous and attractive women are the forte of modern advertising

4. By saying that women depicted in an advertisement is **'not a woman'** the author implies that:
   A. in real life women are less attractive
   B. the depiction of women in advertisement is grossly artificial and unreal
   C. in real life women are more dominant
   D. in advertisement, a woman is a mere commercial symbol

5. In the last sentence of the paragraph, the word **'doll'** is meant to express
   A. tenderness   B. delicacy
   C. contempt   D. beauty

PASSAGE-17

Everything that men do or think concerns either the satisfaction of the needs they feel or the need to escape from pain. This must be kept in mind when we seek to understand spiritual or intellectual movements and the way in which they develop, for feeling and longing are the motive forces of all human striving and productivity—however nobly the latter may display themselves to us.

What, then, are the feelings and the needs which have brought mankind to religious thought and to faith in the widest sense? A moment's consideration shows that the most varied emotions stand at the cradle of religious thought and experience.

In primitive peoples it is, the fear that awakens religious ideas—fear of hunger, of wild animals, of illness and death. Since the understanding of causal connections is usually limited on this level of existence, the **human soul forges a being**, more or less like itself, on whose will and activities depends the experiences which it fears. One hopes to win the favour of this being by deeds and sacrifices which according to the tradition of the race are supposed to appease the being or to make him well disposed to man. I call this the religion of fear.

This religion is considerably stabilized, though not caused, by the formation of the priestly caste which claims to mediate between the people and the being they fear and so attains a position of power. Often a leader or a despot will combine the functions of the priesthood with his own temporal rule for the sake of greater security; or an alliance may exist between the interests of the political power and the priestly caste.

1. Who motivates man's action or thinking?
   A. To satisfy his needs or to escape pain
   B. His desire for progress or to rule
   C. His spiritual urge
   D. To carry out the dictates of his religious faith

2. What feeling prompted primitive man to create religion?
   A. Love
   B. Anger
   C. Fear
   D. Spiritual revelation

3. How did priests come to acquire political power?
   A. By joining hand with the despotic rulers
   B. By protecting the believers against despotic rulers
   C. By generating fear of the unknown in the minds of rulers
   D. By giving religious blessing to political movements

4. How did religion become firmly established?
   A. Through the constant fear of death
   B. Through the perpetuation of faith in God
   C. Through the establishment of religious practices
   D. Through the growth of a priestly class

5. **'Human soul forges a being'** means:
   A. that ghosts and witches are a creation of human mind
   B. that the concept of God is a creation of human mind
   C. Both (A) and (B)
   D. Neither (A) nor (B)

PASSAGE-18

Several years ago my parents, my wife, my son and I ate at a restaurant. After a wonderful dinner, the waiter set the bill in the middle of the table. That's what it happened, my father did not reach for the bill.

Conversation continued. Finally, it dawned on me, I was supposed to pay the bill. After hundreds of restaurant meals with my parents after a lifetime of thinking of my father as the one with the money, it had all changed. I reached for the bill and my view of myself suddenly altered. I was an adult.

Some people mark off their lives in years, I measure mine in small events—in **rites of passage**. I did not become a young man at a particular age, like 13, but rather when a boy strolled into the shop where I worked and called me "mister". The realization hit me like a punch ; I was suddenly a mister.

I never thought that I would fall asleep in front of the television set as my father did. Now it's what I do best. I never thought I would prefer to stay at home, but now I find myself **foregoing parties**. I used to think that people who watched birds were weird, but this summer I found myself watching them, and may be I'll get a book on the subject. I yearn for a religious conviction that I never thought I'd want to feel close to my ancestors long gone, and echo my father in arguments with my son, I still lose.

One day I became a father, and not too long after that I picked up the bill for my own father. I thought then it was a rite of passage for me. But one day, when I was little older, I realized it was one for him too.

1. Which of the following does the author consider a rite of passage for him?
   A. Becoming thirteen years old
   B. Going to a restaurant with his parents, wife and son
   C. Being called 'mister' by the boy in the shop
   D. Working in a shop as a young boy

2. The author's father expected his son to pay the restaurant bill because:
   A. he did not have enough money
   B. he acknowledged that his son was now an adult
   C. it was the first time the family was eating out together
   D. the waiter had set the bill in the middle of the table

3. **'Rites of passage'** for the author generally refers to:
   A. events that mark the passage of time
   B. imitating his father as he grows older
   C. slowing down in his pace of living
   D. the act of growing old with time

4. In the fourth paragraph the author makes the point that as people grow older they:
   A. become lazier and less adventurous in their behaviour
   B. have to take on many more financial responsibilities
   C. turn to their children more for help and advice
   D. behave in the same way as their elders even if they never thought they would

5. In the fourth paragraph, **'foregoing parties'** means:
   A. going early to parties
   B. hosting many parties
   C. giving up parties
   D. going to many parties

PASSAGE-19

Mountaineering is now looked upon as the king of sports. But men have lived amongst the mountains since prehistoric times and in some parts of the world, as in the Andes and Himalayas, difficult mountain journeys have inevitably been part of their everyday life. However, some of the peaks were easily accessible from most of the cities of Europe. It is quite interesting that while modern mountaineers prefer difficult routes for the greater enjoyment of sport, the early climbers looked for the easiest ones, for **the summit was the prize they all set their eyes on**. Popular interest in mountaineering increased considerably after the ascent of the Alpine peak of Matterhorn in 1865 and Edward Whymper's dramatic account of the climb and fatal accident which occurred during the descent.

In the risky sport of mountaineering, the element of competition between individuals or teams is totally absent. Rather one can say that the competition is between the team and the peaks themselves. The individuals making up a party must climb together as a team, for they depend upon one another for their safety. Mountaineering can be dangerous unless reasonable precautions are taken. However, the majority of fatal accidents happen to parties which are inexperienced or not properly equipped. Since many accidents are caused by bad weather, the safe climber is the man who knows when it is time to turn back, however, tempting it may be **to press on** and try to reach the summit.

1. People living in the Andes and the Himalayas made mountain journeys because:
   A. it was a kind of sport
   B. they had to undertake them in their day-to-day life
   C. they lived in prehistoric times
   D. of the challenge offered by the difficult journey

2. Mountaineering is different from other sports because:
   A. it is risky and dangerous
   B. it can be fatal
   C. it is most thrilling and exciting
   D. there is no competition between individuals

3. '..... the summit was the prize they all set their eyes on.' In the context of the passage, this means:
   A. reaching the top was their exclusive concern
   B. they kept their eyes steadily on reaching the summit
   C. they cared for nothing but the prize of reaching the summit
   D. they chose a route from which they could see the summit clearly

4. Mountaineers climb as a team because:
   A. the height is too much for one individual
   B. the competition is between the team and the peak
   C. they have to rely on each other for safety
   D. there is no competition among them

5. 'To press on' in the last sentence of the passage means:
   A. to struggle in a forceful manner
   B. to force upon others
   C. to work fearlessly
   D. to continue in a determined manner

PASSAGE-20

Human analytical abilities remain vastly superior to anything demonstrated elsewhere in the animal kingdom. Virtually in all studies of animal intelligence and language skills, performance plummets as more elements are added to a task and as an animal has to remember these elements for long periods. By contrast, humans can call on vast working memory.

Many evolutionary scholars suspect that as ancient human groups became larger, the need to keep track of ever more complex social interactions was what really pushed the human brain toward superiority. Both dolphins and chimps have very complex interactions, but the intricacy of their social world pales beside the lattice of entanglements that characterised human society as early. Homosapiens bonded together to gather food and defend themselves. In Somalia today, warring clans identify friend or foe by demanding that those accosted recite their ancestry going back many generations. It is easy to see how similar challenges in antiquity might have driven the development of brainpower.

It does not lessen the grandeur of the human intellect to argue that it evolved partly in response to social pressures or that these pressures also produced similar abilities in "lesser" creatures. Instead, the fact that nature may have broadly sown the seeds of consciousness, suggests a world enlivened by many different minds. There may even be practical applications. Studies of animal cognition and language have yielded new approaches to communicating with handicapped and autistic children. Some scientists are pondering ways to turn intelligent animals like sea lions and dolphins into research assistants in marine studies or into lifeguards who can save the drowning upon command.

If the notion that animals might actually think poses a problem, it is an ethical one. The great philosophers, such as Descartes, used their belief that animals cannot think as a justification for arguing that they do not have moral rights. It is one thing to treat animals as mere resources if they are presumed to be little more than living robots, but it is entirely different if they are recognised as fellow sentient beings. Working out the moral implication makes a perfect puzzle for a large-brained, highly social species like our own.

1. Does the author believe that the grandeur of the human intellect is lessened by the fact that the same evolutionary pressure produced similar abilities in animals as in humans?
   A. Perhaps yes   B. Perhaps no
   C. Yes   D. No

2. What could be some of the practical applications of animal intelligence?
   A. To use dolphins for solving difficult mathematical problems
   B. To use some animals for guarding and supervising other animals
   C. To develop new approaches to communicate with handicapped and mentally ill children
   D. All of these

3. In many studies of animal intelligence and language skills, the performance significantly drops
   A. as we move from humans to animals
   B. membered for long periods
   C. as we move from animals with large brains to those with small brains
   D. as the time allowed to develop these skills is reduced

4. What makes a perfect puzzle for a large-brained highly social species like humans, according to the author?
   A. Determining the moral implications of the fact that animals might actually think
   B. discovering the real reason why nature developed the ability to think in animals
   C. Deciding what should be the ideal relationship between humans and animals
   D. To answer the question if animals are different from humans

5. What really pushed the human brain towards superiority?
   A. The need to keep track of ever more complex social interactions
   B. The need to develop efficient methods of gathering food
   C. The need to find better methods of defending themselves
   D. The need to evolve faster than other species

6. What is the ethical problem posed by the notion that animals might actually think?
   A. It is difficult to accept that humans are also animals
   B. animals should perhaps not be used in laboratory experiments
   C. Animals cannot perhaps be treated as mere resources
   D. It has to be correctly assessed as to how much can an animal actually think

7. Why did early Homosapiens bond together?
   A. They formed social groups as they were social animals
   B. To gather food and to defend themselves
   C. To maintain genetic purity
   D. They were more comfortable with similar people

Answers

PASSAGE-1

1	2	3	4	5	6	7
A	D	A	A	A	C	B

PASSAGE-2

1	2	3	4	5	6	7
C	C	A	D	A	D	C

PASSAGE-3

1	2	3	4	5	6	7
A	A	D	A	B	C	D

PASSAGE-4

1	2	3	4	5	6	7
D	C	D	C	A	D	B

PASSAGE-5

1	2	3	4	5	6
B	A	D	C	D	C

PASSAGE-6

1	2	3	4	5	6	7
A	C	B	C	B	C	B

PASSAGE-7

1	2	3	4	5	6	7
B	C	C	B	D	B	C

PASSAGE-8

1	2	3	4	5
A	D	A	C	D

PASSAGE-9

1	2	3	4	5
A	C	D	A	C

PASSAGE-10

1	2	3	4	5
C	D	A	A	D

PASSAGE-11

1	2	3	4	5
C	C	A	B	D

PASSAGE-12

1	2	3	4	5
D	A	C	B	C

PASSAGE-13

1	2	3	4	5
B	C	B	D	C

PASSAGE-14

1	2	3	4	5
C	C	B	C	C

PASSAGE-15

1	2	3	4	5
A	C	C	D	C

PASSAGE-16

1	2	3	4	5
B	C	B	B	D

PASSAGE-17

1	2	3	4	5
A	C	A	D	D

PASSAGE-18

1	2	3	4	5
C	A	A	D	C

PASSAGE-19

1	2	3	4	5
B	C	A	B	D

PASSAGE-20

1	2	3	4	5	6	7
A	C	B	A	A	C	B

❑ ❑ ❑

Synonyms and Antonyms 10

English is the most popular language of the world. It comprises thousands of words. No one can remember all the words and their meanings but everyone must try to read and learn the maximum number of words and their Synonyms. Learning the Antonyms is also equally important.

Directions (Qs. 1 to 32): *In the following questions, each word is followed by four options A, B, C and D. Select the option which best expresses the **meaning** of the given word.*

1. ABSURD
   A. Foolish   B. Simple
   C. Courageous D. Silly

2. ABANDON
   A. Lose   B. Profit
   C. Vacate D. Foil

3. ADULATION
   A. Embarrassment
   B. Fawning
   C. Veneration
   D. Praise

4. ABDICATE
   A. Rude   B. Soft
   C. Imperious D. Give up

5. BAFFLE
   A. Abet   B. Enlighten
   C. Foil   D. Taciturnity

6. BUOYANT
   A. Support   B. Unworthy
   C. Desponding D. Cheerful

7. BLEMISH
   A. Eccentric B. Disgrace
   C. Fair   D. Youth

8. BOOTY
   A. Buxom   B. Loot
   C. Delicate D. Daub

9. CUPIDITY
   A. Shrewd   B. Basic
   C. Avarice D. Parody

10. CORRIGIBLE
    A. Amendable B. Oppose
    C. Devise   D. Illicit

11. CONNIVE
    A. Overlook B. Grow
    C. Censure   D. Defect

12. CAJOLE
    A. Pause B. Lenient
    C. Blast D. Lure

13. HAUGHTY
    A. Imperial B. Imperious
    C. Umpire   D. Brave

14. OPPORTUNE
    A. Timely   B. Short lived
    C. Occasional D. Temper

155

15. EXTERMINATE
    A. Extensore   B. Rubbing
    C. Soothing   D. Extirpate
16. VENERABLE
    A. Watchful   B. Lawful
    C. Respectful   D. Hateful
17. VORACIOUS
    A. Funny   B. Venturous
    C. Gluttonous   D. Hungry
18. INSOLVENT
    A. Rich   B. Poor
    C. Bankrupt   D. Penniless
19. REPEAL
    A. Pass   B. Cancel
    C. Sanction   D. Dishonour
20. LYNCH
    A. Murder   B. Shoot
    C. Killed   D. Hang
21. COMBAT
    A. Fight   B. Conflict
    C. Shoot   D. Quarrel
22. LAMENT
    A. Condone
    B. Console
    C. Complain
    D. Contribution
23. DEBACLE
    A. Disgrace   B. Defeat
    C. Collapse   D. Decline
24. SHIVER
    A. Fear   B. Tremble
    C. Shake   D. Ache
25. TORTURE
    A. Terror   B. Harassment
    C. Torment   D. Tranquility
26. LAUDABLE
    A. Lovable
    B. Commendable
    C. Profitable
    D. Oblivious
27. FIXED
    A. Sterile   B. Static
    C. Stubborn   D. Parennial
28. FANCIFUL
    A. Romantic   B. Beautiful
    C. Imaginative D. Egoistic
29. QUEER
    A. Unfamiliar   B. Cute
    C. Curious   D. Strange
30. OPPRESS
    A. Prosecute   B. Trouble
    C. Persecute   D. Perilous
31. ZEST
    A. Anticipation
    B. Optimistic
    C. Cruel
    D. Enthusiasm
32. SUFFICIENT
    A. Fit   B. Proper
    C. Adequate   D. Vast

Directions (Qs. 33 to 100): *In each of these questions, you find a sentence, a part of which is bold. For the bold part, four words/phrases are suggested. Choose the word/phrase* **nearest in meaning** *to the bold part.*

33. His descriptions are **vivid**.
    A. Detailed
    B. Categorical
    C. Clear
    D. Ambiguous
34. Friends have always **deplored** my unsociable nature.
    A. Deprived   B. Implored
    C. Denied   D. Regretted
35. Despite his enormous wealth, the businessman was very **frugal** in his habits.
    A. Reckless

B. Law-abiding
C. Unpredictable
D. Economical

36. He was **engrossed** in writing a story.
    A. Absolved B. Absorbed
    C. Interested D. Engaged

37. People fear him because of his **vindictive** nature.
    A. Violent B. Cruel
    C. Revengeful D. Irritable

38. He always has a very **pragmatic** approach to life.
    A. Practical B. Proficient
    C. Potent D. Patronizing

39. He was not at all **abashed** by her open admiration.
    A. Delighted
    B. Piqued
    C. Embarrassed
    D. Livid

40. Rahul was amazed at how **affable** his new employer was.
    A. Demanding
    B. Polite
    C. Repulsive
    D. Quality-conscious

41. Since our plans are **amorphous** we shall send you the detailed programme at a later date.
    A. Impractical
    B. Prohibitive
    C. Inimical
    D. Formless

42. Preeti's **arduous** efforts had sapped her energy.
    A. Over-ambitious
    B. Strenuous
    C. Sterile
    D. Apocryphal

43. The manager's **articulate** presentation of the advertising campaign impressed his employers.
    A. Well-prepared
    B. Effective
    C. Superficial
    D. Banal

44. I do not wish to be **beholden** to anyone in this office.
    A. Dependent
    B. Opposed
    C. Obligated
    D. Sycophant

45. We must prevent the **proliferation** of nuclear weapons.
    A. Use B. Increase
    C. Expansion D. Extension

46. The debate has **instigated** a full official enquiry into the incidence.
    A. Initiated B. Incited
    C. Forced D. Caused

47. The workers were full of **applause** for the new policy of the management.
    A. Approval B. Adulation
    C. Praise D. Eulogy

48. Her **ostensible** calm masked a deepseated fear.
    A. Illusory B. Apparent
    C. Dubious D. Visible

49. Sonu is an **inveterate** liar.
    A. Effective B. Habitual
    C. Frequent D. Familiar

50. The underworld still makes solid profit out of **illicit** liquor.
    A. indigenous
    B. illegitimate
    C. illegal
    D. country

51. When youngesters do not have good role-models to **emulate** they start searching for them amongst Sportsmen of Filmstars.
    A. imitate
    B. modify
    C. molify
    D. inhabit

52. The **abberration** in the Indian Economy can be attributed to short-sightedness of its political masters.
    A. procrastination
    B. privilege
    C. deviation
    D. steadfastness

53. The claims of students look hollow when they **attribute** their poor performance to difficulty of examination.
    A. infer
    B. impute
    C. inhere
    D. inundate

54. As soon as he finished his speech, there was **spontaneous** applause from the audience.
    A. well-timed
    B. willing
    C. instinctive
    D. instantaneous

55. The soldier proved his **mettle** in the battlefield.
    A. persistence
    B. stamina and strength
    C. courage and endurance
    D. heroism

56. He listened of my request with **indifference**.
    A. disinterest
    B. concern
    C. displeasure
    D. caution

57. The accident occurred due to his **lapse**.
    A. trick
    B. interval
    C. error
    D. ignorance

58. Being a member of this Club, he has certain **rights**.
    A. status
    B. truth
    C. virtues
    D. privileges

59. He is **averse** to the idea of holding elections now.
    A. convinced
    B. angry
    C. agreeable
    D. opposed

60. Silence is **mandatory** for meditation to be effective.
    A. compulsory
    B. necessary
    C. required
    D. needed

61. The underworld still makes solid profit out of **illicit** liquor.
    A. indigenous
    B. illegitimate
    C. illegal
    D. country

62. When I look back over the wartime years I cannot help feeling that time is an inadequate and even **capricious** measure of their duration at one moment they seem so long, at another so short.
    A. misleading
    B. whimsical
    C. erratic
    D. unpredictable

63. The tablet **alleviated** the pain, and the patient was soon feeling much better.
    A. mitigated
    B. moderated
    C. removed
    D. lightened

64. The leader nodded his **approbation**.
    A. understanding
    B. approval
    C. admiration
    D. appreciation

65. We should always try to maintain and promote communal **amity**.
    A. bondage

B. contention
C. friendship
D. understanding

66. Many species of animals have become **extinct** during the last hundred years.
    A. aggressive
    B. non-existent
    C. scattered
    D. feeble

67. True religion does not require one to **proselytise** through guile or force.
    A. translate   B. hypnotise
    C. attack   D. convert

68. That the plan is both inhuman and **preposterous** needs no further proof.
    A. heartless   B. impractical
    C. absurd   D. abnormal

69. She **baffled** all our attempts to find her.
    A. defeated
    B. thwarted
    C. foiled
    D. circumvented

70. Instead of putting up a united front against of common enemy, the medieval states frittered away their energy in **internecine** warfare.
    A. mutually destructive
    B. baneful
    C. pernicious
    D. detrimental

71. The bullet wound proved to be **fatal** and the soldier died immediately.
    A. grievous   B. dangerous
    C. serious   D. deadly

72. Whatever opinion he gives is **sane**.
    A. rational   B. obscure
    C. wild   D. arrogant

73. He **corroborated** the statement of his brother.
    A. confirmed   B. disproved
    C. condemned   D. seconded

74. Whatever the **verdict** of history may be, Chaplin will occupy a unique place in its pages.
    A. judgement   B. voice
    C. outcome   D. prediction

75. The attitude of the Western countries towards the Third World countries is rather **callous** to say the least.
    A. passive   B. unkind
    C. cursed   D. unfeeling

76. The story is too fantastic to be **credible**.
    A. believable
    B. false
    C. readable
    D. praiseworthy

77. Catching snakes can be **hazardous** for people untrained in the art.
    A. tricky   B. harmful
    C. difficult   D. dangerous

78. After the **dismal** performance of the team in the series concluded yesterday, the captain offered his resignation to the president of the club.
    A. poor   B. sorrowful
    C. minimum   D. short

79. The small boy was able to give a **graphic** description of the thief.
    A. picture   B. drawing
    C. vivid   D. broad

80. The prisoner has been **languishing** in the jail for the last many years.
    A. convicted B. suffering
    C. attempting D. avoiding
81. Some of the Asian countries have been **enmeshed** in an inescapable debt trap.
    A. entangled B. hit
    C. struck D. ensured
82. In spite of their efforts, the team of scientists could not make much **headway** to solve the problem.
    A. progress B. thinking
    C. efforts D. start
83. On scrutiny the police officer found out that the documents provided by the landlord were totally **fabricated**.
    A. forged B. historical
    C. prepared D. genuine
84. The soldier displayed **exceptional** courage and saved the Major from the enemy's hand.
    A. avoidable B. unusual
    C. strange D. abnormal
85. He found a **lucrative** assignment.
    A. good B. profitable
    C. excellent D. significant
86. The novel was so interesting that I was **oblivious** of my surroundings.
    A. precarious B. unmindful
    C. aware D. watchful
87. The great dancer impressed the appreciative crowd by her **nimble** movements.
    A. unrhythmic B. lively
    C. quickening D. clear
88. The president of the party **deprecated** the move of the Government to introduce electroal reforms in a haste.
    A. welcomed B. denied
    C. protested D. humiliated
89. It took him a long time to **come round** after the operation.
    A. recover B. walk
    C. move D. eat
90. Few teachers have been spared the problem of an **obstreperous** pupil in the class.
    A. sullen B. unruly
    C. lazy D. awkward
91. His visit to foreign countries brought about a **sea-change** in his outlook and his attitude to people.
    A. complete change
    B. partial change
    C. favourable change
    D. unfavourable change
92. Swift is known in the world of letters for his **misogynism**.
    A. hate for mankind
    B. hate for womankind
    C. love for the reasonable
    D. love for womankind
93. He was warned at the **outset** of his career.
    A. end B. beginning
    C. middle D. entrance
94. The time I spent in the library was a most **rewarding** one.
    A. profitable B. paying
    C. serviceable D. precious
95. That young is quite **sanguine** about the result of his competitive examination.
    A. depressed B. pessimistic
    C. anxious D. optimistic

96. The courage shown by the soldiers at this moment of crisis is **exemplary**.
    A. suitable B. clear
    C. elementary D. admirable

97. The notice said that the meeting would begin **precisely** at 9.30 a.m.
    A. approximately B. exactly
    C. accurately D. concisely

98. The inspector was a **vigilant** young man.
    A. intelligent B. ambitious
    C. watchful D. smart

99. A **rupture** in the relationship of the two brothers is quite apparent.
    A. break B. damage
    C. breach D. gap

100. "I have learnt a great deal working in factories, and for a time I've been a weaver. Here are my **testimonials**, Mr. Davis."
    A. witnesses B. testaments
    C. tokens D. credentials

Directions (Qs. 101 to 121): *In the following questions choose the word which is the exact **opposite** of the given word.*

101. DEAR
    A. Priceless B. Free
    C. Worthless D. Cheap

102. FLAGITIOUS
    A. Innocent B. Vapid
    C. Ignorant D. Frivolous

103. LIABILITY
    A. Property B. Assets
    C. Debt D. Teasure

104. VIRTUOUS
    A. Wicked B. Corrupt
    C. Vicious D. Scandalous

105. ENCOURAGE
    A. Dampen B. Disapprove
    C. Discourage D. Warn

106. MORTAL
    A. Divine B. Immortal
    C. Spiritual D. Eternal

107. LEND
    A. Borrow B. Cheat
    C. Pawn D. Hire

108. COMIC
    A. Emotional B. Tragic
    C. Fearful D. Painful

109. ADDITION
    A. Division
    B. Enumeration
    C. Subtraction
    D. Multiplication

110. MINOR
    A. Big B. Major
    C. Tall D. Heavy

111. REPEL
    A. Attend
    B. Concentrate
    C. Continue
    D. Attract

112. ARTIFICIAL
    A. Red B. Natural
    C. Truthful D. Solid

113. CAPACIOUS
    A. Limited B. Caring
    C. Foolish D. Changeable

114. PROVOCATION
    A. Vocation B. Pacification
    C. Peace D. Destruction

115. METICULOUS
    A. Mutual B. Shaggy
    C. Meretricious D. Slovenly

116. ABLE
    A. Disable B. Inable
    C. Unable D. Misable

117. COMFORT
    A. Uncomfort
    B. Miscomfort
    C. Discomfort
    D. None of these
118. GAIN
    A. Loose   B. Fall
    C. Lost   D. Lose
119. SYNTHETIC
    A. Affable B. Natural
    C. Plastic D. Cosmetic
120. ACQUITTED
    A. Freed   B. Burdened
    C. Convicted D. Entrusted
121. STRINGENT
    A. General
    B. Vehement
    C. Lenient
    D. Magnanimous

Directions (Qs. 122 to 150): *Each of the following items consists of a sentence followed by four words. Select the* ***antonym*** *of the word occuring in the sentence in bold letters, as per the context.*

122. What the critic said about this new book was **absurd**.
    A. Interesting B. Impartial
    C. Sensible   D. Ridiculous
123. The issue raised in the forum can be **ignored**.
    A. Removed   B. Considered
    C. Set aside D. Debated
124. After swallowing it the frog has become **lethargic**.
    A. Aggressive B. Dull
    C. Active   D. Hungry
125. For the first time I saw him speaking **rudely** to her.
    A. Softly   B. Gently
    C. Politely D. Slowly
126. Dust storms and polluted rivers have made it **hazardous** to breathe the air and drink the water.
    A. Convenient B. Risky
    C. Wrong   D. Safe
127. Only hard work can **enrich** our country.
    A. Impoverish B. Improve
    C. Increase   D. Involve
128. He is man of **extravagant** habits.
    A. Sensible   B. Careful
    C. Economical D. Balanced
129. They employ only **diligent** workers.
    A. Unskilled B. Lazy
    C. Careless D. Idle
130. His success in the preliminary examination made him **complacent**.
    A. Discontented
    B. Self-satisfied
    C. Curious
    D. Militant
131. In this competition, he has become the **victor**.
    A. Beaten
    B. Frustrated
    C. Disappointed
    D. Vanquished
132. His behaviour at social gatherings is **laudable**.
    A. Condemnable B. Impolite
    C. Unpleasant D. Repulsive
133. The characters in this story are not all **fictitious**.
    A. Common B. Factual
    C. Real   D. Genuine

134. The **reluctance** of the officer was obvious.
    A. Eagerness
    B. Hesitation
    C. Enjoyment
    D. Unwillingness
135. He is a **generous** man.
    A. Stingy
    B. Uncharitable
    C. Selfish
    D. Ignoble
136. He showed a marked **antipathy** to foreigners.
    A. Profundity   B. Fondness
    C. Objection   D. Willingness
137. The authorities took the corrective action with **celerity**.
    A. Reluctance
    B. Delay
    C. Promptness
    D. Lack of judgement
138. It seems **churlish** to refuse such a generous offer.
    A. Wise   B. Sensible
    C. Polite   D. Immature
139. A **conscientious** editor, he checked every definition for its accuracy.
    A. Novice   B. Careless
    C. Unscientific D. Biased
140. Sharma's **craven** refusal to join the protest was criticised by his comrades.
    A. Strategic
    B. Bold
    C. Diplomatic
    D. Well-thought
141. The dictator **quelled** the uprising.
    A. Fostered   B. Defended
    C. Supported   D. Fomented
142. People are unwilling to **follow** the rules.
    A. Waive
    B. Neglect
    C. Dispose
    D. Disregard
143. That was an **impudent** remark.
    A. Gentle
    B. Mild
    C. Modest
    D. Unassuming
144. His sudden appearance on the scene was **fortuitous**.
    A. Circumstantial
    B. Unfortunate
    C. Sudden
    D. Calculated
145. The batsman gave a **sterling** performance.
    A. A risky
    B. A vital
    C. An ordinary
    D. A match-saving
146. While facing that situation he turned out to be **dauntless**.
    A. Tactful   B. Stoical
    C. Bashful   D. Cowardly
147. We went to the first floor through the **rickety** wooden stairs.
    A. Stable
    B. Old
    C. Narrow
    D. Uncomfortable
148. They made a **profligate** use of scarce resources.
    A. Proper
    B. Extravagant
    C. Effective
    D. Thrifty

149. The consultant analysed the proposal carefully before he decided to **jettison** it.
 A. Abandon B. Strengthen
 C. Accept D. Modify

150. The politician was **flummoxed** by the question put to him.
 A. Comfortable
 B. Annoyed
 C. Delighted
 D. Disconcerted

Answers

1	2	3	4	5	6	7	8	9	10
D	C	D	D	C	D	B	B	C	A
11	12	13	14	15	16	17	18	19	20
C	D	B	A	D	C	C	C	B	C
21	22	23	24	25	26	27	28	29	30
A	C	C	B	C	B	B	C	D	C
31	32	33	34	35	36	37	38	39	40
D	C	C	D	D	B	C	A	C	B
41	42	43	44	45	46	47	48	49	50
D	B	A	C	B	B	C	B	B	C
51	52	53	54	55	56	57	58	59	60
A	C	B	C	C	A	C	D	D	A
61	62	63	64	65	66	67	68	69	70
C	B	A	B	C	B	D	C	C	A
71	72	73	74	75	76	77	78	79	80
D	A	A	A	D	A	D	A	C	B
81	82	83	84	85	86	87	88	89	90
A	A	A	B	B	B	C	C	A	B
91	92	93	94	95	96	97	98	99	100
A	B	B	A	D	D	B	C	A	D
101	102	103	104	105	106	107	108	109	110
D	A	B	C	C	B	A	B	C	B
111	112	113	114	115	116	117	118	119	120
D	B	A	B	D	C	C	D	B	C
121	122	123	124	125	126	127	128	129	130
C	C	B	C	C	D	A	C	C	A
131	132	133	134	135	136	137	138	139	140
D	A	C	A	A	B	B	C	D	B
141	142	143	144	145	146	147	148	149	150
D	D	A	D	C	D	A	D	C	A

Words Commonly Confused 11

There are many words in English which seem or sound similar but are completely different in their meanings and cause confusion and errors in their usage. Try some questions on such words here. Many homonyms and homophones are also included here in the questions.

Directions: *Select the right word between option A and B to fill in the blank. If both words seem right to you, select 'C' and if None of them is right, select 'D'.*

1. If .... is lost everything is lost.
   A. character
   B. conduct
   C. Any one of these
   D. None of these

2. There is a film .... board in India to certify the films.
   A. censure
   B. censor
   C. Any one of these
   D. None of these

3. I have applied for two days .... leave.
   A. casual
   B. causal
   C. Any one of these
   D. None of these

4. It is a/an .... to think that honesty does not pay.
   A. error
   B. mistake
   C. Any one of these
   D. None of these

5. In the Second World .... atom bombs were dropped on Nagasaki and Hiroshima.
   A. war
   B. battle
   C. Any one of these
   D. None of these

6. Lord Rama went into .... for fourteen years.
   A. banishment
   B. exile
   C. Any one of these
   D. None of these

7. India Gate is a war ....
   A. memorable
   B. memorial
   C. Any one of these
   D. None of these

8. The .... gate of the building was closed.
   A. main
   B. mane
   C. Any one of these
   D. None of these

9. She was awarded a gold .... for bravery.
   A. meddle
   B. medal
   C. Any one of these
   D. None of these

10. .... is followed by thunder.
    A. Lightning
    B. Lightening
    C. Any one of these
    D. None of these

11. I have not received any .... from my father for the past two months.
    A. latter
    B. letter
    C. Any one of these
    D. None of these

12. Avoid using this .... as it is very narrow.
    A. lain
    B. lane
    C. Any one of these
    D. None of these

13. The lawyer quoted many .... in support of his argument.
    A. precedents
    B. presidents
    C. Any one of these
    D. None of these

14. The doctor has .... this medicine for my father.
    A. prescribed
    B. proscribed
    C. Any one of these
    D. None of these

15. Trespassers will be ....
    A. persecuted
    B. prosecuted
    C. Any one of these
    D. None of these

16. My brother has no .... experience of factory life.
    A. practical
    B. practicable
    C. Any one of these
    D. None of these

17. Theory .... practice.
    A. proceeds
    B. precedes
    C. Any one of these
    D. None of these

18. I .... the house where my sister was born.
    A. recollect
    B. remember
    C. Any one of these
    D. None of these

19. The .... of mango trees are very deep.
    A. roots
    B. routes
    C. Any one of these
    D. None of these

20. Mohan is .... of his success.
    A. sanguinary
    B. sanguine
    C. Any one of these
    D. None of these

21. A .... man like Mr. Malhotra should not have used such words.
    A. sensible
    B. sensitive
    C. Any one of these
    D. None of these

22. We sat in the .... of a tree.
    A. shade
    B. shadow
    C. Any one of these
    D. None of these

23. My eyes are ....
    A. soar
    B. sore

C. Any one of these
   D. None of these
24. Our new house is very ....
   A. spacious
   B. specious
   C. Any one of these
   D. None of these
25. I will tell a .... to those who complete their homework.
   A. storey
   B. story
   C. Any one of these
   D. None of these
26. She has not sent a/an .... to my letter.
   A. reply
   B. answer
   C. Any one of these
   D. None of these
27. Shyam is .... to drinking.
   A. devoted
   B. addicted
   C. Any one of these
   D. None of these
28. He is the ....boy that stole your pen.
   A. very
   B. vary
   C. Any one of these
   D. None of these
29. This child is the .... survivor of this accident.
   A. sole
   B. soul
   C. Any one of these
   D. None of these
30. We should not .... others' things.
   A. steel
   B. steal
   C. Any one of these
   D. None of these
31. Might is ....
   A. right
   B. write
   C. Any one of these
   D. None of these
32. The whole shop was .... to the ground by the fire.
   A. raised
   B. razed
   C. Any one of these
   D. None of these
33. The Niti Aayog is drawing the next five year ....
   A. plan
   B. plane
   C. Any one of these
   D. None of these
34. Rajputs belong to a .... race.
   A. marshal
   B. martial
   C. Any one of these
   D. None of these
35. Give me a blade to .... my nails.
   A. pair
   B. pare
   C. Any one of these
   D. None of these
36. .... were issued by the court to summon the suspects.
   A. Ardours
   B. Orders
   C. Any one of these
   D. None of these
37. This is a .... problem, you cannot solve it easily.
   A. knotty
   B. naughty
   C. Any one of these
   D. None of these

38. Arvind has purchased a new .... of shoes for two hundred rupees.
   A. pare
   B. pair
   C. Any one of these
   D. None of these

39. Madhu is full of youthful ....
   A. ardour
   B. order
   C. Any one of these
   D. None of these

40. My sister's child is very ....
   A. knotty
   B. naughty
   C. Any one of these
   D. None of these

41. Do not be tempted by .... gains.
   A. momentary
   B. momentous
   C. Any one of these
   D. None of these

42. About thirty .... lost their lives in an accident at Raniganj colliery.
   A. minors
   B. miners
   C. Any one of these
   D. None of these

43. Iron is a very useful ....
   A. metal
   B. mettle
   C. Any one of these
   D. None of these

44. I went to the bank and got my .... cashed.
   A. check
   B. cheque
   C. Any one of these
   D. None of these

45. We have revised our .... in English.
   A. course
   B. corse
   C. Any one of these
   D. None of these

46. Please convey my .... to your brother.
   A. compliments
   B. complements
   C. Any one of these
   D. None of these

47. I can work for twelve hours ....
   A. continually
   B. continuously
   C. Any one of these
   D. None of these

48. I write my .... daily.
   A. diary
   B. dairy
   C. Any one of these
   D. None of these

49. Chicken pox is an infectious ....
   A. decease
   B. disease
   C. Any one of these
   D. None of these

50. Vasco da Gama .... the sea route to India in 1498.
   A. invented
   B. discovered
   C. Any one of these
   D. None of these

51. The Moon .... from behind a cloud.
   A. immersed
   B. emerged
   C. Any one of these
   D. None of these

52. Many Indians .... are settled in Sri Lanka.
    A. emigrants
    B. immigrants
    C. Any one of these
    D. None of these
53. We went on an .... to Kashmir.
    A. incursion
    B. excursion
    C. Any one of these
    D. None of these
54. Real .... is found only in hard work.
    A. felicity
    B. facility
    C. Any one of these
    D. None of these
55. The poor man had to .... his meals.
    A. forego
    B. forgo
    C. Any one of these
    D. None of these
56. My final year examination .... on 21st April.
    A. begins
    B. commences
    C. Any one of these
    D. None of these
57. Recently there was a bus .... in Patna.
    A. collision
    B. collusion
    C. Any one of these
    D. None of these
58. The .... is very fine today.
    A. weather
    B. climate
    C. Any one of these
    D. None of these
59. Anand was rewarded for his good ....
    A. character
    B. conduct
    C. Any one of these
    D. None of these
60. Everyone made fun of him as his manner of speaking was ....
    A. childlike
    B. childish
    C. Any one of these
    D. None of these
61. Lalitha was .... for her objectionable remarks.
    A. censured
    B. censored
    C. Any one of these
    D. None of these
62. The judge made a/an .... of judgement.
    A. error
    B. blunder
    C. Any one of these
    D. None of these
63. The .... from Kalka to Simla is very steep.
    A. assent
    B. ascent
    C. Any one of these
    D. None of these
64. Her remarks were not .... to the occasion.
    A. apposite
    B. opposite
    C. Any one of these
    D. None of these
65. He is a very famous ....
    A. artisan
    B. artist
    C. Any one of these
    D. None of these

66. The teacher .... her to appear for the paper again.
    A. allowed
    B. permitted
    C. Any one of these
    D. None of these

67. You should .... from telling lies.
    A. refrain
    B. abstain
    C. Any one of these
    D. None of these

68. I .... that you are innocent, but I am helpless.
    A. admit
    B. confer
    C. Any one of these
    D. None of these

69. My brother .... his right to the family property.
    A. waved
    B. waived
    C. Any one of these
    D. None of these

70. The .... carry blood in our body.
    A. veins
    B. vanes
    C. Any one of these
    D. None of these

71. What .... will you pursue in your life?
    A. vacation
    B. vocation
    C. Any one of these
    D. None of these

72. This lake .... with fish.
    A. teems
    B. teams
    C. Any one of these
    D. None of these

73. Do not .... at pretty girls.
    A. stair
    B. stare
    C. Any one of these
    D. None of these

74. Akbar was a man of deep ....
    A. insight
    B. incite
    C. Any one of these
    D. None of these

75. Kanpur is an ....city.
    A. industrious
    B. industrial
    C. Any one of these
    D. None of these

76. This is a very .... book.
    A. idle
    B. ideal
    C. Any one of these
    D. None of these

77. He has .... much wealth.
    A. hoarded
    B. horde
    C. Any one of these
    D. None of these

78. The princess had a very kind ....
    A. hart
    B. heart
    C. Any one of these
    D. None of these

79. There is a big .... in our school.
    A. haul
    B. hall
    C. Any one of these
    D. None of these

80. We should be determined to achieve our ....
    A. goal
    B. gaol

C. Any one of these
D. None of these

81. I always .... what I say.
    A. mean
    B. mien
    C. Any one of these
    D. None of these

82. We must .... to God daily.
    A. prey
    B. pray
    C. Any one of these
    D. None of these

83. The .... is the prettiest of all the flowers.
    A. rose
    B. rows
    C. Any one of these
    D. None of these

84. The .... of democracy in India is not little.
    A. roll
    B. role
    C. Any one of these
    D. None of these

85. This is not a .... line.
    A. straight
    B. strait
    C. Any one of these
    D. None of these

86. To .... is a crime.
    A. gambol
    B. gamble
    C. Any one of these
    D. None of these

87. Capt. Singh received .... wounds in the battlefield.
    A. fatal
    B. fateful
    C. Any one of these
    D. None of these

88. She has a very .... impression of the picture.
    A. feint
    B. faint
    C. Any one of these
    D. None of these

89. I found her in ....misery.
    A. abject
    B. object
    C. Any one of these
    D. None of these

90. The committee .... a resolution condemning terrorism in the country.
    A. adapted
    B. adopted
    C. Any one of these
    D. None of these

91. You .... to do your duty.
    A. ought
    B. aught
    C. Any one of these
    D. None of these

92. The accused was released on ....
    A. bale
    B. bail
    C. Any one of these
    D. None of these

93. One must not go against the .... of morality.
    A. cannons
    B. canons
    C. Any one of these
    D. None of these

94. She had very little time to .... votes.
    A. canvass
    B. canvas
    C. Any one of these
    D. None of these

95. Dayanand Saraswati was the .... guide of many people.
    A. spiritual
    B. spirited
    C. Any one of these
    D. None of these
96. Aarti should not approve of her .... ways.
    A. wilful
    B. willing
    C. Any one of these
    D. None of these
97. Rajesh .... many instances in support of his argument.
    A. sited
    B. cited
    C. Any one of these
    D. None of these
98. The .... drops on the petals of the rose looked beautiful.
    A. due
    B. dew
    C. Any one of these
    D. None of these
99. Please .... my white shirt red.
    A. die
    B. dye
    C. Any one of these
    D. None of these
100. This is not a .... surface.
    A. plain
    B. plane
    C. Any one of these
    D. None of these

Answers

1	2	3	4	5	6	7	8	9	10
A	B	A	B	A	B	B	A	B	A
11	12	13	14	15	16	17	18	19	20
B	B	A	A	B	A	B	B	A	B
21	22	23	24	25	26	27	28	29	30
A	A	B	A	B	A	B	A	A	B
31	32	33	34	35	36	37	38	39	40
A	B	A	B	B	B	A	B	A	B
41	42	43	44	45	46	47	48	49	50
A	B	A	B	A	A	B	A	B	B
51	52	53	54	55	56	57	58	59	60
B	A	B	A	B	B	A	A	B	B
61	62	63	64	65	66	67	68	69	70
A	A	B	A	B	B	A	A	B	A
71	72	73	74	75	76	77	78	79	80
B	A	B	A	B	B	A	B	B	A
81	82	83	84	85	86	87	88	89	90
A	B	A	B	A	B	A	B	A	B
91	92	93	94	95	96	97	98	99	100
A	B	B	A	A	A	B	B	B	A

One Word Substitutes 12

There are many words in English language which can be perfectly used for a number of words. These words help in expressing ideas in a short and correct manner for the right occasion. Such words not only enhance the vocabulary but also enable you to economise in the use of words to a great extent.

Directions: *In questions given below choose the options which can be substituted for the given words/sentences.*

1. An assembly of listeners
   A. Audience   B. Nostrum
   C. Ostracise   D. Obituary

2. That which cannot be heard
   A. Audible   B. Pregnant
   C. Inaudible   D. Bobemian

3. A person who hates mankind
   A. Philanthropist
   B. Misanthropist
   C. Nihilist
   D. Theist

4. Animals that suckle their young ones
   A. Mammals   B. Pisces
   C. Amphibian   D. Birds

5. Murder of infants
   A. Regicide   B. Suicide
   C. Homicide   D. Infanticide

6. Short lived or fleeting
   A. Permanent   B. Ephemeral
   C. Effeminate D. Optimist

7. A person whose thoughts are turned inward and who never opens his heart to others
   A. Extrovert   B. Introvert
   C. Sceptic   D. Ambivert

8. Word for word
   A. Verbatim   B. Compound
   C. Synonym   D. Oral

9. A truth which is often repeated
   A. Aesthetics B. Truism
   C. Verbose   D. Truant

10. Belief in the role of a strong dictator is
    A. Fanaticism B. Fascism
    C. Nepotism   D. Dogmatism

11. A person who does things only for pleasure
    A. Professional B. Radical
    C. Amateur   D. Empiric

12. A person who practices celibacy
    A. Celibate   B. Mature
    C. Married   D. Widower

13. That which can be easily carried
    A. Portable
    B. Impregnable
    C. Invisible
    D. Apostate

14. One who flirts with ladies
    A. Solvent   B. Gentleman
    C. Philanderer   D. Popular
15. An office for which no salary is paid
    A. Hospitable   B. Free
    C. Honorary   D. Gratis
16. One who firmly believes in fate or destiny
    A. Honorary   B. Gratis
    C. Dermatologist   D. Fatalist
17. A word which has the same meaning as another
    A. Contemporary   B. Substitute
    C. Synonym   D. Antonym
18. Allowance due to a wife from her husband on legal separation
    A. Wage
    B. Compensation
    C. Debt
    D. Alimony
19. Four children born at the same time
    A. Forte
    B. Twins
    C. Fortis
    D. Quadruplets
20. An insect with many legs
    A. Biped   B. Butterfly
    C. Centipede   D. Quadruped
21. Birds moving from one place to another
    A. Migratory   B. Respiratory
    C. Obituary   D. Transitory
22. To change hostility into friendship
    A. Surrogate   B. Castigate
    C. Placate   D. Complicate
23. The study of the art of printing is
    A. Typography
    B. Phenology
    C. Astrology
    D. Graphology
24. One who studies the history of development of mankind is
    A. Anthropologist
    B. Botanist
    C. Economist
    D. Historian
25. A handwriting which cannot be easily read
    A. Lucid   B. Edible
    C. Illegible   D. Legible
26. Government in which all religions are honoured is called
    A. Fanatic   B. Ascetic
    C. Secular   D. Catholic
27. One who does not show favour to anyone is called
    A. Impartial
    B. Unfavourable
    C. Prejudiced
    D. Rude
28. To throw light on something difficult
    A. Amplify   B. Expand
    C. Explain   D. Elucidate
29. A style that is full of words is known as
    A. Elegant
    B. Complicated
    C. Verbose
    D. Bombastic
30. A book or paper written by hand is known as
    A. Script
    B. Manuscript
    C. Draft
    D. Hand-written
31. A disease which ends in death is known as
    A. Life-suck   B. Cancer
    C. Fatal   D. Deadly

32. Those are practised by statesmen is called
    A. Diplomacy
    B. Viewpoint
    C. Statesmanship
    D. Politics
33. What we say about a man after his death is called
    A. Epitome   B. Elegy
    C. Posthumous D. Epitaph
34. One who looks at the dark side of things is known as
    A. A pessimist
    B. An iconoclast
    C. An optimist
    D. A fatalist
35. The act of speaking through one's thoughts when alone
    A. Autologue B. Dialogue
    C. Monologue D. Soliloquy
36. To congratulate someone in a formal manner
    A. Solemnise B. Celebrate
    C. Facilitate D. Felicitate
37. A disease of the mind causing an uncontrollable desire to steal
    A. Kleptomania
    B. Schizophrenia
    C. Claustrophobia
    D. Megalomania
38. A person pretending to be somebody he is not
    A. Liar   B. Magician
    C. Imposter   D. Rogue
39. One who dabbles in fine arts for the love of it and not for monetary gains
    A. Dilettante
    B. Professional
    C. Connoisseur
    D. Amateur
40. A prima facie case is such
    A. As it turns out to be at the end
    B. As it seems at first sight
    C. As it seems to the court after a number of hearings
    D. As it is made to seem at first sight
41. Tending to move away from the centre or axis
    A. Centripetal B. Awry
    C. Centrifugal D. Axiomatic
42. A drawing on transparent paper
    A. Transparency B. Blue print
    C. Red print   D. Negative
43. Something that relates to everyone in the world
    A. Usual   B. General
    C. Universal D. Common
44. Continuing fight between parties, families, clans, etc.
    A. Quarrel B. Skirmish
    C. Feud   D. Enmity
45. Extreme old age when a man behaves like a fool
    A. Senility
    B. Superannuation
    C. Imbecility
    D. Dotage
46. One who does not believe in existence of God
    A. Stoic   B. Egoist
    C. Atheist D. Naive
47. That which is preceptible by touch is
    A. Tenacious B. Contagious
    C. Tangible D. Contingent
48. Words used in ancient times but no longer in general use now
    A. Ancient B. Extinct
    C. Archaic D. Antiquated

49. Incapable of being seen through
    A. Potable   B. Ductile
    C. Opaque   D. Obsolete

50. A fixed orbit in space in relation to earth
    A. Geo-centric
    B. Geological
    C. Geo-stationary
    D. Geo-synchronous

51. A long vehement speech
    A. Abuse   B. Abhor
    C. Tirade   D. Vulgar

52. The body at the state of growth between boyhood and youth, is
    A. Youth
    B. Adolescent
    C. Mature
    D. Adult

53. The doctor who specializes in the treatment of nervous system
    A. Neurologist
    B. Oculist
    C. Opticum
    D. Obstetrician

54. A person who has an extensive knowledge
    A. Illiterate   B. Innocent
    C. Erudite   D. Scholar

55. The science or art of conducting negotiations between nations
    A. Erratic   B. Wandering
    C. Diplomacy   D. Epicure

56. One who relies on experiment not on theory
    A. Theoretical   B. Empiric
    C. Practical   D. Scientist

57. One incredulous of human goodness
    A. Naxalite   B. Hedonist
    C. Cynic   D. Stoic

58. That which cannot be explained
    A. Ennui
    B. Interesting
    C. Emancipate
    D. Inexplicable

59. Animals which like to live in flocks
    A. Isolate   B. Gregarious
    C. Voracious   D. Precarious

60. A person blindly attached to any opinion, system or party
    A. Fatalist   B. Bourgeois
    C. Bigot   D. Fallible

61. One who is well versed in the knowledge of plants and vegetables
    A. Botanist
    B. Vegetarian
    C. Scientist
    D. Non-vegetarian

62. A place where one lives permanently
    A. Bourgeois   B. Refugee
    C. Domicile   D. Confiscate

63. A battle or a match which neither party wins
    A. Detergent   B. Caucus
    C. Equal   D. Draw

64. A piece of writing full of words or using more words than required
    A. Vociferous   B. Verbose
    C. Sadist   D. Voracity

65. The violation or profaning sacred things
    A. Pantheism
    B. Sceptic
    C. Sacrilege
    D. Opportunist

66. One who eats only vegetables and abstains from meat of animals
    A. Gentle
    B. Mercenary
    C. Non-vegetarian
    D. Vegetarian

67. One who cannot be easily pleased
    A. Sycophant   B. Reserved
    C. Flatterer   D. Fastidious
68. A supporter of the cause of women
    A. Feminist   B. Effeminate
    C. Loquacious D. Sophist
69. A person who hates women
    A. Monogamy
    B. Misogamist
    C. Misogynist
    D. Gynaecologist
70. Without payment or free of cost
    A. Hedonist   B. Stoic
    C. Precious   D. Gratis
71. A person who changes sides
    A. Ductile   B. Anarchist
    C. Communist   D. Turncoat
72. A letter or a document which does not bear the name of its writer
    A. Acknowledge
    B. Pseudonym
    C. Elite
    D. Anonymous
73. Incapable of being effaced, or cancelled or obliterated
    A. Obviously   B. Delegate
    C. Indelible   D. Delible
74. An associate in an office or institution
    A. Accomplice B. Crew
    C. Colleague   D. Tyro
75. A person's first public speech
    A. Maiden speech
    B. Inaugural
    C. Libertine
    D. Final speech
76. That which is endless
    A. Irrefutable
    B. Underscore
    C. Refutable
    D. Interminable
77. One skilled in the disease of the eyes
    A. Neurologist
    B. Dentist
    C. Oculist
    D. Obstetrician
78. The study of energy is
    A. Geography   B. Biology
    C. Physics   D. Chemistry
79. Words inscribed on a tomb
    A. Alibi
    B. Epitaph
    C. Writ
    D. Monument
80. One who manages funerals
    A. Undertaker B. Anarchist
    C. Agnosite   D. Belligerent
81. A style in which a writer seeks to display his knowledge is known as
    A. Superficial
    B. Pedantic
    C. Showy
    D. Extravagant
82. One who keeps guard is known as a
    A. Soldier
    B. Policeman
    C. Gate-keeper
    D. Watchman
83. One who is insensible to kind thought is known as
    A. Unsympathetic
    B. Unkind
    C. Callous
    D. Inconsiderate
84. An address poem is called
    A. Elegy   B. Sonnet
    C. Ode   D. Epic

85. One who does a job for monetary consideration is known as
    A. Materialist
    B. Trader
    C. Mercenary
    D. Businessman
86. That which cannot be changed
    A. Unchanged   B. Revocable
    C. Changeless D. Irrevocable
87. Money paid to employees on retirement is called
    A. Advance   B. Deposit
    C. Gratuity D. Pension
88. To make the facts known is called
    A. Message
    B. Information
    C. Intimation
    D. News
89. Property inherited from one's father is called
    A. Ancestry B. Patrimony
    C. Legacy   D. Matrimony
90. Ordinary and common-place remarks
    A. Satire   B. Humour
    C. Examples D. Platitude
91. One who is not easily pleased by anything
    A. Precarious B. Maiden
    C. Medieval   D. Fastidious
92. Malafide case is one
    A. Which is undertaken after a long delay
    B. Which is not undertaken at all
    C. Which is undertaken in bad faith
    D. Which is undertaken in good faith
93. The absence of Law and order
    A. Revolt   B. Rebellion
    C. Anarchy   D. Mutiny
94. To slap with a flat object
    A. Gnaw   B. Chop
    C. Swat   D. Hew
95. A person who tries to deceive people by claiming to be able to do wonderful things
    A. Magician
    B. Trickster
    C. Impostor
    D. Mountebank
96. A government by the nobles
    A. Bureaucracy
    B. Autocracy
    C. Aristocracy
    D. Democracy
97. The custom or practice of having more than one husband at the same time
    A. Polyphony
    B. Polychromy
    C. Polygyny
    D. Polyandry
98. To issue a thunderous verbal attack
    A. Animate   B. Invigorate
    C. Fulminate D. Languish
99. Present and opposing arguments or evidence
    A. Reprimand B. Criticise
    C. Rebut   D. Rebuff
100. Deriving pleasure from inflicting pain on others
    A. Sadism
    B. Malevolence
    C. Bigotry
    D. Masochism
101. The policy of extending a country's empire and influence
    A. Imperialism
    B. Communism
    C. Internationalism
    D. Capitalism

102. One who knows everything
    A. Omnipotent B. Scholar
    C. Omniscient D. Literate
103. One who eats everything
    A. Irresistible
    B. Insolvent
    C. Omnivorous
    D. Omniscient
104. The act of violating the sanctity of the church is
    A. Sacrilege
    B. Desecration
    C. Heresy
    D. Blasphemy
105. A school-boy who cuts classes frequently is a
    A. Sycophant B. Defeatist
    C. Truant D. Martinet
106. The part of a government which is concerned with making of rules
    A. Bar B. Court
    C. Legislature D. Tribunal
107. That which cannot be corrected
    A. Indelible
    B. Illegible
    C. Incorrigible
    D. Unintelligible
108. That which cannot be believed
    A. Implausible
    B. Unreliable
    C. Incredible
    D. Incredulous
109. A small shop that sells fashionable clothes, cosmetics etc.
    A. Booth B. Store
    C. Stall D. Boutique
110. A large sleeping-room with many beds
    A. Hostel B. Bedroom
    C. Basement D. Dormitory
111. One who talks too much
    A. Pregnable B. Quite
    C. Illogical D. Garrulous
112. One that lives on another
    A. Parasite
    B. Eligible
    C. Independent
    D. Rudimentary
113. A material through which water cannot pass
    A. Fragile
    B. Fireproof
    C. Pillion
    D. Waterproof
114. The murderer of a King
    A. Regicide B. Fanatic
    C. Suicide D. Fratricide
115. Talking to one's self
    A. Egotism B. Soliloquy
    C. Egoism D. Ennui
116. One who is given to sensual enjoyments
    A. Cynic B. Epicurean
    C. Fanatic D. Eccentric
117. A lover of books
    A. Brittle
    B. Bibliophile
    C. Biographer
    D. Philosopher
118. That which is bound to happen
    A. Wavering B. Inevitable
    C. Opaque D. Doubtful
119. A place where birds are kept
    A. House B. Zoo
    C. Stable D. Aviary
120. One who walks on foot
    A. Rider
    B. Omnipotent
    C. Pedestrian
    D. Traveller

121. The crime of literary theft
    A. Panacea   B. Partiality
    C. Plagiarism   D. Pluralism
122. A medicine that induces sleep is known as
    A. Poppy   B. Opium
    C. Poison   D. Narcotic
123. A word no longer in use is called
    A. Non-existent   B. Ancient
    C. Obsolete   D. Out-dated
124. Nations engaged in war are known as
    A. Enemies
    B. Belligerents
    C. Mongers
    D. Neutrals
125. A line of persons waiting
    A. Queue   B. Masses
    C. Passengers   D. Gathering
126. A dramatic performance
    A. Mascot   B. Mosque
    C. Mask   D. Masses
127. A person who speaks many languages
    A. Polyglot
    B. Bilingual
    C. Linguist
    D. Monolingual
128. The raison d'etre of a controversy is
    A. The finesse with which participants handle it
    B. The unending hostility the parties concerned have towards each other
    C. The enthusiasm with which it is kept alive
    D. The reason or justification of its existence
129. To walk with slow or regular steps is to
    A. Stride   B. Pace
    C. Advance   D. Limp
130. A person of good understanding, knowledge and reasoning power
    A. Literate   B. Expert
    C. Intellectual   D. Snob
131. Teetotaller means
    A. One who abstains from taking wine
    B. One who abstains from theft
    C. One who abstains from malice
    D. One who abstains from meat
132. Very pleasing to eat
    A. Sumptuous   B. Tantalising
    C. Palatable   D. Appetising
133. Parts of a country behind the coast or a river's banks
    A. Archipelago   B. Swamps
    C. Isthmus   D. Hinterland
134. Giving undue favours to one's own kith and kin
    A. Worldliness
    B. Corruption
    C. Nepotism
    D. Favouritism
135. One who sacrifices his life for a cause
    A. Soldier
    B. Revolutionary
    C. Martyr
    D. Patriot
136. A person who eats human beings
    A. Cannibal   B. Nostrum
    C. Cynosure   D. Animal
137. A thing fit to be eaten
    A. Farrier   B. Edible
    C. Eradicate   D. Audible

138. That which cannot be limited
    A. Optimist
    B. Mimicry
    C. Inimitable
    D. Genealogy
139. A territory ruled by a monarch
    A. Aristocracy   B. Monarchy
    C. Democracy   D. Plutocracy
140. That which is not subject to death
    A. Mortal   B. Earthy
    C. Immature   D. Immortal
141. A victory gained at too great an expense
    A. Bloody   B. Pyrrhic
    C. Decisive   D. Celibacy
142. The doctor who specializes in the treatment of corns
    A. Oculist   B. Podiatrist
    C. Cardiologist D. Optician
143. A person who feels sorry for a wrong he has done
    A. Compunctious
    B. Overt
    C. Illiterate
    D. Literate
144. A person who advocates extreme Patriotism
    A. Atheism   B. Chauvinism
    C. Socialism   D. Democracy
145. To ponder over to meditate
    A. Alleviate   B. Expedite
    C. Ruminate   D. Ascetic
146. One who is habitually silent
    A. Chatter box B. Taciturn
    C. Indifferent D. Verbose
147. A letter which is not claimed by anyone
    A. Wasted letter B. Epigram
    C. Dead letter   D. Epicure
148. A well-experienced person
    A. Veteran   B. Tyro
    C. Outlandish D. Novice
149. Medical examination of a dead body
    A. Psychologist
    B. Post-mortem
    C. Dissection
    D. Caesarian
150. One who is all powerful
    A. Wait   B. Embezzle
    C. Omnipotent D. Effigy
151. The killing of one man by another man
    A. Insecticide B. Suicide
    C. Homicide   D. Fillicide
152. A drug which produces sleep or stupor, torpor, etc.
    A. Amulet   B. Narcotic
    C. Yawning   D. Insomnia
153. Science of the study of old age is called
    A. Exbiology
    B. Anthropology
    C. Genetics
    D. Gerontology
154. That which cannot be understood
    A. Infallible
    B. Unintelligible
    C. Incorrigible
    D. Intelligible
155. Anything that destroys the effect of poison
    A. Poison-free B. Preserver
    C. Antidote   D. Saver
156. One who is at home in all countries
    A. Universal
    B. International
    C. Cosmopolitan
    D. Metropolitan

157. A person who has no regard for others' feeling is known as
    A. Boastful B. Haughty
    C. Inconsiderate D. Unkind
158. A place where bees are kept is called
    A. A hive
    B. A sanctuary
    C. An apiary
    D. A mole
159. An expression of mild disapproval
    A. Denigration B. Reproof
    C. Warning D. Denigration
160. A voice loud enough to be heard
    A. Laudable
    B. Oral
    C. Audible
    D. Applaudable
161. A style in which a writer makes a display of his knowledge
    A. Ornate B. Pompous
    C. Pedantic D. Verbose
162. One who is fond of fighting
    A. Militant B. Belligerent
    C. Bellicose D. Aggressive
163. To take secretly in small quantities
    A. Theft
    B. Defalcation
    C. Pilferage
    D. Robbery
164. One who is honourably discharged from service
    A. Relieved
    B. Emancipated
    C. Emeritus
    D. Retired
165. An actor who plays humorous parts
    A. Fool B. Joker
    C. Clown D. Comedian
166. A building for storing threshed grain
    A. Store B. Granary
    C. Hangar D. Dockyard
167. To cause troops, etc., to spread out in readiness for battle
    A. Align B. Disperse
    C. Deploy D. Collocate
168. One who is determined to exactfull vengeance for wrongs done to him
    A. Vindictive B. Usurer
    C. Vindicator D. Virulent
169. List of the business or subjects to be considered at a meeting
    A. Plan B. Agenda
    C. Schedule D. Time-table
170. A person who brings goods illegally into the country
    A. Smuggler B. Importer
    C. Exporter D. Fraud
171. To talk without respect for something sacred or holy
    A. Vulgarity B. Rudeness
    C. Obscenity D. Blasphemy
172. Communication between mind and mind
    A. Tell-tale B. Telephone
    C. Telepathy D. Amistice
173. A player, who acts, not by speaking, but wholly by gesticulations
    A. Pantomine B. Patent
    C. Paronyms D. Patricide
174. To set free from restraint or bondage
    A. Detest B. Manipulate
    C. Emancipate D. Conjecture

175. An elderly unmarried woman
    A. Spinster   B. Vandal
    C. Adult   D. Bachelor
176. One who makes or compiles a dictionary
    A. Lexicographer
    B. Photographer
    C. Publisher
    D. Manuscript
177. One who is deprived of the protection of law
    A. Iconoclast B. Citizen
    C. Belligerent D. Outlaw
178. A vain boasting fellow
    A. Gallant   B. Fool
    C. Braggart   D. Chivalrous
179. A general pardon of political offenders
    A. Arson   B. Amnesty
    C. Emergency D. Arsenal
180. A woman of very fair complexion with light hair and light blue eyes
    A. Pretty   B. Blonde
    C. Beauty   D. Braggart
181. The principle of living and acting for the welfare of others
    A. Egoism
    B. Misogynism
    C. Asceticism
    D. Altruism
182. The study of earthquakes is
    A. Zoology   B. Physiology
    C. Seismology D. Etymology
183. The study of religion is
    A. Philology B. Astrology
    C. Philosophy D. Theology
184. An object which has no life
    A. Animate   B. Living
    C. Movable   D. Inanimate
185. A round about way of speaking
    A. Circumlocution
    B. Gourmet
    C. Flamboyant
    D. Eccentric
186. A person who cannot pay his debts
    A. Arsonist   B. Agnostic
    C. Solvent   D. Bankrupt
187. One who is irreverent towards God
    A. Fatalist   B. Bigot
    C. Blasphemers D. Fanatic
188. One who is incapable of being tired
    A. Indefatigable
    B. Extempore
    C. Opportunist
    D. Fatigable
189. A list of books
    A. Epilogue   B. Epigram
    C. Catalogue D. Phrase
190. Animals living on plants
    A. Cliche
    B. Celibate
    C. Herbivorous
    D. Carnivorous
191. That which cannot be passed through
    A. Present   B. Passage
    C. Impassable D. Passable
192. A thing through which rays of light cannot pass
    A. Transparent B. Species
    C. Waif   D. Opaque
193. A thing which is not fresh
    A. Old   B. New
    C. Juicy   D. Stale

194. A place for invalids and convalescents
    A. Irony
    B. Hospitable
    C. Dipsomania
    D. Sanatorium

195. A child born after the death of his father
    A. Posthumous   B. Consort
    C. Censer   D. Premature

196. A person interested in reading books and nothing else
    A. Student
    B. Book-worm
    C. Book-keeper
    D. Scholar

197. A man of odd habits
    A. Introvert   B. Moody
    C. Eccentric   D. Cynical

198. A tank for fishes or water plants
    A. Pyrrhic   B. Expiate
    C. Aviary   D. Aquarium

199. Person anxious for or trying to provoke war
    A. warhead   B. wary
    C. warmonger   D. extremist

200. Young and ambitious professional-person, working in a city
    A. yokel   B. yankee
    C. zippy   D. yuppie

Answers

1	2	3	4	5	6	7	8	9	10
A	C	B	A	D	B	B	A	B	B
11	12	13	14	15	16	17	18	19	20
C	A	A	C	C	D	C	D	D	C
21	22	23	24	25	26	27	28	29	30
A	C	A	D	C	C	A	D	C	B
31	32	33	34	35	36	37	38	39	40
C	A	D	A	D	D	A	C	D	B
41	42	43	44	45	46	47	48	49	50
C	A	C	C	D	C	C	C	C	C
51	52	53	54	55	56	57	58	59	60
C	B	A	C	C	B	C	D	B	C
61	62	63	64	65	66	67	68	69	70
A	C	D	B	C	D	D	A	C	D
71	72	73	74	75	76	77	78	79	80
D	D	C	C	A	D	C	C	B	A
81	82	83	84	85	86	87	88	89	90
B	D	C	C	C	D	C	C	B	A
91	92	93	94	95	96	97	98	99	100
D	C	C	C	B	C	D	C	C	A
101	102	103	104	105	106	107	108	109	110
A	C	C	A	C	C	C	C	D	D
111	112	113	114	115	116	117	118	119	120
D	A	D	A	B	B	B	B	D	C

121	122	123	124	125	126	127	128	129	130
C	D	D	B	A	B	C	D	B	C
131	132	133	134	135	136	137	138	139	140
A	C	D	C	C	A	B	C	B	D
141	142	143	144	145	146	147	148	149	150
B	B	A	B	C	B	C	A	B	C
151	152	153	154	155	156	157	158	159	160
C	B	D	B	C	C	C	C	B	C
161	162	163	164	165	166	167	168	169	170
C	C	C	D	C	B	C	A	B	A
171	172	173	174	175	176	177	178	179	180
D	C	A	C	A	A	D	C	B	B
181	182	183	184	185	186	187	188	189	190
D	C	D	D	A	D	C	A	C	C
191	192	193	194	195	196	197	198	199	200
C	D	D	D	A	B	C	D	C	D

❏ ❏ ❏

Idioms, Phrases & Proverbs 13

An idiom is a group of words established by usage as having a meaning different from the individual words. A phrase is a small group of words standing together as an idiomatic expression. A proverb is a short pithy saying in general use, stating a general truth or piece of advice.

Directions: *Pick out from the given alternatives the one that gives the correct meaning of the idiom/phrase/proverb.*

1. Above board
   A. A voyage
   B. Beyond doubt
   C. Uncertainty
   D. Honest and frank

2. A bed of roses
   A. always successful
   B. a comfortable situation
   C. very easy
   D. transient pleasure

3. Add fuel to the fire
   A. to activate the flames of an existing controversy
   B. to spread a rumour
   C. to increase the differences
   D. to speed up the work

4. A sleeping partner
   A. one who does not work
   B. unenthusiast
   C. lethargic
   D. exuberant

5. Apple of discord
   A. the cause of separation
   B. the basis of differentiation
   C. the cause of friction
   D. the state of confusion

6. A man of straw
   A. a characterless person
   B. worthless person
   C. an indecisive person
   D. unreliable person

7. Apple of one's eye
   A. a very loving person
   B. recalcitrant
   C. a person full of malevolence
   D. a person who is very dear to one

8. A hard nut to crack
   A. a difficult problem
   B. a difficult situation
   C. an intolerable person
   D. a skinflint

9. Apple-pie order
   A. handling two work simultaneously
   B. extremely neat and tidy
   C. two persons handling the same work
   D. in a haphzard way

10. To pin one's faith
    A. to be sure of somebody's favour
    B. to be unsure of favour
    C. to be insincere to others
    D. to deceive a close friend
11. At arm's length
    A. one arm distance
    B. to keep one at distance
    C. to be indifferent
    D. an intimate relationship
12. A fish out of water
    A. a dangerous situation
    B. death
    C. being in a position which is disagreeable
    D. a lonely person
13. At one's wits end
    A. to be in an embarrassing situation
    B. to be in a state of utter perplexity
    C. to satisfy one's own desire
    D. to abrogate
14. A black sheep
    A. scoundrel
    B. ruthless
    C. vagabond
    D. a traitorous person
15. At sixes and sevens
    A. in a state of confusion or disorder
    B. returning to an earlier or primitive form or state
    C. in a state of retrospection
    D. in the days of childhood
16. A labour of love
    A. a hard-working staff
    B. work done only for love
    C. To believe in work and not in reward
    D. an unpaid servant
17. A Herculean task
    A. unmanageable assignment
    B. confusing and tiring procedure
    C. work requiring extra ordinary strength to be done
    D. almost impossible to acheive something
18. A bolt from the blue
    A. an unexpected and calamitous blow.
    B. a retaliating attack
    C. tumult
    D. a sudden pleasant surprise
19. At the mercy of
    A. totally in the power of
    B. to leave everything on God
    C. to surrender
    D. the supremacy of God's will
20. At the eleventh hour
    A. at the time of death
    B. moment just after the work is completed
    C. moment just after the work is assigned
    D. at the last moment
21. A hornet's nest
    A. a dangerous situation
    B. a house built after great difficulty
    C. an unpleasant situation
    D. a difficult task
22. At the bottom of
    A. secret cause of
    B. at another's support
    C. to find a base
    D. a heavy loss
23. At daggers drawn
    A. a dual
    B. at enmity
    C. a hot debate
    D. one confronted with his rival

24. A man of parts
    A. a man of superior ability
    B. a highly responsible man
    C. a workaholic person
    D. a man of pretension
25. A man of words
    A. a garrulous person
    B. a trustworthy person
    C. a gregarious person
    D. a boastful person
26. An out and outer
    A. a traitor
    B. a man living in the border area
    C. a first rate person
    D. at an extreme point
27. To make an ass of oneself
    A. to bahave foolishly
    B. to laugh at oneself
    C. to make someone fool
    D. a ridiculous person
28. The Augustan Age
    A. an age of Great Kings
    B. the period of highest purity and refinement in any national literature.
    C. a golden age in music
    D. a period of prudent writers
29. In open arms
    A. to welcome cordially
    B. to be brave
    C. fighting openly
    D. ambitions to have all sorts of worldly pleasures
30. All the sundry
    A. all except one
    B. only intellectuals
    C. the whole elite class
    D. everyone without distinction
31. Backstairs influence
    A. improper influence
    B. the ultimate outcome
    C. retarded development
    D. indirect influence
32. Bad blood
    A. active hostility
    B. retribution
    C. very ill
    D. retaliation
33. Beat a retreat
    A. grand and pompous
    B. to withdraw
    C. to warn
    D. not to come straight to the point
34. To have a bee in one's bonnet
    A. to be obsessed with one idea
    B. prejudiced
    C. to have a single penny
    D. None of the above
35. Behind the scenes
    A. the hidden cause
    B. self-contained
    C. influencing events secretly
    D. one's contribution which is yet to be considered
36. To bell the cat
    A. to bring others to one's own opinion.
    B. to harm an enemy
    C. try to render a common enemy harmless
    D. to come to a common conclusion
37. Between the devil and the deep sea
    A. about to die
    B. to be on a wrong path
    C. to be in a dilemma
    D. between two dangers

38. To blow hot and cold in the same breath
    A. to condemn and criticize
    B. a hot discussion
    C. to consider all the aspects
    D. to be imperious and amiable by terms
39. Blow one's own trumpet
    A. to be self-centered
    B. to indulge in self-praise
    C. self-contained
    D. to neglect other's opinion
40. A bolt from the blue
    A. an unexpected event
    B. an expected event
    C. A chain of events
    D. A series of events
41. To burn the candle at both ends
    A. to expend ones energy without regard to health
    B. to live lavishly
    C. to get exhausted
    D. to torture
42. To bury the hatchet
    A. to forgive someone
    B. to forget past quarrels and animosity
    C. to keep the intention secret
    D. to defeat utterly
43. By the sweat of one's brow
    A. very furious
    B. hard labour
    C. short-tempered
    D. to feel insulting
44. Bear the palm
    A. to help voluntarily
    B. to form a team
    C. to be victorious
    D. a joint venture
45. Blow over
    A. pass off
    B. to propagate
    C. to spread a rumour
    D. to ditch or deceive someone
46. Blood is thicker than water
    A. to favour the near ones
    B. thought of approaching death is more severe than the actual death
    C. kinship is stronger than friend ship
    D. Blood and water are equally important
47. By word of mouth
    A. loquacious
    B. verbosity
    C. orally
    D. theoretically
48. By leaps and bounds
    A. very quickly
    B. by any means
    C. by illegal means
    D. vicariously
49. To back out
    A. a narrow-escape from a danger
    B. to attack from behind
    C. to support someone indirectly
    D. to retreat cautiously from a difficult position
50. To bear down upon
    A. to humiliate
    B. to take a responsibility
    C. to interfere deliberately
    D. to approach deliberately
51. Between two fires
    A. subject to a double attack
    B. between two rivals
    C. between two extreme difficulties
    D. a difference of opinions

52. To make no bones
    A. to make no excuse
    B. not to hesitate
    C. to make no commitments
    D. to make no monetary gains
53. To carry coals to Newcastle
    A. to bestow a gift which is not really necessary
    B. to place a thing to a wrong place
    C. to transfer something from one place to another
    D. to recognise the value of a person
54. Cats' paw
    A. a person who is used as a tool by another person
    B. very slowly and quietly
    C. very cleverly
    D. to share a responsibility
55. To catch a tartar
    A. to overcome a serious problem
    B. to attack one who turns out to be stronger than is expected
    C. to achieve the goal
    D. to struggle hard
56. Cheek of jowl
    A. very soft
    B. close together
    C. intimate relationship
    D. low in status
57. A chip of the old block
    A. a symptom of a serious disease
    B. a child of a parent
    C. a part of a whole
    D. offsprings who display characteristics of their parents
58. To cool one's heels
    A. to be kept waiting
    B. to give a cold response to somebody
    C. to follow somebody
    D. to answer all the queries of somebody
59. To cleanse the Augean stables
    A. to clean something which has not been cleaned for a long time
    B. to wind up a joint business
    C. to remove the stains of blood
    D. to remove the traces of murder
60. A cry in wilderness
    A. The cry of the poors
    B. a warning that goes unheeded
    C. A speech made by a less important leader
    D. A cry out of deep sorrow
61. To cut one's coat according to one's cloth
    A. to work according to one's capacity
    B. to allot portfolio according to one's capability
    C. to live within one's means
    D. to live as one desires.
62. Chicken hearted
    A. coward
    B. brave
    C. kind
    D. mortal
63. Cut the Gordian knot
    A. to solve a difficulty
    B. to escape a hurdle
    C. to perform the inaugural ceremony
    D. to break the silence
64. To clip one's wings
    A. to lessen one's power
    B. to defame
    C. to dismiss
    D. to punish

65. To come round
    A. to agree with another's point of view
    B. to come back to the point of origin
    C. a circular movement
    D. to wander
66. To call to order
    A. a command
    B. to rebuke for improper or incorrect behaviour
    C. to obey an order
    D. to show superiority
67. To cover one's tracks
    A. to maintain the secrecy
    B. to hide one's weaknesses
    C. to carefully hide all traces of one's actions
    D. to conceal the falsity
68. To eat the calf in the cows belly
    A. infanticide
    B. to leave the work unfinished
    C. to reject a plan of an important project
    D. to be too ready to anticipate
69. To cap the globe
    A. to surpass everything
    B. to acheive great success
    C. to discover something new
    D. to travel around the world
70. To throw up one's cards
    A. To make a last effort
    B. to cease to struggle
    C. to end up the game
    D. to come out victorious
71. To let the cat out of the bag
    A. to disclose a secret
    B. to set free
    C. a person without a shelter
    D. to permit the thief to run away
72. To cave in
    A. to interfere
    B. to prohibit
    C. to find a way
    D. to give way
73. To chuck up
    A. to abandon
    B. to decorate
    C. to summarize
    D. to cut into pieces
74. A dead letter
    A. a delayed report
    B. a false report
    C. something exaggerated
    D. something which is null and void
75. To die in harness
    A. to die in office
    B. to die with great pain
    C. a premature death
    D. a cruel murder
76. At the drop of a hat
    A. without fail
    B. without delay
    C. against the self-respect
    D. against the will
77. Day in and day out
    A. always
    B. forever
    C. to break a promise done earlier
    D. to remain busy always
78. Ducks and drakes
    A. various hindrances
    B. to spend lavishly
    C. by all efforts
    D. to spend miserly
79. Champ at
    A. to pounce at
    B. be impassioned
    C. be composed
    D. be eager or impatient

80. Burn one's fingers
    A. to get oneself into trouble
    B. to commit a blunder
    C. a heavy monetary loss
    D. to be in great rage
81. Down in the dumps
    A. in a solitary mood
    B. in a bad mood
    C. to be in an unfavourable situation
    D. to decline
82. To beg the question
    A. to beg the pardon
    B. to request for some extra time to finish the work
    C. unanswerable
    D. to assume in the premises something which is to be proved
83. To do a thing on the sly
    A. to do a thing stealthily, without drawing attention to it
    B. a good work went unnoticed
    C. work done under pressure
    D. a highly risky job
84. To have had one's day
    A. to be past one's prime
    B. to have visited only once
    C. poverty
    D. the childhood days
85. To carry the day
    A. to be victorious
    B. an on-going discussion
    C. a memorable day
    D. a miserable phase of life
86. A day after the fair
    A. a delayed decision
    B. too late to see anything
    C. just after the occurence of the event
    D. the passing of good days
87. At death's door
    A. on the point of expiring
    B. on the point of gun
    C. to show bravery
    D. a gradual deterior
88. To pay the debt of nature
    A. to die
    B. to give birth
    C. to safeguard the natural things
    D. to avoid environmental pollution
89. To do up
    A. to finish off
    B. to mend
    C. to improve
    D. to make tidy
90. To do away with
    A. to break
    B. to destroy
    C. to get rid of
    D. to forget
91. To have to do with
    A. to be interested in
    B. to do something under compulsion
    C. work done unenthusiastically
    D. to complete
92. To egg on
    A. just a beginning
    B. to urge on
    C. to develop something
    D. an initial stage
93. To face the music
    A. to face the consequences
    B. to get filled with ecstasy
    C. to be lucky
    D. to lead a happy life
94. To end in smoke
    A. all efforts in vain
    B. the end of life

C. to come to nothing
D. to end the enmity

95. Eye to eye with
    A. agree completely
    B. a confrontation
    C. full of anger
    D. a quarrel between the two persons

96. To eat humble pie
    A. to harass a humble person
    B. a celebration or a treat without any cause
    C. to confess that one is in the wrong
    D. food provided to the needy or poor

97. Easy come easy go
    A. what is gained without difficulty is spent without much thought
    B. anything which is surplus
    C. without any difficulty
    D. to achieve something without any struggle

98. To eat out one's heart
    A. to break one's heart
    B. to deceive someone
    C. to get deceived
    D. to suffer intensely

99. To see with half an eye
    A. to see with great ease
    B. to dislike
    C. to see stealthily
    D. to feel jealous

100. A fair-weathered friend
     A. A friend always eager to help
     B. A friend who deserts one in times of adversity
     C. a selfish friend
     D. a true friend

101. A far cry
     A. an unfulfilled desire
     B. a very low voice
     C. remote from
     D. a distant place

102. To feather one's nest
     A. to provide for one's own comfort
     B. to be proud
     C. to succeed again
     D. to decorate one's house

103. To fish in troubled waters
     A. to be in trouble
     B. to make capital out of other's troubles
     C. to be in trouble because of other's fault
     D. to laugh at other's trouble

104. To follow suit
     A. to follow the command
     B. to obey the rules
     C. to work in accordance with
     D. to behave in the same manner

105. To get the hang of a thing
     A. to understand the implications of something
     B. to get a trace of theft
     C. to find a new resource
     D. to have some indications

106. To get wind of
     A. to get news about something much before the event actually takes place
     B. to forget the event that had taken place
     C. to spread a rumour
     D. to have some idea of a conspiration

107. French leave
    A. a long leave
    B. a small leave
    C. absence from one's place of work without prior information.
    D. to leave the place forever

108. To steal a march upon
    A. to outshine somebody
    B. to rob
    C. to move forward
    D. to crush the enemy

109. A fly in the ointment
    A. to poison one's ear
    B. one that causes a massive loss
    C. something that decreases the value or quality of a person or thing
    D. a deterioration in quality

110. A long face
    A. a sad or mournful countenance
    B. a very shameful defeat
    C. a shameful act
    D. an ugly face

111. To set one's face against
    A. to criticise openly
    B. to oppose with determination
    C. a biased disapproval
    D. to show disappointment

112. To fall away from
    A. to decline
    B. to desert
    C. to avoid
    D. to leave

113. To fall flat
    A. to cause no amusement or interest
    B. to lie down
    C. to defeat the opponent
    D. to plead

114. To live on the fat of the land
    A. to depend solely on agriculture
    B. to live in a posh locality
    C. to live in outskirt of the city
    D. to have every luxury

115. To fight for one's own hand
    A. to fight for one's own right
    B. to struggle for livelihood
    C. to struggle for one's pesonal interests
    D. to fight for compensation against physical injury

116. To have a finger in the pie
    A. to be mixed up in any affair
    B. to interfere in other's work
    C. to have a share in the profit
    D. to be a member of an organisation

117. Neither fish, flesh nor good red herring
    A. an unsuccessful person
    B. having no pronounced character
    C. a person of unpleasing personality
    D. a person living in poverty

118. To fly in the face of
    A. to be superfluous
    B. to support directly
    C. to oppose directly and in a reckless fashion
    D. to show superiority upon others

119. To put one's foot on another's neck
    A. to crush or stumble upon him
    B. to crush one's progress
    C. to put the blame of one on another person
    D. to retaliate

120. In full cry
    A. in full volume
    B. in hot pursuit
    C. a verbosity
    D. manifestation of grief
121. To give a piece of one's mind
    A. to rebuke
    B. to give an idea
    C. to present one's view
    D. to judge one's intelligence on the basis of his work or contributions
122. Gift of the gab
    A. the ability of verbosity
    B. the ability of writing creatively
    C. the ability to speak in an impressive manner
    D. a man of versatile genius
123. To give the cold shoulder
    A. to give support
    B. to be indifferent
    C. to express anger silently
    D. to behave in a cold manner with someone
124. To give devil his due
    A. to give an evil person credit for whatever good he has done
    B. to punish one who has committed sin
    C. an evil person meeting a tragic end
    D. to give devil his share
125. To give up the ghost
    A. to die
    B. to sacrifice
    C. to murder
    D. to convert from vicious to virtuous
126. To give wide berth to
    A. to give more space
    B. to keep far away from
    C. to appreciate more than what one deserves
    D. to maintain a distance
127. To go to pieces
    A. to tear
    B. to feel disheartened
    C. to be wrecked completely
    D. to dismantle
128. To have too many irons in the fire
    A. to be engaged in too many things
    B. to handle more than one work at the same time
    C. to have lot of energy
    D. to have various plans in the mind
129. To put a spoke in one's wheel
    A. to obstruct one in his work
    B. to assist one in his work
    C. to interfere one in his work
    D. to increase the strength of a team
130. On the rack
    A. in a dilemma
    B. tortured by anxiety
    C. highly curious
    D. to be in a disadvantageous position
131. To get into hot water
    A. an acute pain
    B. to be in trouble
    C. to face a short-tempered person
    D. to be in hypertension
132. Fish and blood
    A. by extreme means
    B. by unlawful ways
    C. human nature
    D. life-like

133. From hand to mouth
    A. to harm and humiliate
    B. to be a bankrupt
    C. to spend all that is earned
    D. to feed someone
134. Go through fire and water
    A. Joy and sorrow come together
    B. to overcome all difficulties
    C. to face the misfortune
    D. to be prepared to face any difficulty
135. Hit the nail on the head
    A. to take revenge openly
    B. to insult on the face
    C. to do a wrong thing
    D. to do exactly the right thing
136. Put the cart before the horse
    A. to reverse the natural order
    B. to put obstruction
    C. to cause problem for others
    D. to stop one's advancement
137. Pay back in one's own coin
    A. to save money
    B. to treat in the same way as one has been treated
    C. to get the return of the investment
    D. to give a befitting reply
138. Rest one's oars
    A. to be satisfied with what one has already achieved
    B. to be in a pleasant mood
    C. to feel exhausted
    D. to live lavishly
139. Spick and Span
    A. Brand new
    B. throughout
    C. a short duration
    D. transient
140. To stand on ceremony
    A. to stick to order
    B. to attend a ceremony
    C. to stand at-ease
    D. To behave in a stiff, strictly correct way
141. To worm out
    A. to detect a germ
    B. to discover the cause
    C. to remove the fault
    D. to discover by persistent questioning
142. Red letter day
    A. a day of great importance
    B. an Independence day
    C. the day on which bloodshed had taken place
    D. a memorable day
143. To be all the rage
    A. to be vigorous
    B. to be very popular
    C. a man of bad reputation
    D. to be furious
144. To take time by the forelock
    A. to act immediately
    B. to take time to act
    C. a mental exercise
    D. delay in taking decisions
145. To rub the wrong way
    A. to go on wrong path
    B. to annoy
    C. to wander
    D. to go stray
146. To make up to
    A. to amend
    B. try to rectify a wrong
    C. to modify
    D. to substitute

147. To bring home the bacon
    A. to come to a common conclusion
    B. to invent
    C. to be successful in an undertaking
    D. to discover
148. To be in a brown study
    A. to spend the leisure
    B. to brood
    C. to be absent minded because of deep thought
    D. to introspect
149. To go on a wild goose chase
    A. try to achieve something unknown
    B. to have faith in a general belief
    C. to say the same which is said by the majority
    D. to follow blindly
150. To go to all lengths
    A. to take all necessary steps
    B. try to achieve something by all possible means
    C. to visit all places
    D. to consider details minutely
151. To bite one's lips
    A. to feel shameful
    B. to feel shy
    C. to be furious
    D. to be in doubt
152. To lead by the nose
    A. to be a leader
    B. to be self-dependent
    C. to control absolutely
    D. to feel superior on others
153. A rift in the lute
    A. Any action or thing that causes discord or disharmony
    B. an unpleasant music
    C. a crack in a musical instrument
    D. a discord caused in an intimate relationship
154. To pocket one's pride
    A. to be less proud
    B. to flatter
    C. to add more prestige to oneself
    D. to earn lot of money
155. Platonic love
    A. a passion
    B. a spiritual love devoid of sensuality
    C. infatuation
    D. attraction
156. To put one's cards on the table
    A. to give suggestions
    B. to give opinion
    C. to submit something
    D. to conceal nothing
157. To rest on one's laurels
    A. to depend on others
    B. to look out for possible success among rivals
    C. to remember the past events
    D. To bask in one's past glory
158. Scot-free
    A. unharmed and unfinished
    B. to let out
    C. to escape
    D. to release
159. To steer clear of
    A. to avoid
    B. to make lucid and transparent
    C. to purify
    D. to get rid of
160. To smell a rat
    A. to have some idea of the actual matter
    B. to suspect something wrong
    C. to be sceptic
    D. to feel hungry

161. To sow one's wild oats
    A. to get into the habit of squandering
    B. to lead a dissipated life in one's youth
    C. to spoil the child from very early age
    D. to disseminate more than collection
162. A square peg in a round hole
    A. to keep a right thing on a right place
    B. an adjustment
    C. a disport
    D. a misfit
163. Storm in a tea cup
    A. a hot discussion
    B. a dislocation
    C. dissonance over a paltry matter
    D. excitement over a trivial matter
164. To have the wrong son by the ear
    A. to have captured the wrong person
    B. to discourage someone
    C. to have believed the wrong person
    D. to be in a bad company
165. A Spanish castle
    A. A highly decorated house
    B. something unprecedented
    C. something visionary and unreal
    D. something unparalleled
166. To stand in good stead
    A. to be useful
    B. to stand for some good cause
    C. to be powerful than the opponent
    D. to be in a favourable situation
167. To take the bull by the horns
    A. to face an opponent directly
    B. to aim rightly
    C. to give proper training
    D. to give a lesson to the opponent
168. Tall stories
    A. exaggerated narration
    B. irrelevant narration
    C. persuasive expressiveness
    D. verbose elucidation
169. To throw down the gauntlet
    A. to surrender
    B. to challenge someone
    C. to be a traitor
    D. to be a dastard
170. Tooth and nail
    A. harsh
    B. fierily
    C. fiercely
    D. ferociously
171. To turn over a new leaf
    A. to take a new path
    B. to change one's ambition
    C. to re-start something
    D. to change completely
172. Under the thumb of
    A. under the control of
    B. to be all powerful
    C. completely opponent to
    D. to be under suppression of
173. To run riot
    A. to roam wildly without restraint
    B. to go violent
    C. to be supercilious
    D. to be aimless
174. To take after
    A. to follow
    B. to depart
    C. to look after
    D. to resemble
175. A white lie
    A. a mendacity
    B. a misconception
    C. an innocent falsehood
    D. a conceit

176. The run of one's teeth
    A. very much hungry
    B. the approach of old age
    C. to chew fast
    D. as much as one can eat
177. A white elephant
    A. expensive to maintain but not useful
    B. a showpiece
    C. a sense of prestige
    D. something rare
178. To sail close to the wind
    A. to approach the destination
    B. to go very near to danger
    C. to overcome some grave problem
    D. to be brave
179. To bring one to the scratch
    A. to make someone pauper
    B. to compel one to go against the law
    C. to cause one to come to a decision
    D. to cause one to be realistic
180. With a pinch of salt
    A. to prove
    B. to disprove
    C. to authenticate
    D. to have a doubt whether it is altogether true
181. A wild goose chase
    A. a formal debate
    B. something outwardly fair but inwardly corrupt
    C. a challenge among the fools
    D. a fruitless search
182. Yeoman's service
    A. excellent service
    B. job exclusively for the youth
    C. right job for the right person
    D. social service
183. To skip over
    A. to overlook
    B. to pass unnoticed
    C. to jump to the conclusion
    D. to take a leap
184. With an eye to
    A. With a definite object in mind
    B. to be vigilant
    C. to have vast knowledge
    D. to be imaginative
185. To save one's skin
    A. to be unwilling to work
    B. to be selfish
    C. to get off without bodily hurt
    D. to be miser
186. A wolf in sheep's clothing
    A. a self-contradictory person
    B. a plebeian
    C. a hypocritical person
    D. a poltroon
187. To turn up trumps
    A. to bring a sudden change
    B. to bring to climax
    C. to finish the game
    D. to prove successful
188. The tug of war
    A. the cause of discord
    B. the hardest part of any undertaking
    C. the basis of discrimination
    D. the rules and conditions of a game
189. To draw a veil over
    A. to bury
    B. to forget
    C. to conceive
    D. to conceal
190. To pour out the vials of one's wrath
    A. to be arrogant
    B. to express one's disappointment
    C. to give vent to one's anger
    D. to face the consequences of one's anger

191. To wax fat and kick
    A. to become unruly and hard to manage through too great prosperity
    B. to manage improperly
    C. to become too prosperous
    D. to be wild
192. Upon the whole
    A. taking everything into consideration
    B. to come to a probable conclusion
    C. making a round - about statement
    D. an overview of the matter
193. Maiden speech
    A. speech made by a woman
    B. first speech
    C. a speech in favour of woman
    D. a memorable speech
194. Of the first order
    A. perfect
    B. the first command made by the authority
    C. the order made by the Head of the country
    D. authentic
195. A leap in the dark
    A. a rash experiment
    B. moving towards unknown place
    C. uncertainty
    D. making efforts to succeed in any field
196. Far and away
    A. beyond imagination
    B. completely beyond comparison
    C. unreal
    D. spiritual
197. To split hairs
    A. to struggle hard
    B. to observe minutely
    C. to argue unnecessarily about trivial matters
    D. to dissect
198. To fall in with
    A. to fall in love
    B. to develop intimacy
    C. to lag behind
    D. to meet with
199. To hark back
    A. to return to a subject which has been dropped
    B. to return back to the original point
    C. to retaliate
    D. to rebuke
200. To knuckle under
    A. to escape   B. to hide
    C. to deny   D. to submit

Answers

1	2	3	4	5	6	7	8	9	10
D	B	A	A	C	B	D	A	B	A
11	12	13	14	15	16	17	18	19	20
B	C	B	A	A	B	C	A	A	D
21	22	23	24	25	26	27	28	29	30
C	A	B	A	B	C	A	B	C	D
31	32	33	34	35	36	37	38	39	40
A	A	B	A	C	C	D	D	B	A

41	42	43	44	45	46	47	48	49	50
A	B	B	C	A	C	C	A	D	D
51	52	53	54	55	56	57	58	59	60
A	B	A	A	B	B	D	A	A	B
61	62	63	64	65	66	67	68	69	70
C	A	A	A	A	B	C	D	A	B
71	72	73	74	75	76	77	78	79	80
A	D	A	D	A	B	A	B	D	A
81	82	83	84	85	86	87	88	89	90
B	D	A	A	A	B	A	A	D	C
91	92	93	94	95	96	97	98	99	100
A	B	A	C	A	C	A	D	A	B
101	102	103	104	105	106	107	108	109	110
C	A	B	D	A	A	C	A	C	A
111	112	113	114	115	116	117	118	119	120
B	B	A	D	C	A	B	C	A	B
121	122	123	124	125	126	127	128	129	130
A	C	D	A	A	B	C	A	A	B
131	132	133	134	135	136	137	138	139	140
B	C	C	D	D	A	B	A	A	D
141	142	143	144	145	146	147	148	149	150
D	A	B	A	B	B	C	C	A	B
151	152	153	154	155	156	157	158	159	160
C	C	A	A	B	D	D	A	A	B
161	162	163	164	165	166	167	168	169	170
B	D	D	A	C	A	A	A	B	C
171	172	173	174	175	176	177	178	179	180
D	A	A	D	C	D	A	B	C	D
181	182	183	184	185	186	187	188	189	190
D	A	B	A	C	C	D	B	D	C
191	192	193	194	195	196	197	198	199	200
A	A	B	A	A	B	C	D	A	D

Change of Voice 14

A sentence in active voice focuses on the person or thing doing the action. A sentence in passive voice focuses on the person or thing affected by the action.

Directions: *In these questions, the sentences have been given in Active/Passive voice. From the given options, choose the one which best expresses the given sentence in Passive/Active voice.*

1. There is no time to waste.
    A. There is no time to be wasted.
    B. No time to be wasted there.
    C. No time to be wasted by there.
    D. No time is to be wasted.
2. Take medicine in time.
    A. In time medicine to be taken.
    B. Medicine should be taken in time.
    C. Medicine in time will be taken.
    D. Medicine has to be in time taken.
3. He reads a novel.
    A. A novel was read by him.
    B. A novel has read by him.
    C. A novel is being read by him.
    D. A novel is read by him.
4. They had cleared the dues.
    A. The dues had been cleared.
    B. The dues had cleared by them.
    C. The dues had being cleared.
    D. The dues is cleared.
5. I invite you on the dinner.
    A. On the dinner, you have been invited.
    B. On the dinner, you are inviting.
    C. You are inviting by me on the dinner.
    D. You are invited by me on the dinner.
6. We chose him our leader.
    A. He was chosen our leader.
    B. He has been chosen our leader.
    C. He had chosen our leader.
    D. He have been chosen our leader.
7. Who made a maiden century?
    A. By whose was a maiden century made?
    B. By whom was a maiden century make?
    C. By whom was a maiden century made?
    D. By whom had a maiden century made?

8. I may help him in her project.
   A. He might be helped by me in her project.
   B. He may be helped in her project by me.
   C. He might be helped in her project by me.
   D. In her project, he may be help by me.
9. Take medicine in time.
   A. Medicine should be taken in time.
   B. Medicine will be taken in time.
   C. Medicine will be took in time.
   D. Medicine shall take in time.
10. I am solving the questions.
    A. The questions are being solved by me.
    B. The questions are been solved by me.
    C. The questions are be solved by me.
    D. The question are solved by me.
11. They have built a perfect dam across the river.
    A. Across the river a perfect dam was being built.
    B. A perfect dam has been built by them across the river.
    C. A perfect dam should have been built by them.
    D. Across the river was a perfect dam.
12. I cannot accept your offer.
    A. Your offer cannot be accepted by me.
    B. I cannot be accepted by your offer.
    C. The offer cannot be accepted by me.
    D. Your offer cannot be accepted.
13. The doctor advised the patient not to eat rice.
    A. The patient was advised by the doctor not to eat rice.
    B. The patient was advised by the doctor that he should not eat rice.
    C. The patient was being advised that he should not eat rice by the doctor.
    D. The patient has been advised not to eat rice by the doctor.
14. You can play with these kittens quite safely.
    A. These kittens can be played with quite safely.
    B. These kittens can play with you quite safely.
    C. These kittens can be played with you quite safely.
    D. These kittens can be played with quite safely.
15. They will inform the police.
    A. The police will be informed by them.
    B. The police will inform them.
    C. The police are informed by them.
    D. Informed will be police by them.
16. The invigilator was reading out the instructions.
    A. The instructions were read by the invigilator.
    B. The instuctions were being read out by the invigilator.
    C. The instructions had been read out by the invigilator.
    D. The instructions had been read by the invigilator.

17. You need to clean your shoes properly.
    A. Your shoes are needed to clean properly.
    B. You are needed to clean your shoes properly.
    C. Your shoes need to be cleaned properly.
    D. Your shoes are needed by you to clean properly.

18. You should open the wine about three hours before you use it.
    A. Wine should be opened about three hours before use.
    B. Wine should be opened by you three hours before use.
    C. Wine should be opened about three hours before you use it.
    D. Wine should be opened about three hours before it is used.

19. He is said to be very rich.
    A. He said he is very rich.
    B. People say he is very rich.
    C. He said it is very rich.
    D. People say it is very rich.

20. Could you buy some stamps for me?
    A. Stamps should be bought.
    B. You are requested to buy some stamps.
    C. You are ordered to buy some stamps.
    D. Stamps could be bought.

21. She spoke to the official on duty.
    A. The official on duty was spoken to by her.
    B. The official was spoken to by her on duty.
    C. She was spoken to by the official on duty.
    D. She was the official to be spoken to on duty.

22. A child could not have done this mischief.
    A. This mischief could not be done by a child.
    B. This mischief could not been done by a child.
    C. This mischief could not have been done by a child.
    D. This mischief a child could not have been done.

23. I remember my sister taking me to the museum.
    A. I remember I was taken to the museum by my sister.
    B. I remember being taken to the museum by my sister.
    C. I remember myself being taken to the museum by my sister.
    D. I remember taken to the museum by my sister.

24. After driving Professor Kumar to the museum she dropped him at his hotel.
    A. After being driven to the museum, Professor Kumar was dropped at his hotel.
    B. Professor Kumar was being driven dropped at his hotel.
    C. After she had driven Professor Kumar to the museum she had dropped him at his hotel.
    D. After she was driving Professor Kumar to the museum she was dropping him at his hotel.

25. Darjeeling grows tea.
    A. Tea is being grown in Darjeeling.
    B. Let the tea be grown in Darjeeling.
    C. Tea is grown in Darjeeling.
    D. Tea grows in Darjeeling.
26. Who is creating this mess?
    A. Who has been created this mess?
    B. By whom has this mess been created?
    C. By whom this mess is being created?
    D. By whom is this mess being created?
27. They greet me cheerfully every morning.
    A. Every morning I was greeted cheerfully.
    B. I am greeted cheerfully by them every morning.
    C. I am being greeted cheerfully by them every morning.
    D. Cheerful greeting is done by them every morning to me.
28. She makes cakes every Sunday.
    A. Every Sunday are cakes made by her.
    B. Cakes are made by her every Sunday.
    C. Cakes make her every Sunday.
    D. Cakes were made by her every Sunday.
29. James Watt discovered the energy of steam.
    A. The energy of steam discovered James Watt.
    B. The energy of steam was discovered by James Watt.
    C. James Watt was discovered by the energy of steam.
    D. James Watt had discovered energy by the steam.
30. Do you imitate others?
    A. Are others being imitated by you?
    B. Are others imitated by you?
    C. Have others been imitated by you?
    D. Were others being imitated by you?
31. Nobody has answered my question.
    A. My question has been answered by somebody.
    B. My question has not been answered by anybody.
    C. My question was not answered.
    D. My question remains unanswered.
32. The judge delivered the sentence at the courtroom yesterday.
    A. The sentence been delivered yesterday by the judge.
    B. The sentence was delivered by the judge at the courtroom yesterday.
    C. The sentence was being delivered at the courtroom yesterday by the judge.
    D. Yesterday, the sentence had been delivered at the courtroom by the judge.
33. Shut all the doors and windows in the night.
    A. Let all the doors and windows be shut in the night.
    B. All the doors and windows may be shut in the night.
    C. Let all the doors and windows remain shut in the night.
    D. All the doors and windows be shutted in the night.

34. People use computer for various purposes.
    A. Computers are being used by people for various purposes.
    B. Computers have been used by people for various purposes.
    C. Computers are used by people for various purposes.
    D. Computers will be used by people for various purposes.
35. The problem has been treated by numerous experts.
    A. Numerous experts have been treating the problem.
    B. Numerous experts have treated the problem.
    C. Numerous experts had been treating the problem.
    D. Numerous experts treated the problem.
36. Help the poor.
    A. The poor should be helped.
    B. The poor would be helped.
    C. The poor must be helped.
    D. The poor will be helped.
37. Bring a glass of water.
    A. A glass of water will be brought.
    B. A glass of water should be brought.
    C. Let, a glass of water be brought.
    D. Let, a glass of water will be brought.
38. He gave me a beautiful flower pot.
    A. A beautiful flower pot was given to me by him.
    B. A beautiful flower pot had given to me by him.
    C. A beautiful flower pot had been giving by him.
    D. I was giving him a beautiful flower pot.
39. Is he answering the question?
    A. The question is answered by him.
    B. The question is being answered by him.
    C. Is the question being answered by him?
    D. Is the question being answering by him?
40. Who gave you this letter?
    A. This letter was given to you by whom?
    B. This letter had given to you by whom?
    C. Was this letter given to you?
    D. By whom was this letter given to you?
41. The professor teaches students.
    A. Students are being taught by the professor.
    B. Students are taught by the professor.
    C. The professor is being taught by students.
    D. Students are being teaching by students.
42. M.S. Dhoni has created a world record.
    A. A world record has been created by M.S. Dhoni.
    B. A world record has created by M.S. Dhoni.
    C. A world record is created by M.S. Dhoni.
    D. A world record is being created by M.S. Dhoni.

43. Srishti sings a lovely song.
    A. A lovely song had sung by Srishti.
    B. A lovely song was sung by Srishti.
    C. A lovely song is sung by Srishti.
    D. A lovely song is sang by Srishti.

44. He was drawing a picture.
    A. A picture was drawn by him.
    B. A picture was being drawn by him.
    C. A picture was drawing by him.
    D. A picture was drew by him.

45. We made him leader.
    A. He was made leader by us.
    B. He was maded leader.
    C. He made leader by us.
    D. He was made leader.

Answers

1	2	3	4	5	6	7	8	9	10
A	B	D	A	D	A	B	B	A	D
11	12	13	14	15	16	17	18	19	20
B	A	A	D	A	B	C	D	B	B
21	22	23	24	25	26	27	28	29	30
A	C	B	A	C	D	B	B	B	B
31	32	33	34	35	36	37	38	39	40
B	B	A	C	B	A.	C	A	C	D
41	42	43	44	45					
B	A	C	B	D					

❑❑❑

Change of Speech 15

The exact words spoken by the speaker are known as Direct Speech. The words spoken by somebody and expressed by someone else with some modification are known as Indirect Speech.

Directions (Qs. 1 to 13): *Select the correct indirect speech for the following sentences:*

1. I said to him, "I shall help you."
   A. I told him that I can help him.
   B. I told him that I would help him.
   C. I told him that I will help him.
   D. I told him that I shall be helping him.

2. My Teacher said to me, "The earth revolves round the sun."
   A. My teacher told me that the earth revolves round the sun.
   B. My teacher told me that the earth revolve round the sun.
   C. My teacher told me that the earth had been revolving round the sun.
   D. My teacher told me that the earth has been revolving round the sun.

3. I said to my friend, "My father daily goes for a walk."
   A. I told my friend that my father daily goes for a walk.
   B. I told my friend that my father daily went for a walk.
   C. I told my friend that my father has to go for a walk.
   D. I told my friend that my father had gone for a walk.

4. He said to me, "May God bless you!"
   A. He requested that God can bless me.
   B. He prayed that God can bless me.
   C. He prayed that God might bless me.
   D. He prayed that God will bless me.

5. The patient said, "Thank you, doctor."
   A. The patient thanked the doctor.
   B. The patient requested the doctor with thanks.
   C. The patient told the doctor thanks.
   D. The patient suggested the doctor thanks.

6. Satish said, "No, I shall not talk to him."
   A. Satish told that he should not talk to him.
   B. Satish suggested that he would not have talked to him.
   C. Satish exclaimed with sorrow that he would not talk with him.
   D. Satish refused to talk to him.

7. The child said, "What a lovely place!"
   A. The child exclaimed with sorrow that it was a lovely place.
   B. The child thought that the place was lovely.
   C. The child exclaimed with joy that the place was very lovely.
   D. The child suggested that the place was lovely.

8. He said, "What a fool I have been!"
   A. He told himself with sorrow that he was a fool.
   B. He confessed with regret that he had been a great fool.
   C. He said himself a fool.
   D. He suggested that he could be a fool.

9. He said, "Alas! I am ruined."
   A. He told me that he had been ruined.
   B. He exclaimed with joy that he had been ruined.
   C. He exclaimed with sorrow that he was ruined.
   D. He told me that he should not be ruined.

10. The accused said, "I am not guilty."
    A. The accused exclaimed with sorrow that I am not guilty.
    B. The accused exclaimed with joy that he was not guilty.
    C. The accused stated that he was not guilty.
    D. The accused told me that he has not been guilty.

11. My teacher said, "The earth is round".
    A. My teacher said that the earth was round.
    B. My teacher says that the earth is round.
    C. My teacher said that the earth is round.
    D. My teacher ordered that the earth is round.

12. He said, "What a place it is!"
    A. He said that it was a very fine place.
    B. He said that is a very fine place.
    C. He said that the place is fine.
    D. He exclaimed with joy/surprise that it was a very fine place.

13. Ria said, "Shall I thread the needle?"
    A. Ria asked if she should thread the needle.
    B. Ria asked if she shall thread the needle.
    C. Ria ordered if she should thread the needle.
    D. Ria says that if she would thread the needle.

Directions (Qs. 14 to 33): *Pick out the correct alternative that completes the incomplete sentence which is changed into indirect narration.*

14. She said to me, "I shall see you as soon as I get time."
    She told me:
    A. that she will see me as soon as she will get time.
    B. that she would see me as soon as she would get time.
    C. she would see me whenever she got time.
    D. that she would see me whenever she gets time.

15. My secretary said to me, "Your plane will leave if you do not go at once."
    My secretary told me that:
    A. her plane would leave if she did not go at that time.
    B. her plane would leave if I do not go at once.
    C. my plane would leave if I did not go at that very time.
    D. my plane will leave if I did not go at that time.

16. My mother said to me, "Don't quarrel among yourselves".
    My mother:
    A. forbade me to quarrel among ourselves.
    B. asked me not to quarrel among ourselves.
    C. asked me that not to quarrel among ourselves.
    D. asked me to quarrel not among ourselves.

17. Her father said to her mother, "Excuse the daughter."
    Her father:
    A. requested her mother to excuse the daughter.
    B. asked her mother to excuse the daughter.
    C. asked her mother to have excused the daughter.
    D. asked her mother to have been excused.

18. He said to his friend, "Wait here till father comes."
    He requested his friend:
    A. to wait here till father had come.
    B. that to wait there till his friend came.
    C. to wait there till father came.
    D. to wait here until his friend came.

19. She said to her maid, "Run and catch the thief."
    She ordered her maid:
    A. ran and catch the thief.
    B. that to run and to catch the thief.
    C. ran and caught the thief.
    D. to run and catch the thief.

20. Anita said to Sunita, "What are you doing?"
    Anita asked Sunita:
    A. what she will be doing.
    B. that what she is doing.
    C. that what she was doing.
    D. what she was doing.

21. She said to me, "Are you meeting me today?"
    She enquired of me:
    A. whether I am meeting her that day.
    B. whether I was meeting her today.
    C. whether I was meeting her that day.
    D. I was meeting her that day.

22. Nitish said to me, "When did you buy this pen?"

Nitish asked me:
A. when I was to buy that pen.
B. when I would buy that pen.
C. when I had bought that pen.
D. when I was buying that pen.

23. She said to me, "Are you going to market?"
She enquired of me:
A. I am going to market.
B. I was going to market.
C. if I was going to market.
D. if I had been going to the market.

24. Damini said, "Why did not you change your clothes?"
Damini asked me:
A. why I had not changed my clothes.
B. why I did not change my clothes.
C. why I would not change my clothes.
D. why I have not been changing my clothes.

25. Umesh said to me, "Have you read that novel?"
Umesh asked me:
A. if he was reading that novel.
B. if he had read that novel.
C. if I had read that novel.
D. if I was reading that novel.

26. She said to me, "I shall forgive you."
She told me:
A. that she will forgive me.
B. that she was going to forgive me.
C. that she will not forgive me.
D. that she would forgive me.

27. I said to her, "It was very hot last night."

I told her:
A. that it had been very hot the previous night.
B. that it was very hot the previous night.
C. that it has been very hot the last night.
D. that it had been very hot this night.

28. She said to me, "I thank you for the help you have given."
She:
A. told me that she thanked me for the help I had given.
B. thanked me for the help I have given.
C. thanked to me for the help I have given.
D. thanked me for the help I had given.

29. Mohini said to me, "Trust in God."
Mohini advised me:
A. that I should trust in God.
B. should trust in God.
C. trusted in God.
D. to trust in God.

30. I said to him, "Let us go to school."
I told him:
A. we would go to school.
B. we shall go to school.
C. that we would go to school.
D. that we should go to school.

31. Rajni said, "May God bless you?"
Rajni:
A. exclaimed with wish that God might bless me.
B. expressed a wish that God might bless me.
C. asked God to bless me.
D. shouted with joy to bless me.

32. My mother said to me, "Do not have so many friends."
    My mother forbade me:
    A. to have so many friends.
    B. not to have so many friends.
    C. to have been so many friends.
    D. to possess so many friends.

33. Ram said, "Pay attention to me."
    Ram asked:
    A. pay attention to him.
    B. paid attention to him.
    C. having paid attention to him.
    D. to pay attention to him.

Directions (Qs. 34 to 50): *In questions below, the sentences have been given in Direct/Indirect Speech. Out of the four alternatives suggested select the one which best expresses the given sentence in Indirect/Direct Speech.*

34. She said that her brother was getting married.
    A. She said, "Her brother is getting married."
    B. She told, "My brother is getting married."
    C. She said, "My brother is getting married."
    D. She said, "My brother was married."

35. "Please don't go away", she said.
    A. She said to please her and not go away.
    B. She told me to go away.
    C. She begged me not to go away.
    D. She begged that I not go away.

36. "If you don't keep quiet I shall shoot you", he said to her in a calm voice.
    A. He warned her to shoot if she didn't keep quiet calmly.
    B. He said calmly that I shall shoot you if you don't be quiet.
    C. He warned her calmly that he would shoot her if she didn't keep quiet.
    D. Calmly he warned her that be quiet or else he will have to shoot her.

37. I told him that he was not working hard.
    A. I said to him, "You are not working hard."
    B. I told him, "You are not working hard."
    C. I said, "You are not working hard."
    D. I said to him, "He is not working hard."

38. She said that she would finish the work the next day.
    A. She said, "I will finish the work the next day."
    B. She said, "I will finish the work tomorrow."
    C. She said, "You will finish the work tomorrow."
    D. She said, "I finished the work."

39. She said to him, "Why don't you go today?"
    A. She asked him why he did not go that day.
    B. She said to him that why he don't go today.
    C. She asked him not to go today.
    D. She asked him why he did not go today.

40. "Are you alone, my son?" asked a soft voice close behind me.
    A. A soft voice asked that what I was doing there alone.
    B. A soft voice said to me are you alone son.
    C. A soft voice from my back asked if I was alone.
    D. A soft voice behind me asked if I was alone.

41. My cousin said, "My room-mate had snored throughout the night."
    A. My cousin said that her room-mate snored throughout the night.
    B. My cousin told me that her room-mate snored throughout the night.
    C. My cousin complained to me that her room-mate is snoring throughout the night.
    D. My cousin felt that her room-mate may be snoring throughout the night.

42. He asked Rama if he needed his help then.
    A. He said to Rama, "Do you need my help?"
    B. He told Rama, "Tell me if you need help."
    C. He asked Rama, "Do I need your help?"
    D. He said to Rama, "Do you need my help now?"

43. Nita ordered her servant to bring her a cup of tea.
    A. Nita told her servant, "Bring a cup of tea."
    B. Nita said, "Bring me a cup of tea."
    C. Nita said to her servant, "Bring me a cup of tea."
    D. Nita said to her servant, "Bring her that cup of tea."

44. He exclaimed with joy that India had won the Sahara Cup.
    A. He said, "India has won the Sahara Cup."
    B. He said, "India won the Sahara Cup."
    C. He said, "How! India will win the Sahara Cup."
    D. He said, "Hurrah! India has won the Sahara Cup."

45. The boy said, "Who dare call you a thief?"
    A. The boy enquired who dared call him a thief.
    B. The boy asked who called him a thief.
    C. The boy told that who dared call him a thief.
    D. The boy wondered who dared call a thief.

46. The little girl said to her mother, "Did the sun rise in the East?
    A. The little girl said to her mother that the sun rose in the East.
    B. The little girl asked her mother if the sun rose in the East.
    C. The little girl said to her mother if the sun rises in the East.
    D. The little girl asked her mother if the sun is in the East.

47. Dhruv said that he was sick and tired of working for that Company.
    A. Dhruv said, "I am sick and tired of working for this Company."

B. Dhruv said, "He was tired of that Company."
   C. Dhruv said to me, "I am sick and tired of working for this Company."
   D. Dhruv said, "I will be tired of working for that Company."
48. He said to his father, "Please increase my pocket-money."
   A. He told his father, please increase the pocket-money.
   B. He pleaded his father to please increase my pocket-money.
   C. He requested his father to increase his pocket-money.
   D. He asked his father increase his pocket-money.
49. She said to her friend, "I know where is everyone."
   A. She told that she knew where was everyone.
   B. She told her friend that she knew where was everyone.
   C. She told her friend she knew where is everyone.
   D. She told her friend that she knows where was everyone.
50. His father ordered him to go to his room and study.
   A. His father said, "Go to your room and study."
   B. His father said to him, "Go and study in your room."
   C. His father shouted, "Go right now to your study room."
   D. His father said firmly, "Go and study in your room."

Answers

1	2	3	4	5	6	7	8	9	10
B	A	A	C	A	D	C	B	C	C
11	12	13	14	15	16	17	18	19	20
C	D	A	B	C	A	B	C	D	D
21	22	23	24	25	26	27	28	29	30
C	C	C	A	C	D	A	A	A	D
31	32	33	34	35	36	37	38	39	40
B	A	D	C	C	C	A	B	A	D
41	42	43	44	45	46	47	48	49	50
A	D	C	B	A	B	A	C	B	A

Verbal Analogies 16

Like different people words also have different relationships with each other in comparison to each other. This is called word analogy. Try and master it in the following questions.

Directions: *Each question consists of two words which have a certain relationship to each other followed by four pairs of related words. Select the pair which has the same relationship.*

1. **Useless : Cheap**
   - A. Late : Unpunctual
   - B. Real : Illusive
   - C. Just : Unfair
   - D. Humble : Proud

2. **Loyal : Faithful**
   - A. Treacherous : Devoted
   - B. Just : Fair
   - C. Yield : Suppress
   - D. Uncertain : Sure

3. **Cancel : Confirm**
   - A. Certain : Ambiguous
   - B. Vulgar : Crude
   - C. Reliable : Trustworthy
   - D. Obscure : Anonymous

4. **Gloomy : Bright**
   - A. Pleasant : Delightful
   - B. Funny : Comic
   - C. Condemn : Blame
   - D. Hard : Flexible

5. **Modern : Ancient**
   - A. Happy : Joyful
   - B. Service : Slavery
   - C. Mild : Harsh
   - D. Assumed : Unreal

6. **Dexterous : Clumsy**
   - A. Cheap : Worthless
   - B. Usual : Common
   - C. Zenith : Acme
   - D. True : False

7. **Luscious : Sweet**
   - A. Above : Below
   - B. Absolve : Penalise
   - C. Lucrative : Profitable
   - D. Adopt : Abandon

8. **Fraud : Duplicity**
   - A. Inferior : Cheap
   - B. Delicious : Abhorrent
   - C. Desire : Detest
   - D. Diligent : Lackadiasical

9. **Weired : Ordinary**
   - A. Vacant : Void
   - B. Vivid : Clear
   - C. Vivid : Dim
   - D. Wicked : Unvirtuous

10. **Build : Demolish**
    - A. Abide : Persist
    - B. Compel : Coax
    - C. Odious : Hateful
    - D. Claim : Demand

11. **Passionate : Impassive**
    A. Deter : Discourage
    B. Folly : Stupidity
    C. Polite : Rude
    D. Fanciful : Whimsical

12. **Gauche : Attractive**
    A. True : Exact
    B. Tough : Hard
    C. Tasteful : Palatable
    D. Insipid : Delicious

13. **Existence : Life**
    A. Silence : Noise
    B. Risk : Shield
    C. Enormous : Immense
    D. Rural : Urban

14. **Belief : Suspicion**
    A. Unravel : Unweave
    B. Profuse : Insufficient
    C. Urge : Spur
    D. Use : Occupy

15. **Violent : Calm**
    A. Tranquil : Peaceful
    B. Reticent : Quiet
    C. Even : Smooth
    D. Disdain : Reverence

16. **Lawyer : Court**
    A. Businessman : Market
    B. Chemist : Laboratory
    C. Labourer : Factory
    D. Athlete : Olympics

17. **Corporeal : Spiritual**
    A. Mesa : Plateau
    B. Moron : Savant
    C. Foreigner : Immigrant
    D. Pedagogue : Teacher

18. **Ten : Decimal**
    A. Seven : Septet
    B. Four : Quartet
    C. Two : Binary
    D. Five : Quince

19. **Grain : Salt**
    A. Shard : Pottery
    B. Shred : Wood
    C. Blades : Grass
    D. Chip : Glass

20. **Fish : Shoal**
    A. Audience : Theatre
    B. Elephant : Flock
    C. Whale : Herd
    D. Shark : School

21. **Wan : Colour**
    A. Copulent : Weight
    B. Insipid : Flavour
    C. Pallid : Complexion
    D. Enigmatic : Puzzle

22. **Thrust : Spear**
    A. Mangle : Iron
    B. Scabbard : Sword
    C. Bow : Arrow
    D. Fence : Epee

23. **Indigent : Wealthy**
    A. Angry : Rich
    B. Native : Affluent
    C. Gauche : Graceful
    D. Scholarly : Erudite

24. **Diva : Opera**
    A. Producer : Theatre
    B. Director : Drama
    C. Conductor : Bus
    D. Thespian : Play

25. **Army : Logistics**
    A. Business : Strategy
    B. Soldiers : Students
    C. War : Logic
    D. Team : Individual

26. **Distance : Mile**
    A. Liquid : Litre
    B. Bushel : Corn
    C. Weight : Scale
    D. Fame : Television

27. **After : Before**
    A. First : Second
    B. Present : Past
    C. Contemporary : Historic
    D. Successor : Predecessor
28. **Mundane : Spiritual**
    A. Common : Ghostly
    B. Worldly : Unworldly
    C. Routine : Novel
    D. Secular : Clerical
29. **Filter : Water**
    A. Curtail : Activity
    B. Expurge : Book
    C. Edit : Text
    D. Censor : Play
30. **Pork : Pig**
    A. Rooster : Chicken
    B. Mutton : Sheep
    C. Steer : Beef
    D. Lobster : Crustacean
31. **Pain : Sedative**
    A. Comfort : Stimulant
    B. Grief : Consolation
    C. Trance : Narcotic
    D. Ache : Extraction
32. **Hope : Aspires**
    A. Love : Elevates
    B. Film : Flam
    C. Fib : Lie
    D. Fake : Ordinary
33. **Gravity : Pull**
    A. Iron : Metal
    B. North pole : Directions
    C. Magnetism : Attraction
    D. Dust : Desert
34. **Light : Blind**
    A. Speech : Dumb
    B. Language : Deaf
    C. Tongue : Sound
    D. Voice : Vibration

35. **Symphony : Composer**
    A. Leonardo : Music
    B. Fresco : Painter
    C. Colours : Pallet
    D. Art : Appreciation
36. **Astringent : Pucker**
    A. Car : Engine
    B. Spark : Ignition
    C. Quell : Allay
    D. Sophisticated : Rural
37. **Saga : Heroic**
    A. Epigram : Pithy
    B. Tragedy : Comedy
    C. Editorial : Newspaper
    D. Picture : Book
38. **Obdurate : Flexibility**
    A. Stagger : Amaze
    B. Adamant : Submissiveness
    C. Semite : Jew
    D. Radical : Scorn
39. **Percept : Instructive**
    A. Ribald : Decent
    B. Metaphor : Figurative
    C. Institution : Study
    D. Library : Calmness
40. **Hermit : Gregarious**
    A. Sanguine : Optimistic
    B. Repose : Rest
    C. Ruthless : Merciless
    D. Ascetic : Hedonostic
41. **Braggart : Modesty**
    A. Profound : Intelligence
    B. Opinionated : Over confident
    C. Buffoon : Dignity
    D. Arrogant : Acuity
42. **Posthumous : Death**
    A. Selection : Nomination
    B. Product : Factory
    C. Clay : Mould
    D. Cloudy : Sunny

43. **Prophet : Foreteller**
    A. Precursor : Forerunner
    B. Pretentious : Ambitious
    C. Prodigy : Wonderful
    D. Teacher : Intellectual
44. **Indigent : Wealth**
    A. Yelp : Cry
    B. Yearn : Desire
    C. Wrangle : Argue
    D. Emaciated : Nourishment
45. **Senorita : Woman**
    A. Sophisticated : Self assured
    B. Monologue : Discourse
    C. Semite : Jew
    D. General : Military
46. **Yeoman : Farming**
    A. Clerk : Office
    B. Waiter : Restaurant
    C. Hawker : Business
    D. Apprentice : Engineer
47. **Genuine : Authentic**
    A. Light : Reflection
    B. Image : Shadow
    C. Mirage : Illusion
    D. Vacuum : Transparency
48. **Colour : Bleach**
    A. Buzz : Hum
    B. Echo : Sound
    C. Paper : Burn
    D. Blush : Faint
49. **Labour : Wages**
    A. Capital : Interest
    B. Doctor : Medicine
    C. Ink : Writing
    D. Agree : Oppose
50. **Brusque : Unceremoniousness**
    A. Apparatus : Experiment
    B. Auditor : Lecture
    C. Malaria : Relapse
    D. Obstinate : Intractability
51. **Mature : Regressed**
    A. Intruder : Privacy
    B. Varied : Monotonous
    C. Sufficiency : Adequacy
    D. Train : Compartment
52. **Celerity : Snail**
    A. Curosity : Cat
    B. Cunning : Crow
    C. Humility : Peacock
    D. Obstinacy : Mule
53. **Dilatory : Expeditious**
    A. Direct : Circuitous
    B. Skirmish : Mar
    C. Language : Grammar
    D. Ice : Coolness
54. **Molt : Feathers**
    A. Flutter : Wings
    B. Slough : Skin
    C. Sharpen : Talons
    D. Bare : Fangs
55. **Jeopardy : Peril**
    A. Plead : Insist
    B. Promote : Reward
    C. Rely : Support
    D. Jealousy : Envy
56. **Surfeit : Appetite**
    A. Refine : Taste
    B. Sniff : Nose
    C. Cloy : Palate
    D. Cling : Touch
57. **Aeroplane : Cockpit**
    A. Train : Engine
    B. Train : Compartment
    C. Train : Coach
    D. Train : Wagon
58. **Rider : Bill**
    A. Meter : Electricity
    B. Endorsement : Policy
    C. Purchase : Receipt
    D. Violation : Law
59. **Wax : Wane**
    A. Earth : Orbit
    B. Depth : Shallow

C. Fall : Bottom
D. Zenith : Nadir

60. **Painting : Artist**
    A. Wood : Furniture
    B. Analysis : Critic
    C. Symphony : Composer
    D. Symphony : Poet

61. **Windfall : Jubilation**
    A. Grief : Sorrow
    B. Pratfall : Embarrassment
    C. Bravery : Courageous
    D. Calm : Melancholy

62. **Foresight : Anticipation**
    A. Insomnia : Sleeplessness
    B. Intuition : Happening
    C. Indolent : Incredible
    D. Impromptu: Preparation

63. **Novice : Learner**
    A. Voters : Politicians
    B. Gigolo : Dance
    C. Harbinger : Forerunner
    D. Roster : Duty

64. **Life : Autobiography**
    A. Witness : Truth
    B. Witness : Documents
    C. Culprit : Punishment
    D. Jailor : Prison

65. **Grieve : Sorrow**
    A. Wallow : Misery
    B. Smart : Pain
    C. Weaken : Strength
    D. Afflict : Torment

66. **Cloud : Scud**
    A. Fog : Disperse
    B. Blood : Clot
    C. Mist : Fall
    D. Water : Race

67. **Fire : Ashes**
    A. Heart : Breath
    B. School : Education
    C. Explosion : Debris
    D. Alma mater : Certificate

68. **Ocean : Water**
    A. Mountain : Peak
    B. Cave : Hollow
    C. Glacier : Ice
    D. River : Current

69. **Unctuous : Sincerity**
    A. Urban : Society
    B. Pleasant : Jovial
    C. Wrest : Amusing
    D. Sardonic : Sympathy

70. **Audible : Hear**
    A. Fascinating : See
    B. Palpable : Touch
    C. Distinctive : Smell
    D. Unique : Personality

71. **Article : Newspaper**
    A. Scene : Play
    B. Food : Diet
    C. Account : Diary
    D. Maize : Field

72. **Beginning : Culmination**
    A. Tragedy : Catastrophe
    B. Language : Grammar
    C. Stanza : Poetry
    D. Prologue : Denouement

73. **Ballerina : Ballet**
    A. Stage : Performance
    B. Protagonist : Play
    C. Grief : Tragedy
    D. Ballad : Poem

74. **Bellicose : Quarrelsome**
    A. Boost : Boom
    B. Bonny : Unhealthy
    C. Babel : Babble
    D. Bane : Ruin

75. **Annihilation : Fire**
    A. Ordinance : Parliament
    B. Emergency : Failure
    C. Cataclysm : Flood
    D. Cataclysm : Earthquake

76. **Shovel : Lift**
    A. Break : Pieces

B. Amend : Join
C. Thrust : Dig
D. Push : Fall

77. **Jade : Green**
A. Garnet : Red
B. Rainbow : Sky
C. Mercury : Shine
D. White : Peace

78. **Gamut : Completeness**
A. Square : Perimeter
B. Gas : Volume
C. Conclusion : End
D. Radius : Circle

79. **Truth : Sham**
A. Wariness : Caution
B. Honesty : Deceit
C. Cant : Jargon
D. Abut : Border

80. **Glass : Crockery**
A. Hat : Millinery
B. Books : School
C. Operation Theatre : Hospital
D. Poetry : Books

81. **Install : Officer**
A. Campaign : Candidate
B. Promote : Worker
C. Succeed : Prince
D. Inaugurate : President

82. **Quark : Particle**
A. Proton : Molecule
B. Zinc : Element
C. Light : Photosynthesis
D. Uranium : Fission

83. **Doctor : Disease**
A. Judge : Culprit
B. Politician : Parliament
C. Teacher : Ignorance
D. Policeman : Criminal

84. **Line : Segment**
A. Big : Small
B. Part : Whole
C. Square : Rectangle
D. Circle : Arc

85. **Breeze : Cyclone**
A. Drizzle : Downpour
B. Snowfall : Cold
C. Earthquake : Debris
D. Heat : Sunstroke

86. **Jail : Jailor**
A. Museum : Curator
B. School : Board
C. Life : Wealth
D. Couple : Marriage

87. **Dimwit : Intelligent**
A. Dingy : Decent
B. Felon : Guilty
C. Hoary : Old
D. Harry : Ravage

88. **Grim : Stern**
A. Laud : Blame
B. Zest : Gusto
C. Morbid : Healthy
D. Overt : Concealed

89. **Trap : Spring**
A. Prison : Escape
B. Sentence : Period
C. Alarm : Trigger
D. Convict : Corner

90. **Orgy : Drunken**
A. Wine : Bar
B. Obese : Fast food
C. Oasis : Desert
D. Quicksilver : Mercury

91. **Lunatic : Asylum**
A. The poor : Palace
B. Soldiers : Barracks
C. Flowers : Fields
D. Crops : Garden

92. **Soldier : Rifle**
A. Blacksmith : Anvil
B. Thief : Ladder
C. Watchman : Uniform
D. Barber : Hair

93. **Frog : Tadpoles**
    A. Man : Sons
    B. Woman : Daughters
    C. Cat : Kids
    D. Elephant : Calves

94. **Lizards : Reptiles**
    A. Frogs : Amphibians
    B. Tree : Fruit
    C. Earth : Moon
    D. Man : Woman

95. **Earthworm : Segments**
    A. Tree : Wood
    B. Crocodiles : Scales
    C. Apple : Juice
    D. Earth : Moisture

96. **Mosquito : Malaria**
    A. Rabid dog : Rabies
    B. House fly : AIDS
    C. Cockroach : Influenza
    D. Virus : Diabetes

97. **Fish : Water**
    A. Man : Air
    B. Cat : Mouse
    C. Lion : Flesh
    D. Tree : Roots

98. **Impulsive : Cautious**
    A. Liberty : Bondage
    B. Tyrant : Bully
    C. Tremble : Quake
    D. Vulgar : Indecent

99. **Weighty : Voluminous**
    A. Jolly : Dismal
    B. Loyalty : Perfidy
    C. Wealth : Opulence
    D. Odd : Normal

100. **Innocent : Guilty**
    A. Kill : Produce
    B. Suspect : Doubt
    C. Depress : Discourage
    D. Contract : Condense

Answers

1	2	3	4	5	6	7	8	9	10
A	B	A	D	C	D	C	A	C	B
11	12	13	14	15	16	17	18	19	20
C	D	C	B	D	A	B	C	D	D
21	22	23	24	25	26	27	28	29	30
C	D	C	D	A	A	D	B	D	B
31	32	33	34	35	36	37	38	39	40
B	C	C	A	B	B	A	B	B	D
41	42	43	44	45	46	47	48	49	50
C	A	A	D	B	C	C	D	A	D
51	52	53	54	55	56	57	58	59	60
B	C	A	B	D	C	A	B	D	C
61	62	63	64	65	66	67	68	69	70
B	A	C	A	B	D	C	C	D	B
71	72	73	74	75	76	77	78	79	80
A	D	B	D	C	C	A	C	B	A
81	82	83	84	85	86	87	88	89	90
D	B	C	D	A	A	A	B	C	D
91	92	93	94	95	96	97	98	99	100
B	A	D	A	B	A	A	A	C	A

❏ ❏ ❏

Punctuation 17

Punctuation is the art of placing various stops and marks in a written or printed text. It is designed to separate words, sentences, etc., and to make the meaning of a sentence or passage clear.

Directions: *In the questions given below, select the one alternative out of four which has been applied with correct punctuation marks.*

1. The more we hate one another the worse it will be for everybody
   A. The more we hate one another the worse it will be for everybody.
   B. The more we hate one another, the worse it will be for everybody.
   C. The more we hate one another; the worse it will be for everybody.
   D. The more we hate one another – the worse it will be for everybody.

2. Anita's father Mr Anil Kumar is a teacher
   A. Anita's father Mr Anil Kumar is a teacher.
   B. Anita's father, Mr Anil Kumar is a teacher.
   C. Anita's father Mr Anil Kumar, is a teacher.
   D. Anita's father, Mr. Anil Kumar, is a teacher.

3. Considering all aspects of the matter they decided to give up the plan.
   A. Considering all aspects of the matter, they decided to give up the plan.
   B. Considering, all aspects of the matter, they decided to give up the plan.
   C. Considering all aspects, of the matter, they decided to give up the plan.
   D. Considering all aspects of the matter they decided to give up the plan.

4. The Narmada the Ganga and the Yamuna are three of the largest Indian rivers
   A. The Narmada, the Ganga and the Yamuna are three of the largest Indian rivers
   B. The Narmada, the Ganga, and the Yamuna are three of the largest Indian rivers

C. The Narmada, the Ganga and the Yamuna are three of the largest Indian rivers.
   D. The Narmada, the Ganga and, the Yamuna are three of the largest Indian rivers.
5. What a remarkable victory
   A. What, a remarkable victory.
   B. What a remarkable victory.
   C. What a remarkable victory?
   D. What a remarkable victory!
6. The election many people said would spring a big surprise and they were proved right
   A. The election, many people said, "would spring a big surprise and they were proved right."
   B. "The election," many people said, "would spring a big surprise and they were proved right."
   C. "The election" many people said, "Would spring a big surprise and they were proved right."
   D. "The election" many people said "would spring a big surprise and they were proved right."
7. Are you going he asked we are not I replied
   A. "Are you going?" he asked, "We are not." I replied.
   B. "Are you going?" he asked, "we are not" I replied.
   C. "Are you going?" he asked. "We are not," I replied.
   D. "Are you going?" he asked, "we are not" I replied.
8. Here I am master I am ready to go wherever you want me to go he said
   A. "Here I am, master, I am ready to go," wherever you want me to go he said.
   B. "Here I am master, I am ready to go wherever you want me to go" he said.
   C. "Here I am master, I am ready to go wherever you want me to go", he said.
   D. "Here I am, master, I am ready to go wherever you want me to go", he said.
9. What is your reason for refusing to marry this girl asked his mother
   A. "What is your reason for refusing to marry this girl?" asked his mother.
   B. "What is your reason, for refusing to marry this girl?" asked his mother.
   C. "What is your reason for refusing to marry this girl?" asked his mother
   D. "What is your reason for refusing to marry this girl," asked his mother.
10. He said my brother had an accident on Sunday the 28th April 2013 and is still confined to bed
    A. He said "my brother had an accident on Sunday the 28th April 2013 and is still confined to bed."
    B. He said "My brother had an accident on Sunday the 28th April 2013 and is still confined to bed."
    C. He said, "My brother had an accident on Sunday, the 28th April 2013, and is still confined to bed."

D. He said," My brother had an accident on Sunday, the 28th April 2013 and is still confined to bed."

11. How many r's are there in referred I asked
    A. How many r's are there in referred? I asked.
    B. "How many r's are there, in referred" I asked.
    C. "How many r's are there in referred?" I asked.
    D. "How many rs' are there in referred?" I asked.

12. Friends colleagues relatives none stood by him
    A. Friends, colleagues, relatives none stood by him.
    B. Friends, colleagues, relatives, none stood by him.
    C. Friends, colleagues, relatives, none, stood by him
    D. Friends, colleagues, relatives none, stood by him.

13. He said I am sorry I could not reach in time
    A. He said, "I am sorry I could not reach in time."
    B. He said "I am sorry. I could not reach in time."
    C. He said, "I am sorry. I could not reach in time."
    D. He said "I am sorry I could not reach in time."

14. Never listen to his stories don't believe what he says and always distrust him
    A. Never listen to his stories, don't believe what he says? and always distrust him.
    B. Never listen to his stories, don't believe, what he says? and always distrust him.
    C. Never listen to his stories, do'nt believe what he says and always distrust him.
    D. Never listen to his stories, don't believe what he says and always distrust him.

15. Man proposes God disposes
    A. Man proposes God disposes.
    B. Man proposes, God disposes.
    C. Man proposes, God disposes!
    D. Man proposes God disposes!

16. He asked me what I wanted
    A. He asked me, what I wanted?
    B. He asked me "what I wanted."
    C. He asked me what I wanted.
    D. He asked me "what I wanted!"

17. He said to me lets wait for him
    A. He said to me, "Let's wait for him."
    B. He said to me 'Lets wait for him.'
    C. He said to me, "let's wait for him."
    D. He said to me, "Let's wait for him."

18. In india the ganga and the yamuna are regarded as sacred rivers
    A. In India, the Ganga and the Yamuna are regarded as sacred rivers.
    B. In India, the ganga and the Yamuna are regarded as sacred rivers.
    C. In India, the ganga and the yamuna are regarded as sacred rivers.
    D. In India, the Ganga and the yamuna are regarded as sacred rivers.

19. To err is human to forgive divine
    A. To err is human to forgive divine.
    B. To err is human, to forgive divine.
    C. To err, is human to forgive, divine.
    D. To err is human; to forgive, divine.
20. He was born on August 16, 1944 in Howrah West Bengal
    A. He was born on August 16, 1944 in Howrah West Bengal.
    B. He was born on August 16, 1944, in Howrah West Bengal.
    C. He was born on, August 16 1944 in Howrah West Bengal.
    D. He was born on August, 16 1944, in Howrah West Bengal.
21. He is to tell you the truth is a fool
    A. He is, to tell you the truth, is a fool.
    B. He is to tell you, the truth is a fool.
    C. He is to tell you the truth, is a fool.
    D. He is to tell you the truth is a fool.
22. This in brief is what he said
    A. This in brief is what he said.
    B. This in brief, is what he said.
    C. This, in brief, is what he said.
    D. This, in brief is what, he said.
23. If you need my help write to me
    A. If you need my help write to me.
    B. If, you need my help, write to me.
    C. If you need, my help, write to me.
    D. If you need my help, write to me.
24. They started running for they were getting late
    A. They started running, for they were getting late.
    B. They started running for they were getting late.
    C. They started running for, they were getting late.
    D. They started, running for, they were getting late.
25. The sun having set it became pleasant
    A. The sun having set it became pleasant.
    B. The sun, having set, it became pleasant.
    C. The sun having set, it became pleasant.
    D. The sun, having set it, became pleasant.
26. Mr Sushil please listen to me
    A. Mr Sushil please listen to me.
    B. Mr Sushil, please listen to me.
    C. Mr Sushil please, listen to me.
    D. Mr Sushil, please, listen to me.
27. Wherever you go you face the same difficulties
    A. Wherever you go you face the same difficulties.
    B. Wherever, you go, you face the same difficulties.
    C. Wherever you go, you face, the same difficulties.
    D. Wherever you go, you face the same difficulties.
28. Tell me what I can do for you
    A. Tell me what I can do for you.
    B. Tell me what I can do for you!
    C. Tell me what I can do for you?
    D. Tell me, what I can do for you?

29. May you live long
    A. May you live long.
    B. May you live long?
    C. May you live long!
    D. May, you live long!
30. May God the Greatest bless you
    A. May God the Greatest bless you.
    B. May God, the Greatest bless you!
    C. May God, the Greatest, bless you.
    D. May God, the Greatest, bless you!
31. The sun having risen the fog disappeared
    A. The sun having risen the fog disappeared.
    B. The sun having risen, the fog disappeared.
    C. The sun having risen; the fog disappeared.
    D. The sun, having risen, the fog disappeared!
32. Having done his homework he went to bed
    A. Having done his homework he went to bed.
    B. Having done, his homework he went to bed.
    C. Having done, his homework, he went to bed.
    D. Having done his homework, he went to bed.
33. He is indeed a foolish boy
    A. He is indeed, a foolish boy.
    B. He is indeed a foolish boy.
    C. He is, indeed, a foolish boy.
    D. He, is indeed, a foolish boy.
34. Naresh my younger brother has gone to Patna
    A. Naresh, my younger brother, has gone to Patna.
    B. Naresh, my younger brother has gone to Patna.
    C. Naresh my younger brother, has gone to Patna.
    D. Naresh! my younger brother has gone to Patna.
35. Well I shall look into the matter
    A. Well I shall look into the matter.
    B. Well, I shall look into the matter.
    C. Well I shall, look into the matter.
    D. Well I shall, look into, the matter.
36. All right you can go
    A. All right you can go.
    B. All right you, can go.
    C. All right, you can go.
    D. All right! you can go.
37. Carry on your work I am watching you
    A. Carry on your work I am watching you.
    B. Carry on, your work, I am watching you.
    C. Carry on, your work, I am watching you.
    D. Carry on your work, I am watching you.
38. He was a kind bold man and we all praised him.
    A. He was a kind bold man and we all praised him
    B. He was a kind, bold man and we all praised him.
    C. He was a kind bold, man and we all praised him.
    D. He was, a kind bold man, and we all praised him.

39. He said Honesty is the best policy
    A. He said Honesty is the best policy.
    B. He said, Honesty is the best policy.
    C. He said "Honesty is the best policy."
    D. He said, "Honesty is the best policy."
40. What a beautiful flower it is
    A. What a beautiful flower it is.
    B. What a beautiful flower it is?
    C. What a beautiful flower it is!
    D. What! a beautiful flower it is.
41. Hurry up the train leaves at six o'clock
    A. Hurry up; the train leaves at six o'clock.
    B. Hurry up, the train leaves at six O'clock.
    C. Hurry up! the train leaves at six o'clock.
    D. Hurry up, the train leaves at six o'clock.
42. It is a sin to waste food said the father
    A. It is a sin to waste food said the father.
    B. 'It is a sin to waste food' said the father.
    C. "It is a sin to waste food" said the father.
    D. "It is a sin to waste food," said the father.
43. This is his fathers car
    A. This is his fathers' car
    B. This is his father's car
    C. This is his father's car.
    D. This is his fathers' car.
44. The man asked the taxi driver will you take me to the airport
    A. The man asked the taxi driver, will you take me to the airport?
    B. The man asked the taxi driver, "Will you take me to the airport?"
    C. The man asked the taxi driver, "Will you take me to the airport."
    D. The man asked the taxi driver, "will you take me to the airport!"
45. Bring me a glass of water said the teacher I am feeling very thirsty
    A. "Bring me a glass of water," said the teacher, "I am feeling very thirsty."
    B. "Bring me a glass of water" said the teacher, "I am feeling very thirsty."
    C. "Bring me a glass of water" said the teacher "I am feeling very thirsty."
    D. "Bring me a glass of water, said the teacher, "I am feeling very thirsty."
46. Ram said I am in a hurry I cannot spare time
    A. Ram said, "I am in a hurry" "I cannot spare time."
    B. Ram said "I am in a hurry I cannot spare time."
    C. Ram said, "I am in a hurry, I cannot spare time."
    D. Ram said, "I am in a hurry I cannot spare time."
47. How have you found so much wealth asked Anil's wife
    A. "How have you found so much wealth!" asked Anil's wife.
    B. "How have you found so much wealth?" asked Anil's wife.

C. "How have you found so much wealth." asked Anil's wife.
D. "How have you found so much wealth?", asked Anil's wife.

48. What is the matter why are you crying he asked the child
    A. "What is the matter, why are you crying?" he asked the child.
    B. "What is the matter? why are you crying?" he asked the child.
    C. "What is the matter" "why are you crying?" he asked the child.
    D. "What is the matter? Why are you crying?" he asked the child.

49. I am going to marry and I want a house to live in said the young man
    A. "I am going to marry and I want a house to live in", said the young man.
    B. "I am going to marry" and "I want a house to live in" said the young man.
    C. "I am going to marry and I want a house to live in" said the young man.
    D. "I am going to marry and I want a house to live in." said the young man.

50. What harm is there if we admit the error the lawyer said
    A. "What harm is there, if we admit the error?" the lawyer said.
    B. "What harm is there if, we admit the error?" the lawyer said.
    C. "What harm is there if we admit the error?" the lawyer said.
    D. "What harm is there? if we admit the error". the lawyer said.

Answers

1	2	3	4	5	6	7	8	9	10
B	D	A	C	D	B	C	D	A	D
11	12	13	14	15	16	17	18	19	20
C	B	A	D	B	C	A	A	D	B
21	22	23	24	25	26	27	28	29	30
A	C	D	A	C	B	D	A	C	D
31	32	33	34	35	36	37	38	39	40
B	D	C	A	B	C	D	B	D	C
41	42	43	44	45	46	47	48	49	50
D	D	C	B	A	C	B	D	A	C

FIGURES OF SPEECH 18

It is a common saying that a picture is worth a thousand words. Same goes with the figures of speech as they elaborate and enhance the meaning of words.

Directions (Qs. 1 to 40): *Fill in the blanks with the correct similes.*

1. As deaf as a ....
   A. man   B. bird
   C. stone   D. animal

2. As dry as ....
   A. cloth   B. bone
   C. air   D. sand

3. As easy as ....
   A. ABC   B. 123
   C. PQR   D. XYZ

4. As free as a ....
   A. kite   B. aircraft
   C. bird   D. tiger

5. As gentle as a ....
   A. child   B. woman
   C. man   D. lamb

6. As good as ....
   A. silver
   B. gold
   C. jewellery
   D. ornaments

7. As good as ....
   A. new   B. old
   C. ancient   D. modern

8. As green as ....
   A. grass   B. colour
   C. tree   D. life

9. As hard as a ....
   A. cock   B. glass
   C. rock   D. ice

10. As light as ....
    A. kite   B. feather
    C. bulb   D. hair

11. As mild as ....
    A. silk   B. water
    C. feather   D. milk

12. As neat as a new ....
    A. sin   B. kin
    C. pin   D. tin

13. As old as the ....
    A. air   B. water
    C. river   D. hills

14. As pissed as a ....
    A. rat   B. dog
    C. donkey   D. cat

15. As playful as a ....
    A. toy   B. animal
    C. kitten   D. bird

16. As pretty as a ....
    A. breeze   B. ice
    C. river   D. picture

17. As proud as a ....
    A. crow   B. peacock
    C. vulture   D. eagle
18. As quick as a ....
    A. flash   B. light
    C. air   D. sound
19. As silent as a ....
    A. engine   B. machine
    C. women   D. grave
20. As sly as a ....
    A. cat   B. fox
    C. dog   D. crow
21. As smooth as ....
    A. ice   B. floor
    C. silk   D. road
22. As sober as a ....
    A. judge   B. driver
    C. cop   D. convict
23. As solid as a ....
    A. wood   B. ice
    C. glass   D. rock
24. As straight as an ....
    A. arm   B. ass
    C. arrow   D. abacus
25. As strong as ....
    A. a fox   B. wood
    C. a camel   D. an ox
26. As stubborn as a ....
    A. dog   B. mule
    C. horse   D. elephant
27. As sweet as ....
    A. pie   B. coconut
    C. cucumber   D. gourd
28. As tough as old ....
    A. suit   B. man
    C. boots   D. books
29. As ugly as ....
    A. man   B. woman
    C. moon   D. sin
30. As warm as ....
    A. milk   B. toast
    C. water   D. air
31. As black as ....
    A. coal   B. colour
    C. coat   D. cloud
32. As blind as a ....
    A. cat   B. rat
    C. dog   D. bat
33. As bold as ....
    A. grass   B. brass
    C. ass   D. gas
34. As brave as a ....
    A. horse   B. elephant
    C. lion   D. bull
35. As busy as a ....
    A. man   B. animal
    C. bird   D. bee
36. As cheap as ....
    A. dirt   B. shirt
    C. trouser   D. shoes
37. As clear as ....
    A. shirt   B. picture
    C. crystal   D. sky
38. As cold as ....
    A. ice   B. water
    C. milk   D. breeze
39. As cunning as a ....
    A. ox   B. fox
    C. crow   D. man
40. As dead as ....
    A. button   B. air
    C. water   D. mutton

Directions (Qs. 41 to 70): *In each of the following sentences or verses a Figure of Speech has been used. You have to choose the correct Figure of Speech out of the four choices given under each.*

41. Rivers of blood flowed on the battlefield :
    A. Simile
    B. Metaphor
    C. Hyperbole
    D. Alliteration
42. Camel is the ship of the desert :
    A. Metaphor
    B. Simile
    C. Pun
    D. Personification
43. 'O my love's like a red, red rose, that's newly sprung in June':
    A. Alliteration
    B. Metaphor
    C. Simile
    D. Hyperbole
44. "Opportunity knocks at the door but once."
    A. Hyperbole
    B. Metaphor
    C. Antithesis
    D. Personification
45. "Death lays his icy hand on Kings":
    A. Personification
    B. Antithesis
    C. Metaphor
    D. Oxymoron
46. "The murmurous haunt of flies on summer eves."
    A. Hyperbole
    B. Alliteration
    C. Onomatopoeia
    D. Personification
47. "Milton! thou should'st be living at this hour. "
    A. Personification
    B. Apostrophe
    C. Alliteration
    D. Irony
48. How high his honour holds his haughty head!
    A. Oxymoron
    B. Personification
    C. Alliteration
    D. Irony
49. "Yet Brutus says he was ambitious. And Brutus is an honourable man."
    A. Irony
    B. Oxymoron
    C. Apostrophe
    D. Pun
50. Is life worth living? That depends upon the liver.
    A. Pun
    B. Alliteration
    C. Irony
    D. Metaphor
51. The pen is mightier than the sword.
    A. Simile
    B. Metaphor
    C. Metonymy
    D. Irony
52. A reeling road, a rolling road, that rambles round the shire.
    A. Alliteration
    B. Metonymy
    C. Personification
    D. Apostrophe
53. "The ploughman homeward plods his weary way."
    A. Oxymoron
    B. Synecdoche
    C. Transferred Epithet
    D. Pun
54. To err is human, to forgive divine:
    A. Oxymoron
    B. Antithesis
    C. Transferred Epithet
    D. Pun
55. He passed a sleepless night :
    A. Transferred Epithet
    B. Antithesis
    C. Synecdoche
    D. Oxymoron
56. The best brains assembled there:
    A. Oxymoron

B. Synecdoche
   C. Irony
   D. Pun
57. I have many mouths to feed :
   A. Synecdoche
   B. Irony
   C. Pun
   D. Oxymoron
58. Man proposes, God disposes :
   A. Synecdoche
   B. Antithesis
   C. Pun
   D. Irony
59. O Death! Where is thy sting?
   A. Metaphor
   B. Oxymoron
   C. Personification
   D. Apostrophe
60. "Life is a tale told by an idiot, Full of sound and fury ………"
   A. Simile
   B. Personification
   C. Metaphor
   D. Apostrophe
61. "Thy soul was like a star, and dwelt apart."
   A. Metaphor
   B. Personification
   C. Simile
   D. Onomatopoeia
62. He can devour mountains of food, and drink rivers of whisky.
   A. Onomatopoeia
   B. Hyperbole
   C. Metaphor
   D. Personification
63. "There Honour comes a pilgrim grey" :
   A. Metaphor
   B. Apostrophe
   C. Personification
   D. Onomatopoeia
64. An ambassador is a man who lies abroad for the good of his country:
   A. Metonymy
   B. Personification
   C. Pun
   D. Irony
65. "Husbands had she five on the holy altar" :
   A. Hyperbole   B. Metaphor
   C. Irony   D. Pun
66. His honour rooted in dishonour stood :
   A. Antithesis
   B. Oxymoron
   C. Irony
   D. Personification
67. "Sceptre and crown must tumble down."
   A. Metonymy
   B. Antithesis
   C. Irony
   D. Oxymoron
68. A lie has no legs :
   A. Apostrophe
   B. Pun
   C. Personification
   D. Irony
69. Youth is full of pleasure; Age is full of care:
   A. Antithesis
   B. Pun
   C. Metaphor
   D. Personification
70. The righteous shall flourish as the palm trees :
   A. Simile
   B. Transferred Epithet
   C. Antithesis
   D. Synecdoche

Answers

1	2	3	4	5	6	7	8	9	10
C	B	A	C	D	B	A	A	C	B
11	12	13	14	15	16	17	18	19	20
D	C	D	A	C	D	B	A	D	B
21	22	23	24	25	26	27	28	29	30
C	A	D	C	D	B	A	C	D	B
31	32	33	34	35	36	37	38	39	40
A	D	B	C	D	A	C	A	B	D
41	42	43	44	45	46	47	48	49	50
C	A	C	D	A	C	B	C	A	A
51	52	53	54	55	56	57	58	59	60
C	A	C	B	A	B	A	B	D	C
61	62	63	64	65	66	67	68	69	70
C	B	C	C	C	B	A	C	A	A

❑ ❑ ❑

Clauses 19

A clause is a group of words forming part of a sentence, and having a subject and a predicate of its own. It is a subject-predicate unit. It may combine with other such units in a sentence. Independent clauses are grammatically self-contained.

Directions: *Tick the correct alternative for each of the following clauses in bold letters:*

1. She heard someone singing around **when she was washing clothes**.
   A. Noun clause
   B. Adjective clause
   C. Adverb clause
   D. None of these

2. This is the girl **whose uncle is the personal assistant to the PM**.
   A. Adverb Clause
   B. Adjective Clause
   C. Noun Clause
   D. None of these

3. Do **as you are instructed**.
   A. Adverb Clause
   B. Adjective Clause
   C. Noun clause
   D. None of these

4. He does not know **where his brother has gone**.
   A. Noun Clause
   B. Adverb Clause
   C. Adjective Clause
   D. None of these

5. It is still unknown **why he behaved rudely at the party**.
   A. Adjective clause
   B. Adverb Clause
   C. Noun Clause
   D. None of these

6. I do not know the time **when he gets up in the morning**.
   A. Adjective Clause
   B. Adverb Clause
   C. Noun Clause
   D. None of these

7. I like her **because she is honest**.
   A. Adverb Clause
   B. Adjective Clause
   C. Noun Clause
   D. None of these

8. The boy **who stood first in our class** was given a prize by the Principal.
   A. Adjective Clause
   B. Noun clause
   C. Adverb clause
   D. None of these

9. If **you want to earn a lot of money**, start learning assembling computer.
   A. Adjective clause
   B. Adverb clause
   C. Noun clause
   D. None of these

10. Wait here **until I come back**.
    A. Adjective clause
    B. Noun clause
    C. Adverb clause
    D. None of these

11. She is not **what she seems**.
    A. Noun clause
    B. Adjective clause
    C. Adverb clause
    D. None of these

12. I want to know **where you have put my watch**.
    A. Adverb Clause
    B. Adjective Clause
    C. Noun Clause
    D. None of these

13. It is known to all of us **that he is a stupid fellow**.
    A. Adjective Clause
    B. Adverb Clause
    C. Noun clause
    D. None of these

14. I went to my father finding **that none of us could open that box**.
    A. Adverb Clause
    B. Noun Clause
    C. Adjective Clause
    D. None of these

15. She came back **before it was morning**.
    A. Adjective clause
    B. Adverb clause
    C. Noun Clause
    D. None of these

16. We looked **where mushrooms were growing**.
    A. Adjective Clause
    B. Noun Clause
    C. Adverb Clause
    D. None of these

17. **Where there is a will** there is a way.
    A. Adverb Clause
    B. Adjective Clause
    C. Noun Clause
    D. None of these

18. You may go **wherever you like**.
    A. Adjective Clause
    B. Noun clause
    C. Adverb clause
    D. None of these

19. **As soon as the thief saw a policeman**, he ran away.
    A. Adjective clause
    B. Adverb clause
    C. Noun clause
    D. None of these

20. Wait here **until I come**.
    A. Adjective clause
    B. Noun clause
    C. Adverb clause
    D. None of these

21. He walked out of the house **when the rain stopped**.
    A. Noun clause
    B. Adjective clause
    C. Adverb clause
    D. None of these

22. Her brother danced **while she sang**.
    A. Adverb Clause
    B. Adjective Clause
    C. Noun Clause
    D. None of these

23. You must listen to me **whenever you have finished your home work**.
    A. Adjective Clause
    B. Adverb Clause
    C. Noun clause
    D. None of these
24. We had returned home **before the storm started**.
    A. Noun Clause
    B. Adverb Clause
    C. Adjective Clause
    D. None of these
25. **As long as I'm here** you needn't get afraid of anybody.
    A. Adjective clause
    B. Noun Clause
    C. Adverb Clause
    D. None of these
26. I haven't seen him since I **met him five years ago**.
    A. Adverb Clause
    B. Adjective Clause
    C. Noun Clause
    D. None of these
27. **Just as I was getting out of my car**, I saw a monkey jumping over the wall of the orchard.
    A. Adjective Clause
    B. Adverb Clause
    C. Noun Clause
    D. None of these
28. **As I went out into the courtyard of my house**, I saw a snake in the grass.
    A. Adjective Clause
    B. Noun clause
    C. Adverb clause
    D. None of these
29. She was happy **because she had won a jackpot**.
    A. Adjective clause
    B. Adverb clause
    C. Noun clause
    D. None of these
30. **Since/As you are not going to office**, let's play hockey.
    A. Adjective clause
    B. Noun clause
    C. Adverb clause
    D. None of these
31. I take antihypertensive drugs **so that my blood pressure may remain in control**.
    A. Noun clause
    B. Adjective clause
    C. Adverb clause
    D. None of these
32. He is running fast **so that he may catch the train**.
    A. Adverb Clause
    B. Adjective Clause
    C. Noun Clause
    D. None of these
33. Walk fast **lest you should miss the train**.
    A. Adjective Clause
    B. Adverb Clause
    C. Noun clause
    D. None of these
34. I don't let him run a race **in case he is ill**.
    A. Noun Clause
    B. Adverb Clause
    C. Adjective Cause
    D. None of these
35. We've arranged her a tutor **in order that she may continue her studies**.

A. Adjective clause
B. Noun Clause
C. Adverb Clause
D. None of these

36. He walks **as if or as though he were a king**.
A. Adjective Clause
B. Adverb Clause
C. Noun Clause
D. None of these

37. Do **as I tell you**.
A. Adverb Clause
B. Adjective Clause
C. Noun Clause
D. None of these

38. He can do **as he wishes**.
A. Adjective Clause
B. Noun clause
C. Adverb clause
D. None of these

39. He **is wiser than you**.
A. Adjective clause
B. Adverb clause
C. Noun clause
D. None of these

40. She will work **as fast as she can**.
A. Adjective clause
B. Noun clause
C. Adverb clause
D. None of these

41. He likes to sit calmly **rather than work**.
A. Adverb clause
B. Adjective clause
C. Noun clause
D. None of these

42. **Although he had worked** hard, he failed in the examination.
A. Noun Clause
B. Adjective Clause
C. Adverb Clause
D. None of these

43. **Even if/even though/although you don't like him**, you should greet him in the party.
A. Adjective Clause
B. Adverb Clause
C. Noun clause
D. None of these

44. **However hard you work** you'll not (or won't) get success.
A. Adverb Clause
B. Noun Clause
C. Adjective Clause
D. None of these

45. **If you call him**, he will come to see you.
A. Adjective clause
B. Adverb Clause
C. Noun Clause
D. None of these

46. **If the weather is not good**, the flight may be cancelled.
A. Adjective Clause
B. Noun Clause
C. Adverb Clause
D. None of these

47. **If I had the Sun magazine**, I would show you the picture of Madonna in it.
A. Adverb Clause
B. Adjective Clause
C. Noun Clause
D. None of these

48. **If anybody threatened me**, I would call the police.
A. Adjective Clause
B. Noun clause
C. Adverb clause
D. None of these

49. I would not tell him this **if I were you**.
    A. Adjective clause
    B. Adverb clause
    C. Noun clause
    D. None of these

50. You would have won the race **if you had run fast**.
    A. Adverb clause
    B. Noun clause
    C. Adjective clause
    D. None of these

Answers

1	2	3	4	5	6	7	8	9	10
C	B	A	A	C	A	A	A	B	C
11	12	13	14	15	16	17	18	19	20
A	C	C	B	B	C	A	C	B	C
21	22	23	24	25	26	27	28	29	30
C	A	B	B	C	A	B	C	B	C
31	32	33	34	35	36	37	38	39	40
C	A	B	B	C	B	A	C	B	C
41	42	43	44	45	46	47	48	49	50
A	C	B	A	B	C	A	C	B	A

❏ ❏ ❏

Foreign Words 20

All the words of English are not original English, many of them were extracted from various languages around the globe and then made into English, so one must know their meanings also as many of them are frequently used in day-to-day English and asked about in exams.

Directions: *A few foreign language phrases, which are commonly used, are given below. Select the correct meaning of each phrase.*

1. **Ultra vires**
   A. Beyond the powers
   B. Within the powers
   C. According to law
   D. None of the above

2. **Bona fide**
   A. In good faith
   B. In bad faith
   C. In good behaviour
   D. In bad behaviour

3. **Per jure**
   A. To confess   B. To deny
   C. To hide   D. To lie

4. **Innuendo**
   A. Enquiry
   B. Indirect reference
   C. Innovation
   D. Inorganic

5. **Quid pro quo**
   A. Evidence
   B. Favourable opinion
   C. Revenge
   D. Something in return

6. **De facto**
   A. Actual   B. Factual
   C. Initial   D. Beginning

7. **Amicus Curiae**
   A. An old man
   B. Name given to the poorman
   C. Friend of court or lawyer appointed by a court
   D. A litigant before the court

8. **Pro rata**
   A. At the rate of
   B. At quoted rate
   C. In proportion
   D. Beyond all proportion

9. **Sine die**
   A. Without setting a fixed day
   B. By voice vote
   C. Applying mathematical concepts to solve a difficult problem
   D. Signing legal documents before death

10. **Ab initio**
    A. From the very beginning
    B. High initiative
    C. Thing done later
    D. Without initiative

11. **Intra vires**
    A. Within the powers
    B. Outside the powers
    C. Within the scope of the fundamental rights
    D. Regular

12. **Vice versa**
    A. In verse
    B. Uersatile verse
    C. In consonance with
    D. The other way round

13. **Status quo**
    A. Legally valid
    B. Present condition
    C. Social position
    D. Side remarks

14. **Alibi**
    A. Every where
    B. Else where
    C. No where
    D. Without any excuse

15. **Vox populi**
    A. A famous personality
    B. Popular opinion
    C. A very popular drama
    D. Group of people

16. **Subpoena**
    A. Punishment   B. Summons
    C. Delay   D. Ban

17. **Prima facie**
    A. The most important
    B. That which comes first
    C. At first view
    D. The face that is young

18. **Ipso facto**
    A. In place of
    B. By reason of that fact
    C. By the same source
    D. By the way

19. **Lex tallienis**
    A. The law of the place
    B. The law of the forum
    C. Unwritten law
    D. The law of retaliation

20. **Tour-de-force**
    A. Masterpiece   B. Riche
    C. Traffic   D. Discourse

21. **Ex gratia**
    A. Very grateful
    B. Payment made out of generosity
    C. Extraordinary
    D. Before retirement

22. **Sub judice**
    A. Under consideration of court of law
    B. Beyond jurisdiction of court
    C. Dual view
    D. Same court

23. **Force majeure**
    A. Forced labour
    B. An inevitable event
    C. Majority force
    D. Democracy

24. **Ad Valorem**
    A. According to quality
    B. According to value
    C. According to nature
    D. According to time

25. **Ex facie**
    A. In the light of what is not apparent
    B. In the light of what is apparent
    C. To lose the right
    D. To lose the property

26. **In curia**
    A. In open court
    B. In closed court
    C. In trial court
    D. In High Court

27. **Status quo**
    A. The state in which things are
    B. The past state of affair
    C. To maintain past state of affair
    D. To maintain future state of affair

28. **Ad interim**
    A. In the meantime
    B. In the pastime
    C. In between
    D. In action

29. **Tete-a-tete**
    A. A public conversation
    B. A friend's conversation
    C. A private conversation
    D. A family conversation

30. **Fait Accompli**
    A. Co-accused
    B. Co-conspirator
    C. Accomplished fact
    D. Suplicable

31. **Force majeure**
    A. Superior power
    B. Inferior power
    C. Weak power
    D. Finite power

32. **Lex fori**
    A. The law of the forum or court
    B. The law of the country
    C. The law of nature
    D. The law of God

33. **Lalfeasance**
    A. Wrong doing
    B. Misfortune
    C. By the order
    D. None of these

34. **Quasi**
    A. As if it were
    B. Null
    C. Void
    D. Quashed

35. **Modus operandi**
    A. Way of doing something
    B. Manner of theft
    C. Way of doing theft
    D. Way of worship

36. **Inter alia**
    A. Among other things
    B. Interested in aliens
    C. Alliance invited
    D. All the above

37. **Volte face**
    A. To not face
    B. To face about
    C. To remain absent
    D. To remain present

38. **Ex post facto**
    A. By a subsequent act
    B. By virtue of an office
    C. In itself
    D. Not complete

39. **Inter vivos**
    A. Between dead persons
    B. Between living persons
    C. Between child
    D. Between human beings

40. **Coup d'etat**
    A. A change of government
    B. An abrupt change of government by force
    C. Attack on a country
    D. Formation of a new government

41. **Mala fide**
    A. Generous
    B. Bad intention
    C. Trustworthy
    D. Genuine

42. **De Jure**
    A. Illegal
    B. Heir

C. Concerning law
D. Forbidden

43. **Vini, Vidi, Vice**
    A. Without victory
    B. I came, I fell, I died
    C. She came, she went, the end
    D. I came, I saw, I conquered

44. **In toto**
    A. Unknown
    B. On the whole
    C. Isolated
    D. Part by part

45. **Caveat**
    A. A warning
    B. An injuction
    C. Writ
    D. Certiorari

46. **El Dorado**
    A. An imaginary place
    B. High altitude
    C. A literary man

D. A country full of gold and precious stones

47. **Exempli gratia**
    A. Without examples
    B. Theoretically
    C. Through mass contact
    D. By way of example

48. **Tabula rasa**
    A. Clean slate
    B. Agitated
    C. Deprived
    D. Creative

49. **Raison d'etre**
    A. Logical conclusion
    B. Reason for existence
    C. Free choice
    D. Dubious argument

50. **Vis-a-vis**
    A. Direct
    B. Opposite
    C. Face-to-face
    D. Agree

Answers

1	2	3	4	5	6	7	8	9	10
A	A	D	B	D	A	C	C	A	A
11	12	13	14	15	16	17	18	19	20
A	D	B	B	B	B	C	B	C	A
21	22	23	24	25	26	27	28	29	30
B	A	B	B	B	A	A	A	C	C
31	32	33	34	35	36	37	38	39	40
A	A	A	A	A	A	B	A	B	B
41	42	43	44	45	46	47	48	49	50
B	C	D	B	A	A	D	A	B	C

Odd Words Out 21

Picking odd words out is a common test but if a slight twist is given to this test and the spellings of all the words are jumbled, it becomes cumbersome. Try it here.

Directions: *Each of the following questions has jumbled spellings in all the four options. Rearrange the jumbled alphabet and find the odd word among them.*

1. A. BUC   B. KHICECN
   C. GIP   D. UPP
2. A. BABIRT   B. DROCILCEO
   C. WARTHOREM   D. ANISL
3. A. ERET   B. AELF
   C. SUBH   D. REHB
4. A. TOCORD   B. CEAHETR
   C. GRENINEE   D. VIEDR
5. A. RTOT
   B. SQUETRIAEN
   C. BERDY
   D. NRUGT
6. A. ARNTOE   B. NEASAPTL
   C. RECATDEO   D. TEAUIFBY
7. A. LOPO   B. SHECS
   C. DULO   D. HQASUS
8. A. TRUTO
   B. CRINIPAPL
   C. LUPIP
   D. SROESOPRF
9. A. DONP   B. VIRER
   C. ETRASM   D. OROBK
10. A. NUOTATIOQ   B. TUDY
    C. ATX   D. TCOROI
11. A. OROT   B. ETER
    C. NACBRH   D. WELOFR
12. A. RTMOAIML
    B. NIMENECE
    C. TERPEUPAL
    D. STVRLEAINEG
13. A. NIPACSH   B. TOATPO
    C. RACROT   D. NIGEGR
14. A. NAV
    B. LERPANAEO
    C. COELIPTEHR
    D. SPRANOTRT
15. A. HOATFM   B. NARIME
    C. EDEP   D. CAUNLA
16. A. ORTNATEY
    B. WAYELR
    C. EUDJG
    D. DAIQUITOLR
17. A. RPAROSW
    B. SHINGFIKER
    C. IWIK
    D. RAROPT

18. A. RAOWR   B. GAGEDR
    C. FKIEN   D. RWOSD
19. A. TIATMACMSHE
    B. RALGBEA
    C. NORIGOMETRTY
    D. MEEOTRGY
20. A. HIRSI   B. NRAINIA
    C. ASETREN D. SHINECE
21. A. MECEBEDR B. NUJE
    C. ARANUJY D. CARMH
22. A. ROXEB   B. TLRESEWR
    C. CKEOJY   D. YLAEPR
23. A. RATUME   B. TUODO
    C. EIPRN   D. LOBOM
24. A. RDOAE   B. KILE
    C. EOVL   D. TOVCE
25. A. DREGEY
    B. CIAPAOURS
    C. DNEAER
    D. RIVACIOUAS
26. A. BLUC   B. REAHT
    C. DPASE   D. CAE
27. A. MERIPT   B. WLAOL
    C. EAREG   D. EONFSCS
28. A. OTSOL   B. DOWO
    C. LATEB   D. AHICR
29. A. TIOUNAOFDN
    B. MOTBTO
    C. NABE
    D. SABE
30. A. EHESCE   B. KILM
    C. RUCD   D. EHEG
31. A. REA   B. DANH
    C. EOSN   D. YEE
32. A. MOWR LILBE B. KHECE
    C. REAHT   D. NULG
33. A. NANCNO   B. NUG
    C. TISOPL   D. RWOSD
34. A. AUITGR   B. RAOSD
    C. LIOIVN   D. BALTA
35. A. KOCEHY   B. COCESR
    C. RILIADBSL D. CRICKET
36. A. MISADY   B. ABY
    C. ASY   D. OTY
37. A. VIBLIOUOS
    B. SOOLSCAL
    C. TIGNIGCA
    D. DTUENOUSPS
38. A. MCAE   B. CAPK
    C. IETZHN   D. TUMSIM
39. A. NOZOE   B. XGYEON
    C. EOZN   D. LEIUHM
40. A. LACPEA   B. DEESINCRE
    C. TRIOCPO D. AILVL
41. A. ITE   B. NAPT
    C. RHIST   D. REMBLULA
42. A. ORES   B. NIKP
    C. EDR   D. RAOMON
43. A. NTREGTSH
    B. NIESW
    C. CUSLME
    D. RAGANVT
44. A. ATSG   B. OCKC
    C. RAME   D. ROSHE
45. A. PYOIMA
    B. RAATACTC
    C. MAUCOGAL
    D. NPODYSLITIS
46. A. ERINFD   B. HOTEMR
    C. TROHEBR D. TISESR
47. A. TOHEMR   B. TROHEBR
    C. NUAT   D. CIENE
48. A. SRIPM
    B. GEAOHNX
    C. EONC
    D. DYINECRL

49. A. SHEITRCYM
    B. REOGPHGYA
    C. BUJECST
    D. RIEATURLET
50. A. CENIPL   B. SRUBH
    C. YRAOCN   D. BLUC
51. A. CNLUE   B. NUAT
    C. HOTEMR   D. HEPENW
52. A. RAEA   B. TEIHGH
    C. GETLHN   D. DREATBH
53. A. TCOAR
    B. FOERMREPR
    C. REOH
    D. RIETODRC
54. A. EALD   B. BARLME
    C. NIK   D. LHACK
55. A. KOLO   B. ACSN
    C. WEVI   D. IKNW
56. A. REFCPTE
    B. GNTEROAIVIERT
    C. SRENPTE
    D. RUTUFE
57. A. SHIECL   B. LAIN
    C. XAE   D. PCALESL
58. A. OCKOACRCH B. LFY
    C. MERTITE   D. CNSTIES
59. A. CUDK   B. RAROPT
    C. WROC   D. GIOPEN
60. A. EREH   B. AENR
    C. RHEWE   D. RHETE
61. A. OKOLS   B. TEUBYA
    C. NUEESCTS   D. RAHACTECR
62. A. MNIACIYT
    B. THTACENATM
    C. MINTEY
    D. DIENSHIFPR
63. A. CNIH   B. TOFO
    C. RAYD   D. RUAQT

64. A. AEZL   B. ELAS
    C. ENAKL   D. AEML
65. A. LUJY
    B. METEBPESR
    C. BCTOEOR
    D. MOVBENER
66. A. TAURME   B. BAOULR
    C. EIGDTS   D. PIERN
67. A. ROPEPC   B. LOGD
    C. VIESRL   D. ETESL
68. A. PLPAE   B. GANMO
    C. TOTOAP   D. GRNOEA
69. A. VAUGA   B. PLPAE
    C. NRAGOE   D. AEPR
70. A. RQASEU   B. GRINLTEA
    C. EUBC   D. GECANLRET
71. A. RODO   B. TAGE
    C. BALTE   D. DIWNOW
72. A. NIOL   B. HANTEPR
    C. GIETR   D. FOLW
73. A. LOUPT   B. EIGOPN
    C. WLO   D. RPROSWA
74. A. POASCSM   B. EDELNE
    C. CIRETIODN D. GANEMT
75. A. ARFGT   B. NRACBH
    C. RHOTN   D. OUMUTR
76. A. XAE   B. AELN
    C. CSISORSS   D. VHOESL
77. A. RAROCT   B. RLAIOCN
    C. AEPR   D. YAPAPA
78. A. NIRG   B. GANLBE
    C. AHICN   D. VLOECS
79. A. NROZBE   B. VILESR
    C. AUIQL   D. POPECR
80. A. RSICOHT   B. AWSN
    C. ARNCE   D. WEE
81. A. EHECL   B. DPIESR
    C. CALOFN   D. COUSLT

82. A. TCTIA   B. GLOUPH
    C. ITEL   D. HDES
83. A. RLAIOCN B. THISLWE
    C. TLUFE   D. AINPO
84. A. DPASE   B. TESLPE
    C. VHOETL   D. MAMEHR
85. A. ILOPWL   B. SEDHEBET
    C. KLNEBTA D. RIROMR
86. A. NUAT
    B. NDRAMTHGEOR
    C. CIENE
    D. HEPENW
87. A. BUMD   B. ALEM
    C. NLIBD   D. UINSS
88. A. ARE   B. NULG
    C. NIDEKY   D. GONUTE
89. A. GINEFR   B. NAHD
    C. OET   D. UHMTB
90. A. SONE   B. YEE
    C. ILP   D. OLSE
91. A. EBEF   B. NUTMTO
    C. SENIOVN D. HEWY
92. A. EHAWT   B. EICR
    C. SULPE   D. LOLEPN
93. A. INONO   B. BAAGCEB
    C. JRIABLN D. AEPR
94. A. DURC   B. UTEBRT
    C. EHESCE   D. SOLASEMS
95. A. BALTE   B. AHICR
    C. LTOSO   D. LILOPW
96. A. RHIST   B. KTOCINSG
    C. ITE   D. ACRSF
97. A. NIRG   B. TACWH
    C. GANLBE   D. AIRTA
98. A. ACR   B. ARITN
    C. SUB   D. PHIS
99. A. ANISL   B. RCOPIOSN
    C. PADOLTE D. SIFH
100. A. ROSHE   B. OWC
     C. KONEDY D. KURETY
101. A. MWIS   B. UNR
     C. IST   D. DLISE
102. A. RPILA   B. AMY
     C. RACMH D. ULJY
103. A. UOLMVE B. TOASIRNG
     C. OKOINCG D. LOIINBG
104. A. TICURPE
     B. TOSEPR
     C. GHOTHORAPP
     D. NCEERSY
105. A. NICTIOARDY
     B. VOENL
     C. SHEITS
     D. ZAGAINME
106. A. RIAETCTEG B. AOBCTCO
     C. IPEP   D. IDIB
107. A. TIEK   B. ULTRUVE
     C. WAKH   D. CUKD
108. A. HANTEPR B. LOWF
     C. OILN   D. FUFALBO
109. A. WROCD   B. RWASM
     C. OLCFK D. AETM
110. A. SAUENA B. YORZCA
     C. HTCEIS D. NIPE
111. A. GHITH   B. EHSCT
     C. MILB   D. UTSD
112. A. ETA
     B. FOFECE
     C. SHIKWY
     D. NEMOADLE
113. A. LOTO   B. LURE
     C. LOCO   D. LOPO
114. A. SROUERTS B. BIBORN
     C. RHOTSS D. RKITSS
115. A. RESTEDAYY B. DHRSATYU
     C. NODAMY D. DUNASY

116. A. EREGN   B. DER
     C. ULOCRO   D. GRNOEA
117. A. TBLSEA   B. EOLH
     C. OANCE   D. TSY
118. A. SOEN   B. ESYE
     C. IKSN   D. TETHE
119. A. UENVS   B. MONO
     C. ULTPO   D. RASM
120. A. PAPYH   B. OLOGMY
     C. LIVELY   D. CHEERFUL
121. A. ONCE   B. RICLCE
     C. ARINGLTE D. NECTEAGRL

122. A. EADL   B. ERCURMY
     C. POPECR   D. ORIN
123. A. EITK   B. RIBD
     C. DARAR   D. TEJ
124. A. ENEK
     B. DOULESRH
     C. LNKAE
     D. LAPM
125. A. LEUGDE
     B. MALAITCY
     C. RATSTOPHCEA
     D. ARW

Answers

1	2	3	4	5	6	7	8	9	10
C	A	B	D	D	B	A	C	A	A
11	12	13	14	15	16	17	18	19	20
A	B	A	D	D	D	C	A	A	C
21	22	23	24	25	26	27	28	29	30
B	D	B	D	C	D	D	B	C	B
31	32	33	34	35	36	37	38	39	40
C	C	D	D	C	D	A	B	C	C
41	42	43	44	45	46	47	48	49	50
D	A	D	C	D	A	B	B	C	D
51	52	53	54	55	56	57	58	59	60
C	A	D	B	D	B	B	D	A	C
61	62	63	64	65	66	67	68	69	70
D	C	D	C	A	B	D	C	C	C
71	72	73	74	75	76	77	78	79	80
C	D	C	C	D	B	B	D	C	D
81	82	83	84	85	86	87	88	89	90
C	B	D	B	D	D	D	A	C	D
91	92	93	94	95	96	97	98	99	100
D	D	D	D	D	B	D	D	C	D
101	102	103	104	105	106	107	108	109	110
C	A	A	C	A	B	D	D	D	D
111	112	113	114	115	116	117	118	119	120
D	C	B	B	A	C	C	D	B	B
121	122	123	124	125					
A	B	C	D	D					

Hints for Jumbled Spellings

1. A. Cub   B. Chicken
   C. Pig   D. Pup
2. A. Rabbit   B. Crocodile
   C. Earthworm D. Snail
3. A. Tree   B. Leaf
   C. Bush   D. Herb
4. A. Doctor   B. Teacher
   C. Engineer D. Diver
5. A. Trot   B. Equestrian
   C. Derby   D. Grunt
6. A. Ornate   B. Pleasant
   C. Decorate D. Beautify
7. A. Polo   B. Chess
   C. Ludo   D. Squash
8. A. Tutor   B. Principal
   C. Pupil   D. Professor
9. A. Pond   B. River
   C. Stream D. Brook
10. A. Quotation B. Duty
    C. Tax   D. Octroi
11. A. Root   B. Tree
    C. Branch D. Flower
12. A. Immortal B. Eminence
    C. Perpetual D. Everlasting
13. A. Spinach B. Potato
    C. Carrot D. Ginger
14. A. Van   B. Aeroplane
    C. Helicopter D. Transport
15. A. Fathom   B. Marine
    C. Deep   D. Lacuna
16. A. Attorney B. Lawyer
    C. Judge D. Liquidator
17. A. Sparrow B. Kingfisher
    C. Kiwi   D. Parrot
18. A. Arrow   B. Dagger
    C. Knife D. Sword
19. A. Mathematics B. Algebra
    C. Trigonometry D. Geometry
20. A. Irish   B. Iranian
    C. Eastern D. Chinese
21. A. December B. June
    C. January D. March
22. A. Boxer   B. Wrestler
    C. Jockey D. Player
23. A. Mature   B. Outdo
    C. Ripen D. Bloom
24. A. Adore   B. Like
    C. Love   D. Covet
25. A. Greedy   B. Rapacious
    C. Endear D. Avaricious
26. A. Club   B. Heart
    C. Spade D. Ace
27. A. Permit   B. Allow
    C. Agree D. Confess
28. A. Stool   B. Wood
    C. Table D. Chair
29. A. Foundation B. Bottom
    C. Bane   D. Base
30. A. Cheese   B. Milk
    C. Curd   D. Ghee
31. A. Ear   B. Hand
    C. Nose   D. Eye
32. A. Lower limb B. Cheek
    C. Heart D. Lung
33. A. Cannon   B. Gun
    C. Pistol D. Sword
34. A. Guitar   B. Sarod
    C. Violin D. Tabla
35. A. Tennis   B. Soccer
    C. Billiards D. Cricket
36. A. Dismay   B. Bay
    C. Say   D. Toy

37. A. Oblivious
    B. Colossal
    C. Gigantic
    D. Stupendous
38. A. Acme   B. Pack
    C. Zenith   D. Summit
39. A. Ozone   B. Oxygen
    C. Zone   D. Helium
40. A. Palace   B. Residence
    C. Portico   D. Villa
41. A. Tie   B. Pant
    C. Shirt   D. Umbrella
42. A. Rose   B. Pink
    C. Red   D. Maroon
43. A. Strength   B. Sinew
    C. Muscle   D. Vagrant
44. A. Stag   B. Cock
    C. Mare   D. Horse
45. A. Myopia   B. Cataract
    C. Glaucoma   D. Spondylitis
46. A. Friend   B. Mother
    C. Brother   D. Sister
47. A. Mother   B. Brother
    C. Aunt   D. Niece
48. A. Prism   B. Hexagon
    C. Cone   D. Cylinder
49. A. Chemistry   B. Geography
    C. Subject   D. Literature
50. A. Pencil   B. Brush
    C. Crayon   D. Club
51. A. Uncle   B. Aunt
    C. Mother   D. Nephew
52. A. Area   B. Height
    C. Length   D. Breadth
53. A. Actor   B. Performer
    C. Hero   D. Director
54. A. Lead   B. Marble
    C. Ink   D. Chalk
55. A. Look   B. Scan
    C. View   D. Wink
56. A. Perfect
    B. Interrogative
    C. Present
    D. Future
57. A. Chisel   B. Nail
    C. Axe   D. Scalpel
58. A. Cockroach   B. Fly
    C. Termite   D. Insects
59. A. Duck   B. Parrot
    C. Crow   D. Pigeon
60. A. Here   B. Near
    C. Where   D. There
61. A. Looks   B. Beauty
    C. Cuteness   D. Character
62. A. Intimacy
    B. Attachment
    C. Enmity
    D. Friendship
63. A. Inch   B. Foot
    C. Yard   D. Quart
64. A. Zeal   B. Seal
    C. Kneal   D. Meal
65. A. July   B. September
    C. October   D. November
66. A. Mature   B. Labour
    C. Digest   D. Ripen
67. A. Copper   B. Gold
    C. Silver   D. Steel
68. A. Apple   B. Mango
    C. Potato   D. Orange
69. A. Guava   B. Apple
    C. Orange   D. Pear
70. A. Square   B. Triangle
    C. Cube   D. Rectangle
71. A. Door   B. Gate
    C. Table   D. Window

72. A. Lion B. Panther C. Tiger D. Wolf
73. A. Poult B. Pigeon C. Owl D. Sparrow
74. A. Compass B. Needle C. Direction D. Magnet
75. A. Graft B. Branch C. Thorn D. Tumour
76. A. Axe B. Lean C. Scissors D. Shovel
77. A. Carrot B. Clarion C. Pear D. Papaya
78. A. Ring B. Bangle C. Chain D. Cloves
79. A. Bronze B. Silver C. Quail D. Copper
80. A. Ostrich B. Swan C. Crane D. Ewe
81. A. Leech B. Spider C. Falcon D. Locust
82. A. Attic B. Plough C. Tile D. Shed
83. A. Clarion B. Whistle C. Flute D. Piano
84. A. Spade B. Pestle C. Shovel D. Hammer
85. A. Pillow B. Bedsheet C. Blanket D. Mirror
86. A. Aunt B. Grandmother C. Niece D. Nephew
87. A. Dumb B. Lame C. Blind D. Sinus
88. A. Ear B. Lung C. Kidney D. Tongue
89. A. Finger B. Hand C. Toe D. Thumb
90. A. Nose B. Eye C. Lip D. Sole
91. A. Beef B. Mutton C. Venison D. Whey
92. A. Wheat B. Rice C. Pulse D. Pollen
93. A. Onion B. Cabbage C. Brinjal D. Pear
94. A. Curd B. Butter C. Cheese D. Molasses
95. A. Table B. Chair C. Stool D. Pillow
96. A. Shirt B. Stocking C. Tie D. Scarf
97. A. Ring B. Watch C. Bangle D. Tiara
98. A. Car B. Train C. Bus D. Ship
99. A. Snail B. Scorpion C. Tadpole D. Fish
100. A. Horse B. Cow C. Donkey D. Turkey
101. A. Swim B. Run C. Sit D. Slide
102. A. April B. May C. March D. July
103. A. Volume B. Roasting C. Cooking D. Boiling
104. A. Picture B. Poster C. Photograph D. Scenery
105. A. Dictionary B. Novel C. Thesis D. Magazine
106. A. Cigarette B. Tobacco C. Pipe D. Bidi
107. A. Kite B. Vulture C. Hawk D. Duck
108. A. Panther B. Wolf C. Lion D. Buffalo

109.	A. Crowd	B. Swarm		117.	A. Stable	B. Hole	
	C. Flock	D. Team			C. Canoe	D. Sty	
110.	A. Nausea	B. Coryza		118.	A. Nose	B. Eyes	
	C. Itches	D. Pine			C. Skin	D. Teeth	
111.	A. Thigh	B. Chest		119.	A. Venus	B. Moon	
	C. Limb	D. Stud			C. Pluto	D. Mars	

112. A. Tea
 B. Coffee
 C. Whisky
 D. Lemonade

120. A. Happy B. Gloomy
 C. Lively D. Cheerful

121. A. Cone B. Circle
 C. Triangle D. Rectangle

113. A. Tool B. Rule
 C. Cool D. Pool

122. A. Lead B. Mercury
 C. Copper D. Iron

114. A. Trousers B. Ribbon
 C. Shorts D. Skirts

123. A. Kite B. Bird
 C. Radar D. Jet

115. A. Yesterday B. Thursday
 C. Monday D. Sunday

124. A. Knee B. Shoulder
 C. Ankle D. Palm

116. A. Green B. Red
 C. Colour D. Orange

125. A. Deluge B. Calamity
 C. Catastrophe D. War

❏ ❏ ❏

Do As Directed 22

There are many exams where in place of multiple choice questions we find questions where no choice of words is given and we have to write the answers of the questions ourselves. Some such tests are given in this chapter.

I. Rearrange the words in the following sentences to make them easily intelligible:
 1. meant / from / Gandhiji's / totally / irreligion / secularism / different
 2. to be true / all of them / regarded / equal respect / all religious / to / he / and / gave
 3. identified / Nehru's / cannot be / with Gandhi's / views
 4. little patience / a communal / manifestation / had / as a / he / with religion
 5. organised religion / rejected / he called / he / what

II. Change the voice of the following sentences:
 1. No further letter will be sent.
 2. He watched the progress of the experiment.
 3. He well knew his parents.
 4. He has sent me the vase.
 5. It may save the side.

III. Change the form of the narration of the following sentences:
 1. The postmaster told Ratan that he was going away the next day.
 2. Bill said to Dorset, "How long can you hold him?"
 3. He said, "We'll sell the house and go back to our place."
 4. Rosemary said to Philip, "I picked her in Curzon street."
 5. I said to him, "Let her have a little fun."

IV. Transform the following sentences as directed:
 1. Having done this, he chose out a farm of forty acres. (Change into a compound sentence)
 2. Hardly were his eyes closed when he had a dream. (Use 'as soon as')
 3. He felt too lazy to do any cooking. (Remove too .... to)
 4. How little of the grandiose there was in the palace! (Change into assertive sentence)

5. As soon as he saw the real lion, he was disappointed.
   (Change into negative sentence)

V. Insert appropriate articles in the blanks:
1. I heard .... heavy sound.
2. Is that .... way to drive?
3. What .... surprise it would be!
4. The new law put .... end to old restrictions.
5. I have already filled .... glass.

VI. Fill in the blanks with suitable prepositions:
1. He goes .... swearing.
2. He has always something new to discourse ....
3. He was cured .... blindness.
4. I resigned myself .... despair.
5. She called .... find her little brother.

VII. Fill in the blanks with suitable conjunctions:
1. Iona tried to talk to him again .... he had closed his eyes.
2. Pay the ransom .... get away from him.
3. It was with great difficulty .... I prevented him from following me.
4. She came over .... sat down on his knee.
5. It seemed as .... the rains would never end.

VIII. Use the following words/phrases in meaningful sentences:
1. Distinctly
2. Penetrate
3. Flourish
4. Eccentric
5. Learn by heart
6. Compete with
7. Appalled
8. Complacent

IX. Give one word for each of the following:
1. One who believes in eating, drinking and being merry.
2. A person who makes experiments to turn baser metals into gold.
3. A medicine that counteracts the effect of a poison.
4. A person having strange behaviour and habits.
5. Offensive to taste or smell.

X. Use the following words in sentences of your own as directed:
1. Ring
   (a) Noun ....
   (b) Verb ....
2. Transit
   (a) Noun ....
   (b) Verb ....
3. Word
   (a) Noun ....
   (b) Verb ....
4. Schedule
   (a) Noun ....
   (b) Verb ....
5. Veneer
   (a) Noun ....
   (c) Verb ....

XI. Rewrite the following sentences, correcting them:
1. He is one of the best student in our class.
2. By whom you are taught English?
3. I love my country but work for its progress.
4. No sooner the guard waved the green flag, the train started.
5. This ewe seems ill. So, he should be segregated.

XII. Give the meanings of the following idioms/phrases and use them in sentences of your own.
1. Ask for the moon
   Meaning: ....
   Usage: ....
2. All and sundry
   Meaning: ....
   Usage: ....
3. Act of God
   Meaning: ....
   Usage: ....
4. Add fuel to fire
   Meaning: ....
   Usage: ....
5. Add insult to injury
   Meaning: ....
   Usage: ....

XIII. Complete the following sentences using a Noun clause each as object to the verb:
1. The rich do not realize ....
2. You do not try to understand ....
3. I cannot make out ....
4. Please clarify ....
5. He says ....

XIV. Use the following words in sentences of your own so as to make their meanings clear:
1. Chores
   Chorus
2. Through
   Thorough
3. Leather
   Lather
4. Slander
   Slender
5. Stare
   Stair

XV. Add the suffix as directed to the following words:
   Word   Suffix   New word
1. White + - er   =
2. Bite   + - er   =
3. Evolve + - ed   =
4. Realize + - ing =
5. Phrase + - ed   =

Answers

I. 1. Gandhiji's secularism meant totally different from irreligion.
   2. He regarded all religions to be true and gave equal respect to all of them.
   3. Nehru's views cannot be identified with Gandhi's.
   4. He had little patience with religion as a communal manifestation.

5. He rejected what he called organised religion.

II.
1. We shall not send any further letter, OR We shall send no further letter.
2. The progress of the experiment was watched by him.
3. His parents were well known to him.
4. The vase has been sent (to) me by him.
5. The side may be saved by it.

III.
1. The postmaster said to Ratan, "I am going away tomorrow."
2. Bill asked Dorset how long he could hold him.
3. He said that they would sell the house and go back to their place.
4. Rosemary told Philip that she had picked her in Curzon street.
5. I ordered him to let her have a little fun.

IV.
1. He did this and chose out a farm of forty acres.
2. As soon as he closed his eyes, he had a dream.
3. He felt so lazy that he could not do any cooking.
4. There was very little of the grandiose in the palace.
5. No sooner did he see the real lion, he was disappointed. OR No sooner had he seen the real lion, he was disappointed.

V.
1. a   2. the   3. a
4. an 5. the

VI. 1. on   2. about   3. of
4. to   5. to

VII. 1. when   2. and   3. that
4. and   5. if

VIII.
1. **Distinctly:** Distinctly, he is a brave fellow.
2. **Penetrate:** Water cannot penetrate into a hard surface.
3. **Flourish:** Mosquitoes flourish in dirty water.
4. **Eccentric:** An eccentric person talks in a strange manner.
5. **Learn by heart:** Please learn this lesson by heart.
6. **Compete with:** You have to compete with others at several levels.
7. **Appalled:** I was appalled to see the miserable condition of slum-dwellers.
8. **Complacent:** You should not become/grow complacent after just one victory.

IX. 1. Epicurean   2. Alchemist
3. Antidote   4. Eccentric
5. Nauseous

X.
1. **Ring**
Noun: She is wearing a beautiful ring.
Verb: The peon rings the bell.
2. **Transit**
Noun: Methods of transit by rail have greatly improved.
Verb: A meteorite transited the (disc of the) sun yesterday.
3. **Word**
Noun: What is the meaning of this word?
Verb: Please word your letter carefully.

4. **Schedule**
   Noun: You must do your work according to schedule.
   Verb: The train is scheduled to arrive at 5:05 sharp.

5. **Veneer**
   Noun: It's the colouring of the veneer that suggests the kind of a moth.
   Verb: In this play characters are veneered according to the necessity of the situation.

XI. 1. He is one of the best students in our class.
   2. By whom are you taught English?
   3. I love my country and work for its progress.
   4. No sooner did the guard wave the green flag than the train started.
   5. This ewe seems ill. So, she/it should be segregated.

XII. 1. **Idiom:** Ask for the moon
   Meaning: demand something unattainable
   Usage: I do not ask for the moon if I demand good meals at a restaurant.

   2. **Idiom:** All and sundry
   Meaning: everybody, big and small
   Usage: He invited all and sundry to his son's marriage.

   3. **Idiom:** Act of God
   Meaning: destruction caused by natural forces
   Usage: Man is often helpless before an act of God.

   4. **Idiom:** Add fuel to fire
   Meaning: to accentuate a bad situation
   Usage: I was already upset. He came and told me something depressing. Thus, he added fuel to fire.

   5. **Idiom:** Add insult to injury
   Meaning: to intensify an already volatile situation, that is, to increase difficulties
   Usage: His adverse remarks added insult to injury when the family was already under strain.

XIII. 1. how the poor make both ends meet.
   2. what I say.
   3. what he says.
   4. what you mean.
   5. that God lives everywhere.

XIV. 1. **Chores:** She does her chores conscientiously.
   Chorus: What message does the chorus convey?

   2. **Through:** He passed the examination through hard work.
   Thorough: You must be thorough in doing every good deed.

   3. **Leather:** Leather is used in making shoes.
   Lather: This soap produces a lot of lather.

   4. **Slander:** Do not slander anybody.
   Slender: He has only a slender chance of success.

   5. **Stare:** Do not stare at the child.
   Stair: How did you fall down from the stairs?

XV. 1. Whiter   2. Biter
   3. Evolved   4. Realizing
   5. Phrased

www.ingramcontent.com/pod-product-compliance
Lightning Source LLC
Chambersburg PA
CBHW050555170426
43201CB00011B/1704